MONEYPOWER

Books by Vernon Coleman include:

The Medicine Men (1975)
Paper Doctors (1976)
Stress Control (1978)
The Home Pharmacy (1980)
Aspirin or Ambulance (1980)
Face Values (1981)
The Good Medicine Guide (1982)
Bodypower (1983)
Thomas Winsden's Cricketing Almanack (1983)
Diary of a Cricket Lover (1984)
Bodysense (1984)
Life Without Tranquillisers (1985)
The Story Of Medicine (1985, 1998)
Mindpower (1986)
Addicts and Addictions (1986)
Dr Vernon Coleman's Guide To Alternative Medicine (1988)
Stress Management Techniques (1988)
Know Yourself (1988)
The Health Scandal (1988)
The 20 Minute Health Check (1989)
Sex For Everyone (1989)
Mind Over Body (1989)
Eat Green Lose Weight (1990)
How To Overcome Toxic Stress (1990)
Why Animal Experiments Must Stop (1991)
The Drugs Myth (1992)
Complete Guide To Sex (1993)
How to Conquer Backache (1993)
How to Conquer Pain (1993)
Betrayal of Trust (1994)
Know Your Drugs (1994, 1997)
Food for Thought (1994, revised edition 2000)
The Traditional Home Doctor (1994)
People Watching (1995)
Relief from IBS (1995)
The Parent's Handbook (1995)
Men in Dresses (1996)
Power over Cancer (1996)
Crossdressing (1996)
How to Conquer Arthritis (1996)
High Blood Pressure (1996)
How To Stop Your Doctor Killing You (1996, revised edition 2003)
Fighting For Animals (1996)

Alice and Other Friends (1996)
Spiritpower (1997)
How To Publish Your Own Book (1999)
How To Relax and Overcome Stress (1999)
Animal Rights – Human Wrongs (1999)
Superbody (1999)
Complete Guide to Life (2000)
Strange But True (2000)
Daily Inspirations (2000)
Stomach Problems: Relief At Last (2001)
How To Overcome Guilt (2001)
How To Live Longer (2001)
Sex (2001)
We Love Cats (2002)
England Our England (2002)
Rogue Nation (2003)
People Push Bottles Up Peaceniks (2003)
The Cats' Own Annual (2003)
Confronting The Global Bully (2004)
Saving England (2004)
Why Everything Is Going To Get Worse Before It Gets Better (2004)
The Secret Lives of Cats (2004)
The Cat Basket (2005)
The Truth They Won't Tell You (And Don't Want You To Know) About The EU (2005)
Living in a Fascist Country (2006)
How To Protect and Preserve Your Freedom, Identity and Privacy (2006)
The Cataholic's Handbook (2006)
Animal Experiments: Simple Truths (2006)
Coleman's Laws (2006)
Secrets of Paris (2007)
Cat Fables (2007)
Too Sexy To Print (2007)
Oil Apocalypse (2007)
Gordon is a Moron (2007)
The OFPIS File (2008)
Cat Tales (2008)

novels
The Village Cricket Tour (1990)
The Bilbury Chronicles (1992)
Bilbury Grange (1993)
Mrs Caldicot's Cabbage War (1993)
Bilbury Revels (1994)
Deadline (1994)

The Man Who Inherited a Golf Course (1995)
Bilbury Pie (1995)
Bilbury Country (1996)
Second Innings (1999)
Around the Wicket (2000)
It's Never Too Late (2001)
Paris In My Springtime (2002)
Mrs Caldicot's Knickerbocker Glory (2003)
Too Many Clubs And Not Enough Balls (2005)
Tunnel (1980, 2005)
Mr Henry Mulligan (2007)
Bilbury Village (2008)
Bilbury Pudding (2009)

as Edward Vernon
Practice Makes Perfect (1977)
Practise What You Preach (1978)
Getting Into Practice (1979)
Aphrodisiacs – An Owner's Manual (1983)

with Alice
Alice's Diary (1989)
Alice's Adventures (1992)

with Donna Antoinette Coleman
How To Conquer Health Problems Between Ages 50 and 120 (2003)
Health Secrets Doctors Share With Their Families (2005)
Animal Miscellany (2008)

TACTICS AND STRATEGIES

FOR THE THINKING INVESTOR

MONEYPOWER

THE SECRETS OF POWER OVER MONEY AND THE ESSENTIAL PRINCIPLES OF MACRO INVESTING

Vernon Coleman

Published by Blue Books, Publishing House, Trinity Place, Barnstaple, Devon EX32 9HG, England.

Reprinted 2009

ISBN: 978-1-899726-13-4

A catalogue record for this book is available from the British Library.

Printed by CPI Antony Rowe, Chippenham, Wiltshire

For my wife, Donna Antoinette,
Mistress of my Universe.
With all my love.
All ways and forever.

Note

This book is a general investment guide; an introduction to a wide variety of matters relating to money. The author does not offer specific investment advice of any kind and *Moneypower* is intended as general guidance and to help readers formulate their own, personal, independent investment philosophies.

Contents List

INTRODUCTION

'Have you a good map in this house?'

THE DUKE OF WELLINGTON, SPEAKING TO HIS HOSTESS AS HE LEFT A BALL HELD IN BRUSSELS ON THE EVE OF THE BATTLE OF WATERLOO. AS THE DUKE SPOKE, NAPOLEON AND HIS ARMY WERE JUST NINE MILES AWAY.

Investing isn't taught at school (though it should be – it certainly is more deserving of a place on the education syllabus than sex). When it comes to finding a place to invest their money most people blunder around; accepting advice where it is offered, but never really having the foggiest idea what they are doing. People who wouldn't trust a second-hand car salesman or an estate agent will willingly trust a bank manager or an investment adviser.

Everyone knows the adage: 'If you think education is expensive, try ignorance'. But no one takes it seriously. Primary schools should be teaching pupils about compound interest and the shortcomings of unit trusts instead of organising compulsory lessons on the joys of anal sex. It is through ignorance that so many people end up failing to budget properly. It is through rows about money (not sex) that marriages most commonly fail. It is because people don't have the faintest idea what they are getting into that homes are repossessed. If you don't teach yourself about money then you will stay ignorant because the state's educational system will most certainly leave you ignorant.

Very few people understand just how important money will be in their lives. They see money as merely a tool for purchasing carpets, television sets and motor cars. How dull and prosaic and unimaginative. It's like saying sex is about having children. Money also provides security, freedom and endless opportunities. Money can help you escape from difficult circumstances. Money can sometimes even free you from the many petty tyrannies which rule our lives. Money can enrich your life. Or at least it can do if you know how to use it properly.

Most people fritter away their money. They think of saving as boring. They regard investing as something done exclusively by clever people in expensive suits.

Amazingly few people understand money management which, although it isn't taught in our schools, is one of the most important skills anyone can have. Most people think they can trust the experts; they think that money management is boring, too complex, or beneath them. Most people think that you need years of training to understand shares, bonds and money markets. None of this is true. Most of the most spectacularly successful investors have never had any proper or orthodox training. And if you do decide to manage your own money you will have one huge advantage over everyone else: you will always care more about your money than anyone else will.

I think the future is exceedingly worrying. To survive you will need to understand money; you will need to make the most of what you have available. And so will your children.

* * *

I used to find it terribly difficult to get money matters straight in my head. One problem was the fact that I found myself being bombarded with so much confusing information; so much deceit and deliberate misinformation.

Like most people, I had never had any training in understanding money. I spent the first 20 years of my life at school and although I was taught a great deal of stuff that was never of any value to me (other than in enabling me to pass examinations so that I could learn more useless stuff), I was never given as much as one minute's advice on how to look after or invest my money.

Prudent adults with no formal medical training take a first aid course. How many attend genuinely unbiased investment courses?

* * *

I have wanted to write a book on investing for years; a book describing the things I have learned and the things I have worked out for myself and which have enabled me to be successful as an investor.

This book doesn't offer you the names of shares you can buy to make a fortune. Such a list would, in any case, be out of date by the time you read it. And I would worry that sceptical readers might fear that I was recommending shares I already held so that the price would rise. Nor does this book contain long lists of useful websites or tips on using charts. It doesn't even contain boastful examples of successful investments I've made.

There is nothing in this book about convertibles, preference shares, guaranteed income bonds, contracts for difference, futures, spread betting, corporate bonds or horse racing. Some of these investments are sound and useful. But I believe that to be a successful investor I have to accept that I need to restrict the areas in which I choose to invest. In order to produce a good return I prefer to use the time I'm prepared to allocate to finance on taking an overview. Besides, my experience tells me that this approach is more profitable. (I have in the past made investments in most of the areas I now ignore.)

This is a philosophical book about investing. My aim is to tell you the things I've learned about making money from money.

You remember the old Chinese adage about fishing?

Give a man a fish and you feed him for a day but teach him how to fish and you feed him for a lifetime.

This is a 'teach you how to invest' book.

There isn't a single tip on how to get rich in this book. You can't turn to page 128 and find a list of recommended shares.

I hate those books. They are useless. If the guys writing them really have a list of foolproof shares why are they telling the world? And surely by the time the books come out the shares will have either gone up (and therefore stopped being a bargain) or the companies behind them will have gone bankrupt?

There isn't even a brilliant new investing technique in this book. There are no wonderful but complex plans based on past records and there are no wonderfully unreadable charts created by specially devised computer software. Books on money are often full of graphs and charts which are either forbidding or incomprehensible or both. Not here.

This is intended to be the book on money that you can keep on your shelf and refer to whenever you are getting jittery. It is, I hope, the honest, impartial book about money that you can give your children and grandchildren to read – so that they grow up understanding something about money.

This is a book to last a lifetime. This is a book to teach you things you need to know in order to invest profitably. It's a book that will, I hope, be just as valid in ten, twenty or thirty years as it is today. The advice in it is timeless and hard-won. This book enables you to benefit from my mistakes.

Most of us have to work hard to get rich or even mildly well-off. And once we've become rich we have to work hard to keep it. But we have to work at the right things. As someone once put it: if simply working hard made people rich then the exit gates at most factories would be jammed with people driving home in Rolls Royce or Bentley motor cars.

Your investment capital consists of two things: your accumulated savings on the one hand and your skills, experience, training and wisdom on the other.

Ignore people who tell you (or imply) that making money out of money is unbelievably complicated and inevitably involves the use of complex software programmes, high powered computers and many hours spent staring at computer screens. I know one man who is regarded by many around the world as an investment guru. He spends hours every day hunched in front of his computer screen. He and I used to be good friends but we drifted apart after he cancelled numerous social engagements because he couldn't leave his screen. His reward for all this effort? Sub-average profits and poor health. Too much information can seriously damage your wealth.

Why else am I writing this book?

Four reasons.

First, I find investing fun. And I've found writing about investing fun too. I've spent the best part of a lifetime accumulating the information contained in this book.

Second, I wanted to write down everything I know about money to pass on to my wife. I don't want her to have to trust investment advisers when I get run over by the inevitable bus. This book is, curious as that may sound, a labour of love.

Third, writing books is what I do for a living. What else am I going to do with my time? I don't need to do anything. But I'm not the beach type and I've been thrown out of almost every golf club I've ever joined.

Fourth, I've had a number of letters from readers asking for precisely this book. Indeed, this is, I think, the first time I've written a book in response to popular demand from readers.

I have written this book in the first person because the advice is personal. There are no firm rules. All I can tell you is what has worked for me. And you know the advice is honest because this is the advice I am giving the one I love. There can be no guarantees, but this is the book I wish I'd been given half a century ago.

I hope you will use this book to help you formulate your own investment style.

> *'It is necessary to plan and to organise in order to get rich. Staying poor is very easy; poverty needs no plan.'*
> NAPOLEON HILL

Investing is not primarily a science. There is a smidgen of science in there somewhere, but investing is partly a craft and partly an art. Every investor's needs, views and style must be personal. I hope you will cherry-pick my advice and use it to create your own personal approach to investing.

It is never too late to start investing and to start using money for your benefit. There are wonderful stories about people in their seventies (or even older) suddenly starting to invest – and doing very well on the stock market. Being older means you have all sorts of advantages. Experience, for a start. And not having to worry about feeding and clothing young kids for another.

* * *

Next, two practical points.

First, I haven't included all the research references I've used in this book. You have to take my word for it that I believe everything in this book. I haven't included references for two reasons. First, the book would be twice as big and twice as expensive to print and mail. Second, if you don't believe what I tell you then I don't believe references are going to help either of us very much. The relationship between the author and reader of a non-fiction book has to be one built on trust. There's no specific advice in this book but I hope my experiences, and the general advice here, will help you formulate your own investing philosophy.

Second, you will doubtless find that I have repeated pieces of advice at different points in this book. I've done that not through carelessness but because these are points that I wanted to reinforce – and it seemed to me easier to do it by occasionally repeating advice rather than by cross referring the reader to another part of the book.

* * *

Few, if any, of the so-called experts who appear on your television screen, or who are quoted in your newspaper, know more about the general principles of money than you will by the time you have finished this book. Many of them probably know considerably less. Most are far too close to the action to be able to use strategy or tactics in the way you will.

And you will, of course, have one enormous advantage over them.

They aren't handling their own money.

You are.

And that will, I believe, give you an unbeatable edge.

Vernon Coleman, England 2009

PART ONE

THE DOWNSHIFT PRINCIPLE

'He who knows when he has enough is rich.'
TAO TE JING BY LAO TSU

The latter part of the twentieth century was, without a doubt, the era of greed. Millions of people fought hard not to acquire a decent standard of living but to get everything. Humans went from needs to wants, through luxury to excess. Moral, ethical, environmental, cultural, emotional, spiritual and personal consequences were ignored in the search for more stuff.

Shopping became a hobby, a recreation ('retail therapy', 'shop till you drop') and, for many, an addiction. Work became a constant grind. Instead of going to work to 'earn a living' people were earning but no longer living. Work had become simply a source of money and there could never be enough (or too much) of that. Earning and spending, owing and worrying.

Money became an end rather than a means. Money was no longer a way to buy food and pay for shelter and nor was it something to use to purchase treats and delights. Acquiring money – and then spending it – had become everything. And we were encouraged in this belief by advertisers (who wanted our money themselves) and by politicians (who wanted us to keep spending so that the economy would grow and they could disguise the fact that the state itself had a huge spending problem). To them we are consumers and taxpayers. Nothing more. When the nation's economy hits hard times the citizens are exhorted to go and spend. If things are really bad the government will hand out tax refunds – together with instructions that they are to be spent.

Millions learnt the superficial short-term joys of debt. People didn't just borrow money to buy a home (though they did that in huge quantities). They also borrowed money to buy cars (why share one when you can have one each – besides with two jobs, necessary to bring in the money to pay all the bills, two cars became essential), kitchen equipment, huge flat-screen digital televisions and computers. They borrowed money to make sure that everyone in the house had a mobile telephone of their own. They borrowed money so that they could talk to their neighbours on the telephone (so much more satisfying than leaning on the garden fence which can't possibly be as much fun because it costs nothing). They borrowed money to go on holiday. They borrowed money to buy second homes. And, of course, they borrowed money to buy smart clothes to wear for work. They borrowed money to buy the season ticket for the train to get to work. They borrowed money to pay for expensive snacks bought to eat on the train while rushing from one appointment to the next. They borrowed money to pay the interest on the money they had borrowed.

No one ever slowed down long enough to realise that if they didn't have two jobs they wouldn't need two cars. Born to work. Born to shop. Whoever dies with the most toys is the winner and gets the biggest obituary. (Though those with the most toys have, paradoxically, probably worked so hard to pay for them that they have played with them very little.) Life, liberty and the pursuit of a bigger television set.

Survey after survey has shown that the majority of people find their work boring and stressful. People complain that they have no free time and no time for hobbies. The divorce rate has risen and risen (the vast majority of divorces being caused by arguments over money not sex). Anxiety and depression are often blamed on stress caused by worrying about work and money.

Work and money.

During the last years of the 20th Century, and the first of the 21st Century, our identities became our work and our shopping; our earning and our spending. We became worth what we earned. A top television performer in the USA has a clause in his contract confirming that he will always be paid $1 more than the next highest paid performer at the network. Why? What does it matter to him what anyone else gets paid?

Our self-regard became tied up with the stuff we had bought with the money we'd borrowed. Our status was determined not by what we had done or learnt or contributed, nor even by what we had acquired through our hard work, but by what we had acquired through borrowing. Our success was measured by our capacity to borrow.

Today, we think we are working to pay the bills but we end up spending more than we earn on more than we need. And when our only joy is shopping we make things worse for ourselves. We shop to cheer ourselves up (a new outfit, a bottle of wine, a visit to the hairdresser, a trip to Disneyland). We buy books about hobbies rather than actually spending time doing them ourselves. We watch television programmes about other people experiencing life because we are too busy to experience life ourselves.

> *'No man ever stood the lower in my estimation for having a patch in his clothes; yet I am sure that there is greater anxiety, commonly, to have fashionable, or at least clean and un-patched clothes, than to have a sound conscience.'*
> HENRY DAVID THOREAU

Here are five questions hardly anyone ever asks about money. Try them. Think about them. They sound surprisingly straightforward but you might surprise yourself with your answers.

1. What is money for?
2. Why do you need money?
3. How much do you really need?
4. Are you wasting money?
5. Do you know the real cost of everything you buy?

* * *

Minimise your wastage and cut your expenses. Know where your money goes and you may find that you need less. But don't make false economies.

I usually drive big cars. I keep them and drive them into the ground. There are several reasons for this. I like big cars because I'm tall and my back aches if I spend too long in a tiny car. I also like big, well-made cars because they tend to be tougher and have a better chance of surviving a crash. Finally, I prefer them because they tend to break down less often and to last longer. I hate looking for and buying new cars. It's a tiresome, time consuming chore. One friend buys a new, small car every two years. He sniffily claims that his vehicle is much cheaper to run and better for the environment. He has to change these tinny little things after two years because by then they're not fit for anything much. The cars he buys seem to be made out of some sort of plastic coated reinforced cardboard and they fall apart if kept too long. His cars use less petrol than mine but I don't use my car all that much (I prefer to travel by train) so I don't spend much more on petrol than he does. His cars are cheaper to mend when they break down but they break down a lot more often. Bits are always falling off them and the dealer usually manages to find a clause in the contract which excludes the latest disaster from the guarantee. And what's better for the environment – buying a big, expensive car which lasts or buying loads of smaller, cheaper cars which have to be replaced every couple of years? The slightly surprising truth is that the big, expensive car may sometimes be much, much better for the environment.

* * *

Debt creates shackles. To pay our debts (and the debts our debts themselves accrue) we are forced to continue with work we hate. We cannot afford to quit. We cannot even afford to pause, rethink and replan our lives. Every small threat becomes a major stress. A temporary illness, an inability to work, becomes a huge problem. The threat of unemployment is a nightmare when credit card bills are pouring through the letterbox.

Real dreams, hopes and aspirations are forgotten; pushed aside by plastic dreams, cardboard hopes and tinsel aspirations. The essentials in life are drowned by the non-essentials. In the same way that savings can provide freedom so debt will inevitably produce slavery. We may be affluent but our noses are stuck to the grindstone as we work ever harder to keep the banks and loan companies off our backs. We make our businesses bigger. And then we need accountants, lawyers and other specialists. The man who used to enjoy his work finds that the more successful he becomes the less time he spends doing what he originally wanted to do with his life. He spends all his time in meetings and preparing for meetings. The problem with our recommended lifestyle is that when your life is designed to accumulate then what you have is never enough. More is always better and 'enough' is always a distant, unattainable horizon. If more is better then what we have can never be enough. There is always more more.

* * *

Look around your house. How much stuff have you got that you don't need? How much time and energy are you wasting looking after it and providing storage space for it? How much time are you wasting wondering if you'll ever wear it again, find the manual or find the other bit that makes it work? How much of it could you sell? How much of it could you give away to your local charity shop? How much of it should you throw away? How much cleaner – and clearer – will your life be without all this unnecessary stuff?

Social security has created jealousy, resentment and institutionalised laziness. People who have been unemployed for generations, in families where no one has done a day's work and where everyone is a parasite, live well. They have smart homes, motor cars, huge television sets, satellite channels and crates of beer delivered by the local supermarket once a week. Even the long-term unemployed have become addicted consumers.

Few people need a new car every two years. Most people have more pairs of shoes than they really need. Millions have electrical equipment they never use. Standard of living and quality of life aren't the same thing but we confuse the two.

There have been more shopping malls than high schools in the USA for many years. Three quarters of the people who go shopping are not looking for something in particular. They are simply out 'shopping'.

We all need to get into the habit of asking ourselves why we buy the things we buy. This isn't a judgemental question. I honestly don't give a damn how you spend your money. But it's a question well worth asking. How many jumpers do you really need? Why do so many people insist on having an entirely new outfit if they are planning to attend someone else's wedding? The complaint 'I don't have a thing to wear' has become a social joke.

> *'Desire is the source of all suffering.'*
> THE BUDDHA

Why do people always expect their standard of living to keep going up? It is this bizarre, inexplicable modern phenomenon (the constantly growing greed of progress) which is largely responsible for the mess we are in. This curious anxiety is based on the apparent belief that our happiness will grow if we have more wealth. People don't want better health, or more time to do things they enjoy, as much as they want more money. And more stuff.

Today, most people spend considerably more than they earn and give no real thought to the future. There is a widespread feeling that everything will sort itself out. Perhaps they are relying on inflation to make their debts disappear.

If you did not have so much stuff (to buy and maintain) how much money would you have left over? What could you do with it? Maybe you could take a year off or train yourself to do another job.

Savings help us avoid making bad choices. Savings give us the ability to say 'no' to things we don't want to do. Saving money helps create a force which can be used to power all sorts of things, and to improve our lives in many different ways, but largely, in my view, by giving us freedom.

Frugality is regarded as a rude word. But in reality it means being efficient in finding happiness from the world around. It means using time, money, energy and possessions wisely. We buy on impulse and forget how long we had to work to earn the money to pay for it.

How mad we are to waste money on stuff we neither want nor need. How mad to spend money (bought with our time) on trying to impress people we don't even know. How crazy to buy children so many presents that they become confused and bad tempered because there is too much choice and they don't know what to play with next.

We insure everything. Is it all really necessary? Public liability insurance is wise and essential. But how many people waste money insuring heirlooms they would never replace if they were stolen?

Look through your standing orders. Are you still subscribing to magazines you don't really want? Many people do. It's easy just to let the standing orders go through. (This also applies to other standing orders. Check them all out.)

When we've got rid of all the material clutter, what about the social clutter? The meetings we go to but don't really need to attend. The television programmes we watch for no very good reason. The cocktail parties, organised dinners and power breakfasts we attend because we have been asked, or because other people expect us to be there. These things take so much time, so many hours that will never return, but offer so little real reward.

> *'Men do not desire to be rich, only to be richer than other men.'*
> JOHN STUART MILL

It is, of course, a myth that money produces happiness. I know there are all sorts of witty sayings such as 'I've tried rich and I've tried poor and believe me rich is better', but riches alone do not produce joy.

One big American study showed that there was a negative correlation between 'quality of life' and 'income level'. Poor people had a better quality of life than rich people. It isn't difficult to find evidence of this.

Study after study has shown that very few lottery winners are happier after their wins. Very few, indeed, had any real idea about what to do with the money. A surprising number were less happy after their wins. Those who gave up work entirely felt that their lives no longer had purpose; their self-esteem was lower and they were lonely. Many felt guilty because they had suddenly acquired money they didn't deserve. Isolated and glum many lottery winners turn to alcohol or drugs, or both. Money can help ease pains and can smooth the way through many of life's travails. But when money runs our lives we forget the joy of just walking in the park or sitting on a bench listening to the birds sing and looking at the flowers.

* * *

If you don't understand why you spend money, you will never be able to control your spending and eliminate the unnecessary expenditures. Here are five reasons people buy things which aren't necessities:

1. To make themselves feel good.
2. To impress family and friends.
3. To impress complete strangers.
4. Because they enjoy spending money.
5. Because they have been seduced into spending by a salesman.

* * *

Don't waste your life penny pinching. You aren't going to get rich by buying cheap beans or cheap jam. And cheap doesn't necessarily save you money.

Always figure in the value of your time. For example, if you are travelling somewhere and there's a choice of going by coach or train think about the time it's going to take you. Which journey will take longest? And will one form of transport enable you to do something useful while you are travelling? I can work on trains but I couldn't possibly work on a coach. I get travel sick on coaches and I can't get my long legs between the seats. If I travel by coach I risk getting a deep vein thrombosis and I waste the time I'm travelling. If I travel by train I can go in some comfort and I can work while I travel. The travelling time won't be wasted.

If you buy cheap, new furniture it will probably fall apart, it will never make you feel good and it will be worthless when you come to sell it. If you buy expensive, well-made old furniture it will not fall apart, it will make you feel good when you use it and if you ever want to sell it, it will probably be worth more than you paid for it. The same isn't quite true for clothes (you probably aren't going to be able to sell them at all) but good clothes will always look better, feel better, keep their shape better and last longer. And good clothes will make you feel good too. (There is the added bonus that when you are travelling security guards and waiters will usually treat you better if you are well-dressed than they will if you are dressed in scruffy, cheap clothes. It's just human nature. They know that rich people are more likely to have clout and make their lives miserable if they mess them around too much.)

Buy quality, rather than quantity. When you are buying new stuff remember William Morris: "Don't buy anything that isn't beautiful or useful or preferably both".

Finally, remember: it isn't wrong to spend money on yourself occasionally. Enjoy your money. Enjoy making it. Enjoy having it. And enjoy spending it. What the hell is it for if not to enjoy?

* * *

Many well-off people living in cities don't own cars. The hassle of having a car serviced and repaired, and finding somewhere to park it, mean that it really isn't worthwhile. When they need to move around they use trains and taxis. And if they want a car for the weekend they just hire one. It's often cheaper to do this than to buy a car and cope with all the expense and trouble.

* * *

I never spend money I haven't yet got sitting in my bank account. There are always a million and one things that can go wrong to turn expectations into disappointments. And I don't believe in tempting fate.

* * *

Most investors spend more time thinking about which telephone system to use, or which shoes to buy, than they spend thinking before making an investment or starting a pension. Learn to spend more time on the big stuff and less time on the little stuff. I have known many people who spent their lives saving pennies through thrifty shopping but losing pounds through bad investments.

* * *

No one will ever spend your money as wisely, or with as much care as you will. Apart from leaving enough money to ensure that your dependants are looked after, your aim should be to spend your money (or to give it away) and to die destitute; with just enough money to pay the undertaker and to meet the solicitor's bill.

* * *

Not everyone can be rich. But everyone who wants it can have some independent wealth. The first trick is not to spend all your income. The second is to invest your savings carefully. That's all.

* * *

A friend of mine recently sold his fairly new large car because the cost of petrol had gone up. He bought a much smaller car that does far more miles to the gallon. He lost a lot of money when he sold the big car. I asked him how much mileage he did each year. I then worked out that even if the price of petrol doubled it would still take him eight years for the money he was saving on petrol to match the money he had lost on the car he'd sold.

* * *

Don't lend money to anyone.

Don't lend money to friends if you want to keep them as friends. They will resent you for being able to lend them money. And, if they don't pay you back, you will resent them for cheating you.

And why the hell would you lend money to enemies?

* * *

Consume less and you need to work less.

* * *

Use cash not credit cards. When I stand in a queue at the newsagents I am constantly surprised by the number of people using plastic to buy one magazine or one notebook. Don't these people carry cash? Are they all Royal? Using plastic is stupid for three reasons. First, the more you use your cards the more you are likely to end up with an identity theft problem. Second, if you use cards for all your purchases you will lose track of your spending. If you have to go and get the cash out of the bank then you'll know that your money is disappearing. It's much easier to keep control of your spending if you use cash. Third, if you use plastic then anyone following you can easily see where you are. If someone has access to the credit card company's computers they will easily spot that you're on holiday in Brighton and not at your flat in Leeds. If you are worried about carrying enough cash just split it between two or three wallets. Make sure that the wallet you use in shops only contains a modest amount of cash. Keep the rest of your cash in inside pockets or in a money belt or money pouch of some kind. And carry what I call a 'mugger's wallet' with you. (A mugger's wallet is simply an old wallet which contains a few notes, and a few bits of useless plastic which look like credit cards but aren't. If a mugger demands your wallet, this is the one you hand over.)

* * *

Don't wait for a lucky break. It will probably never come.

* * *

If you want to make money but you also need the stability and security of a salaried job, think about earning money through a supplementary source. Start a business on the side. (But do remember that you must declare the earnings to the Inland Revenue.) Make sure it is something you enjoy. (You'll be much more likely to be successful if you do. And why not also have fun?). And make sure that you don't short change your employer (or steal his telephone or stationery). That's dishonest and apart from anything else there's a risk that if you do this you could end up losing your stable, secure job before your side line has blossomed and is producing a genuine income.

> *'Fill your house with gold and jade,*
> *And it can no longer be fully guarded.*
> *If you set store by your riches and honour,*
> *You will only reap a crop of calamities.'*
> TAO TE JING BY LAO TSU

What's the difference between comfort and luxury?
Is the extra value of the latter worth the extra cost?

> *'This spending of the best part of one's life earning money in order to enjoy a questionable liberty during the least valuable part of it, reminds me of the Englishman who went to India to make a fortune first, in order that he might return to England and live the life of a poet.'*
> HENRY DAVID THOREAU

Here's a question most people never ask: What is money for and how much money do you need? And what do you need it for? Most investment books I have ever seen never touch on this. The authors seem to assume that acquiring money is an end in itself with no purpose necessary other than the accumulation of wealth.

'The first couple of million bucks you make put it away! You don't ever touch that. That's the 'fuck you' money. That way, anybody ever tries to make you do something you don't want to, you can tell 'em, 'fuck you'.'
IRVING (SWIFTY) LAZAR

Money is crucial: it provides freedom, independence, time and 'fuck you' money. Money can give you the opportunity to say 'No' when you want to say 'No'. Money can give you a voice. The more money you have, the more your voice will be heard. But you can only choose to do two things with money: spend it or save it. If you're doing the latter you need to know why. And you need to know what your needs are (and are likely to become) and what you are prepared to do to satisfy those needs. You need a strategy.

'In the dissipation of worldly treasure the frugality of the future may balance the extravagance of the past; but who can say: 'I will take minutes from tomorrow to compensate for those I have lost today.'
BISHOP JACKSON OF EXETER

If you are old and frail you may need money for nursing home fees. If you are young and healthy you may need money to buy a car or a house. Or to travel. If you are in the middle you may need money to mend the roof or to pay for shoes for the kids.

And, however old you are now, you will almost certainly need money to buy health care at some time in your life. Even in Britain, the home of the National Health Service, the quality of 'free' medical care has been deteriorating for decades and it is now commonplace for potentially lifesaving drugs to be withheld from some patients on the grounds of cost. The elderly (by which the authorities seem to mean anyone over the age of 60) are now officially regarded as not worth saving. You will likely need money for drugs, operations and essential dental care.

What do you need money for? And what do you want money for?

They are the most important questions of all and yet they are the questions hardly anyone ever asks. (Needs and wants are, of course, very different. We all need food and shelter. No one needs a yacht. No one needs to own a football club. No one needs to own a diamond encrusted gold watch.)

None of us actually needs very much money.

It's the wanting that is special.

So, what do you want money for?

Necessities? Helping others? Looking after yourself and your loved ones in the future when the state has thrown you on the scrapheap? Luxuries? Do you like travelling first class and enjoy eating expensive delicacies?

> *'Money is like a sixth sense without which you cannot make a complete use of the other five.'*
> W. SOMERSET MAUGHAM

Do you want money because you know it will buy you freedom? Money doesn't just buy foods, shelter and clothing. It doesn't just buy electric nose hair clippers. Money also buys a certain amount of freedom.

If you want money then first you have to know what you want it for. There has to be a purpose. Otherwise you might as well be collecting blades of grass or old newspapers. Money doesn't have any value unless you do something with it. There has to be a reason for wanting money. Money can buy you expensive, hand-made shoes. It can buy you a yacht. It can buy you first class travel. It can buy you (or someone you love) medical treatment that might not otherwise be available. People's reasons for wanting money vary. As far as I am concerned the one thing money can provide which I really value is freedom. Money gives me the freedom to write what I want to write and to make sure that it gets published and marketed without my worrying too much about whether or not it is commercially successful. (In the bad old days most publishers used to operate like this. They published what they wanted to publish – regardless of whether or not it was likely to make money. If they were unlucky they went bust. If they were lucky they published enough commercial successful books to pay for the commercially unsuccessful books. So far, I'm pleased to say, I've managed to ensure that the commercially successful books I write make more than enough money to pay for the commercially unsuccessful books I want to write and publish anyway.)

> *'Money can't buy friends but you can get a better class of enemy.'*
> SPIKE MILLIGAN

So, the questions to ask yourself are very simple.

1. What do you need money for?
2. How much do you need?
3. When are you likely to need it?

Once you have answered these questions you will find it much easier what to do next. Only when you have these answers will you be able to judge what risks you should be taking, what investments you should be making and so on.

Some assets fit certain aims much better than others. For example, if your sole aim is capital preservation putting at least some of your funds into index-linked gilts makes excellent sense.

* * *

Before you begin to think about investing your money you need to ask yourself some fundamental questions.

How much richer are you likely to become through investing your money?

If your investments are successful will you buy a bigger house? A bigger car? Or will you just be able to buy more of what you already have?

Will that make your life better?

How much food can you eat?

How many pairs of shoes do you want? (We know how many you need.)

How much would you be hurt if you lost your money?

When will you be as rich as you need to be?

> *'Being rich is having more money; being wealthy is having time.'*
> MARGARET BONNANO

Be careful you don't spend money buying too much insurance. The extended warranties so beloved by electrical stores are a perfect example of stores using fear to sell us an expensive product we probably don't really need. The small print is usually complicated and far too daunting to read in the time available. And so we hand over another substantial sum for an over-expensive extended warranty. (The fact that many stores now make a considerable portion of their profit from selling these warranties should tell you something about their value to the customer.)

We have been brought up willing to pay to avoid risk. And some risks (the big ones) are always worth insuring against. Most of us need to take out public liability insurance because if a slate falls off our roof and lands on a passer-by the resulting claim for damages could bankrupt us. Most of us need to insure our homes against fire because if our house burns down we won't be able to afford another one. This sort of insurance doesn't usually cost a great deal (because the risks are quite small) but it is worth buying.

But much of the insurance we are sold doesn't fit into that sort of category. Most of the time we insure ourselves against losses which will not seriously embarrass us. To make things worse we take out extra insurance when the manufacturer's guarantee will protect us against the risk of buying a particularly shoddy item. And our excessive zeal for insurance cover means that we end up buying multiple cover for the same risk. The expense of these accumulated policies can be horrendous.

The variety of risks against which one can now take out insurance is apparently unending. Every time you buy one insurance policy the company from which you bought it will try to sell you another policy, covering areas that weren't included in the first policy. The small print invariably means that the insurance company can find an escape clause or a reason to charge another fee for something else.

We should really only buy insurance which is legally required or to insure against losses that we really cannot afford – huge legal costs for example. Most of us – particularly those who are careful and honest – will be better off if we put many other premiums into a special savings account and use that to pay for plumbing costs, heating repairs and so on.

And since it is probably not worthwhile making a claim against an insurance policy unless the claim is considerable it makes sense to agree formally not to make a claim for small sums, in return for a discount on the premium. (Remember, too, that insurance companies now tend to put up premiums when they pay out. A small claim can lead to an annual rise in premiums which matches the one-off payment.)

The careful and honest lose out twice in the current way of things. First, they must pay high premiums to include the cost of all the false claims that will be made, and the cost of all the problems which will arise because of poor maintenance or bad habits. Second, they must struggle to obtain payment and put up with small print clauses which exclude most claims and put huge excesses on the ones which are (eventually and grudgingly) paid.

Finally, remember that insurance companies are routinely dishonest. They lie. A lot. When they tell you the cheque is in the post they are probably lying. When they tell you that the claims form is in the post they are probably lying. When they tell you that your claim is being processed they are probably lying. Insurance companies lie (and make life exceedingly difficult for anyone trying to make a claim) for one very good reason: they hope that if they make things difficult for you then you will get bored and go away without them ever having to give you any money.

* * *

Put money aside for emergencies, the taxman, your old age and medical problems. Who knows when you will need to have a hernia repaired?

I have never taken out insurance against ill health. There are two reasons for this. First, I try to look after my health. This means that if I pay premiums to a medical insurance company I will probably be subsidising all the over-weight, meat-eating smokers who don't take any exercise but do need a lot of medical attention. Second, I long ago worked out that if I put money aside each month I could use that money if I fell ill and needed private treatment. The money I've put aside has been earning its keep for years. On the other hand, premiums paid are money lost for ever. (I have, however, always bought sickness insurance that pays me money if I am too sick to be able to work.)

I first recommended this policy in the 1970's. It has, I'm pleased to say, now become widely accepted.

* * *

Look after your money and one day it will look after you.

* * *

How much money do you really need?

Take a good hard look at your income and expenditure. Do you need more money for the things you want to do with your life? Or could it be that you already have enough income (and enough money saved up) to buy everything you need? Are you, perhaps, simply wasting money on things you neither want nor need. I know a fellow who lives in the country and has a job in the city. He spends six hours a day on trains (three hours each way) and an hour a day on the Underground. That is seven hours a day, five days a week. He says he has the benefit of a London salary while living in a large house in the country. But he spends seven hours a day travelling. Unless there are breakdowns, of course. When there are breakdowns he spends more time travelling.

* * *

The other day I saw a piece of software being advertised for businessmen and women. The idea was that when you paid for a coffee in a café and wanted to claim the expenditure as an expense, either against your company's accounts department or the taxman, you photographed the receipt with your mobile phone and then e-mailed the photograph to the software site, together with a text note serving as an explanatory caption. The receipt would then be stored in photographic form, together with all its colleagues. In due course, the receipt could be printed out and then used to fill in the usual claim form or to substantiate a tax form claim.

Have you ever heard of such nonsense? What better example is there of how we waste our time and our money in an attempt to find ways to use technology in order to complicate fairly simple matters? I keep my receipts in old envelopes and have done so for many decades. If the taxman wants to compare receipts with the totals I've prepared he is quite at liberty to do so. All he has to do is tip the receipts out of the envelope and start rummaging.

(The day after I wrote this I watched in astonishment as a traffic warden photographed an inappropriately parked car with an expensive looking digital camera. Instead of taking out a notepad and writing down the car numberplate, and details of where the vehicle was parked, he took a series of pictures. He photographed the numberplate, the tax disk, the car as a whole, the surroundings and the disabled driver's badge clearly visible on the dashboard.)

> *'Half our life is spent trying to find something to do with the time we have rushed through life trying to save.'*
> WILL ROGERS

You don't have to be rich enough to do anything you want to do. You just have to be rich enough not to have to do things you don't want to do.

* * *

The advantages of having money are pretty obvious. People are sometimes surprised to discover that there are also some pretty vast disadvantages. For one thing most people who have money worry enormously about losing it all. And so hanging on to it becomes a burden. And, in a purely practical sense, there is the fact that means-testing rules mean that if you have worked hard and saved hard you will be denied government help if and when it might otherwise be appropriate.

* * *

Money and plastic surgery have something in common. Neither will solve your problems. If your life is glum it won't get better just because you have bigger breasts or a shapelier nose. Similarly, your life won't automatically be better just because you have money in the bank. Money won't make all your problems and anxieties disappear.

* * *

Some people accumulate vast quantities of money for its own sake. They acquire far more money than they can ever possibly need. Why do they want so much? Often, they seem frightened to spend it once they've got it. It's as though they are frightened that they will lose the game if they spend the wealth they have acquired.

Others spend their wealth on absurd and clearly overpriced dross. This morning I read about one idiot who had spent £100,000 on a bottle of brandy and another who had paid untold millions for a boat with three helipads. It used to be called showing off. Today it's known as conspicuous consumption.

> *'I don't want money. It is only people who pay their bills who want that, and I never pay mine.'*
> OSCAR WILDE

What is your income per hour, after tax? Work it out. Remember it.

Get into the habit of thinking of the things you buy in terms of hours rather than pounds.

If you buy a television set that costs £1,000 and you earn £10 an hour then the television set has cost you 100 hours.

If you buy a book for £10 and your income is £10 an hour then the book has cost you one hour.

Every time you spend money ask yourself how long you have had to work to earn that money. Do this especially when you are spending money on something destined to go down in value.

How much of your life would you give in order to buy a car with a three-speed rear window wiper instead of one with a one-speed rear window wiper? (That was the sole difference between two models of a car I once saw for sale. The extra price was £500.) I suspect you'll soon find yourself less willing to spend money on things you don't really need or want.

Much of this sounds pretty obvious. But it isn't what most people do, so it isn't that obvious.

You have to trade your time (that means your life and your energy) for money. So, what does money mean to you?

If you are 40-years-old you can reasonably expect to have 37 years of life left – that's 329,601 hours. Assuming that half your time is spent maintaining your body (sleeping, eating, washing etc.) you have 164,800 hours left.

* * *

What can money buy you in addition to £100,000 bottles of brandy?

Security

Power

Social acceptance

Comfort

Freedom

Your life (if you need medical treatment which is only available if you pay for it privately.)

* * *

What is rich?

There are some who claim that you aren't rich until you have £50 million or £100 million in the bank. But that seems to me to be nonsensical.

Ignore all those idiotic books by rich people who define 'wealth' by their own success and standards. 'You aren't rich unless you have £50,000,000,' wrote one author I saw. What planet does he call home? What expensive habits do you need to have to require a bank balance of £50,000,000 before you feel 'rich'?

Maybe being rich is just being free of guilt, envy and anxiety about money. Maybe it is not having to buy things you don't want or need because you are comfortable with your life and your world, and immune to the entreaties of advertisers.

* * *

Here are some more questions you should ask yourself:

1. Do you want to be rich?
2. Do you need to be rich?
3. Why do you want or need to be rich?
4. How rich do you want or need to be?
5. In what way would being rich change your life?

Curiously, these are questions very few people ask themselves.

* * *

In the old days people considered themselves rich if they were millionaires.

But having a million doesn't necessarily make you *rich* rich these days. And a million what? A million Zimbabwean dollars wouldn't buy you a loaf of bread. A millionaire used to be someone who had a million pounds or a million dollars. But if you add in houses and pensions there are a lot of millionaires around these days. Not many of them would really call themselves 'rich'.

Perhaps being rich these days is having a million that doesn't include the money tied up in your home or your pension fund.

* * *

Don't ever tell anyone how much you earn, how much stuff you have or how much you are worth. Such confessions will inspire jealousy and contempt rather than admiration. And you're likely to be robbed.

Don't talk about money to other people. Most people aren't interested. Talking about money is more likely to invoke jealousy than to impress people or make them pleased for you.

I know a couple who are very well off. They live in Monaco (don't even think about it incidentally – it's an awful place, and what's the point of being rich if you end up living somewhere that is soulless, simply so that you don't have to pay any tax?) and they can't enjoy their wealth unless everyone they meet knows that they are rich. So, she walks around with jewellery dripping from every place from which you can hang jewellery. They might as well walk around waving a copy of their latest bank statement.

The inevitable result is that they are forever looking over their shoulders for muggers. They won't walk down the street because they are frightened of muggers. They won't sit in the park or on the beach because they are frightened of muggers. (She wouldn't dream of going on the beach without her bracelets, necklaces and earrings. She'd rather go without a bikini than go without jewellery.) Instead of making their lives better, their money (and their taste for conspicuous consumption) has made them prisoners of their own vanity.

Here are the top ten most disgustingly flashy things rich people do:

1. Fly all their relatives to somewhere hot and sticky and then rent a whole hotel.

2. Hire an ageing pop star to perform at their birthday party.
3. Buy such expensive, rattly pieces of jewellery that the newspapers carry pictures of it.
4. Own two private jets and then say it is because one is always in the wrong country.
5. Have a private zoo.
6. Buy a farm or ranch where they pretend to farm.
7. Allow television or magazine cameras into their home. (This is really stupid. Burglars buy these magazines and look through them to find nice things to steal.)
8. Sell their wedding (or any other occasion) to a magazine.
9. Fill a whole garage with expensive motor cars.
10. Have a yacht with more than one helicopter pad.

> *'Unsure of what they stand for, people increasingly rely on money as the criterion of value. What is more expensive is considered better. What used to be a medium of exchange has usurped the place of fundamental values...The cult of success has replaced a belief in principles. Society has lost its anchor.'*
>
> GEORGE SOROS

What is wealth?

Some people say it is being able to live on your capital.

Some say it is being able to live on the income derived from your capital.

And some say it is being able to live on the interest you get on the income derived from your capital.

You are certainly rich if you can live on the interest on the interest on your capital.

If you have £1,000,000 invested and you receive 5% income (after tax and inflation) that's an income of £50,000 a year. At 5% the interest on that £50,000 is £2,500. If you can live on £2,500 a year (before tax) then you are rich. (You are also a very good shopper).

So, if you reckon you would need £10,000 a year before tax to survive then you would need £4 million before you considered yourself rich (if you were planning to live on the interest on the income from your capital). You would not, however, be living the life of someone rich. If you need £50,000 a year to live comfortably then you would need investments of £20 million before you could consider yourself rich.

* * *

If you want to get rich you need to know how much you want, when you want it and how you're going to get it.

* * *

Some people (largely, it has to be said, the people who don't have any) regard money as evil. Having the stuff is a sin, they say. That is balderdash. Money isn't good or bad. How you got it can be good or bad. How it affects you can be good or bad. And what you do with it can be good or bad. But money itself can't be good or bad or anything. It's just money. Money isn't dirty. It's what you do with it that matters. Not how much you have.

* * *

One of the fundamental truths about getting rich is that very few people get rich by earning a salary. Most people who have money acquired it by working for themselves. Their money came in fees, royalties or profits.

To become rich you may need several income streams. (The added advantage of this is that it will give you more security.) Most of the people who are independent because they are wealthy usually have several sources of income. They may have a business, a consultancy, a rental property and a portfolio of shares, for example.

* * *

Financial security is a state of mind.

Lots of people think that having a job with a big company provides more security than working for yourself. It is true that the self-employed have less immediate security. They often don't know where the next job is coming from. But in a downturn big companies often lay off employees. No one can make you redundant if you are self-employed. You may find it harder to get work, and you may have to work longer hours for the same income as before, but you aren't going to be queuing on the docks waiting for a chance to unload ships.

Financial security means knowing that whatever happens you and your family won't starve because you will be able to find a way to earn a living and put bread on the table. I know a millionaire who keeps a bicycle and a bucket in his garage next to his Rolls Royce and his wife's Mercedes sports car. 'If I lose all my money,' he told me once, 'I'll start a window cleaning round and build it up.' The bicycle and the ladder are his ultimate financial security.

Having some savings will provide you with security against bad times, misfortune and mistakes.

But do not trust anyone to look after your financial security blanket for you. Do not trust banks. Do not trust brokers. Do not trust advisers. And, most of all, do not trust your government or any official regulators. The financial world today is riddled with regulations which make life difficult for everyone. The regulations will not, I fear, protect you against thievery, dishonesty or incompetence. The bottom line is that there is no one more interested in your financial security than you are.

* * *

If you want to be rich, are you prepared to do the work?

Most people who make money do so by working hard. Even people who seem to get rich by good fortune (rock stars, actors and sport stars) have usually put in years of hard work before they become overnight successes. (Though it is, of course, a myth that hard work alone is the route to financial success.)

Some people inherit money. Some people marry it. Some people win it. Some people grab huge quantities of it; scooping it up simply because it's there and no one stops them. Some people are given it as bribes. Some people steal it or obtain it through fraud.

But most people who have a lot of money probably got it by working hard.

* * *

Some people would like to be rich but only if they can get there by winning the lottery.

Ah, the lottery.

The tragedy for lottery winners is four fold.

First, the money arrives suddenly: there is no time to get used to it. The very suddenness of its arrival means that many lottery winners are made miserable by their sudden wealth. Apart from splashing out on a new house and a new car and a holiday they don't know what to do with the money. The new house will be far away from anyone they know. They will be lonely and lost. They will probably be scared of scratching the new car (or having it stolen). And the holiday (in a posh hotel) will probably make them feel out of their depth.

Second, their chances of replicating their success are slim to none. If you've become rich through your own efforts then you can probably do it again. If you've won the lottery you are extremely unlikely to be able to win it twice (though many people try). Everyone who is rich is afraid of losing their money. Lottery winners worry more than other rich people because they know that if they lose it they're sunk. They'll never have a second chance.

Third, many lottery winners lose their money because they don't know how to handle the stuff properly. Because they didn't make it themselves, and have never learned the basic principles of money management, they have to put their trust in advisors and managers. And so they often lose all their money. (Or it is taken from them in fees and expenses and poor investments.)

Fourth, lottery winners start off just wanting to be rich. They haven't usually worked out in any detail why they want to be rich. They think that being rich will solve all their problems. It won't, of course. People who work hard for their money are usually driven by something more specific than a vague desire to be able to drive a Ferrari or buy a season ticket for Manchester United football club.

* * *

You are the best investment you'll ever make. Put as much time as you can into improving your knowledge and skills. Remember that imagination and a capacity for hard work are far more important than formal qualifications. And if you have a good business idea, and you have a little capital, doesn't it make sense to invest in yourself? Put your own money into your business and you will retain control. Allow banks or investors to put up all the money and they will take over. If your business becomes successful, they will be the ones to profit.

If you meet someone successful, spend a little time asking them about themselves and their philosophy. Ask them how they succeeded. I read an article yesterday about a would-be billionaire who claimed that his hero was Richard Branson. The two had met by accident at an airport. 'I talked to him for fifteen minutes and told him everything about my plans and my business,' said the young would-be billionaire who didn't seem to realise that he should have been listening, not talking; asking not telling.

The more you understand about money the more you will feel comfortable with it. I felt much more comfortable about money after I sacked an incompetent accountant. For the first time in my life I knew how much I was earning, how much I owed the taxman, how much I had saved and how best I could invest.

> *'A Monday through Friday sort of dying.'*
> STUDS TERKEL

Being rich may mean being financially independent, but it also means being independent of the tyranny of money; the tyranny which forces so many people to spend their lives earning money they don't really need in order to buy things they neither need nor want.

If you didn't have to work so hard, and had more time to yourself, how would you spend it?

Are you getting real value out of your life, out of your job and out of the money you earn?

> *'For most of human history people only worked for two or three hours per day. As we moved from agriculture to industrialisation, work hours increased, creating standards that label a person lazy if he or she doesn't work a forty hour week... The very notion that everyone should have a job only began with the Industrial Revolution.'*
> DR FRITHJOF BERGMANN

Rich is earning more than you are spending.

Rich is earning money while you sleep, watch television and lie in the bath.

Rich is not having to worry about money.

Rich is being able to buy whatever you want without worrying about the price.

Rich is not knowing how much your central heating costs to run.

Rich is having a job you enjoy so much that you don't think of it as work.

> *He squandered health in search of wealth,*
> *To gold became a slave;*
> *Then spent his wealth in search of health,*
> *But only found a grave.*
> INSCRIPTION ON A TOMBSTONE

Most of our lives we allow money to use us. You can, and should, learn to use money. That, after all, is what it is for. Always try to make your money work for you. Don't let it just sit around, lazily. Make it provide you with rents, dividends and so on. Money loves working. And it never gets tired.

* * *

In 2003, 12 million Europeans deliberately took a cut in salary and chose to work shorter hours. They decided that they could earn what they needed by working less.

* * *

Don't waste time envying other people. It's true that some people are extraordinarily lucky. They inherit millions. They win the lottery. Rejoice for them. That's their good fortune. But their good fortune doesn't damage your chances of becoming wealthy enough for your purposes.

> *'There is no wealth but life. Life, including all its powers of love, of joy, and of admiration. That country is the richest which nourishes the greatest number of noble and happy human beings; that man is richest who, having perfected the functions of his own life to the utmost, has also the widest helpful influence, both personal, and by means of his possessions, over the lives of others.'*
> JOHN RUSKIN

Do you want to be really, really rich?

Why?

Why not?

When you can answer those two questions you will understand your attitude to money a little better.

You have to trade your time (that means your life and your energy) for money. So, what does money mean to you?

* * *

Decades ago I wrote a book called *Bodypower* for which I formulated my basic principles of dieting. They were amazingly simple:

Eat when you are hungry and need food.

Stop eating when you are no longer hungry

The same principles can be applied to money.

Earn what you need.

Stop earning when you have enough.

* * *

People usually buy things (such as expensive cars) because they want to appear rich and because they want to convince themselves they are rich and because they believe that looking wealthy and behaving rich will make them rich. In fact the opposite is true. Unless you really are rich, behaving rich will simply make you poor.

* * *

If you didn't have to work so hard, and had more time to yourself, how would you spend it?

Are you getting real value out of your life, out of your job and out of the money you earn?

What have you done with your life that you are proud of? How would you spend the next year if you knew it was going to be your last year?

What are your values? How does your earning money satisfy those values? What about your spending of money?

What do you want from your money?

How much money do you really need?

What do you intend to do with your money when you have it?

* * *

Don't allow yourself to become obsessed with money. If you spend too much time reading, thinking and worrying about money there is a risk that you will lose contact with the important things in life. Money, remember, is there to make life better for you. Once you have some capital it should be working for you, not the other way round. The key is to find your balance of money and happiness. What do you want/need out of life? How much money do you need to do that?

Where do you want to be, and what do you want to be doing, in 5, 10, 15, 20, 25 years time?

How much money might you need then?

> *'Not for to hide it in a hedge,*
> *Nor for a train attendant,*
> *But for the glorious privilege*
> *Of being independent.'*
> ROBERT BURNS

PART TWO

THE NUTS AND BOLTS OF INVESTING

Wealth is not without its advantages, and the case to the contrary, although it has often been made, has never proved widely persuasive.'
JOHN KENNETH GALBRAITH

Acquisitions and Mergers
Alternative Investments
Analysts and Economists
Asset Allocation
Averaging Up and Down
Bank Deposits
Bear and Bull Markets
Bonds and Gilts
Brokers
Bubbles
Cashflow
Charts
Commodities
Company Accounts
Company Reports
Complex Investments
Contrarian Investors
Corporate Pay
Corporate Power
Correlation
Costs
Directors
Diversification
Dividends
Efficient Market Hypothesis
Emerging Markets
Ethical Investing
Exchange Traded Funds (ETFs)
Fashion
Foreign Investments
Fund Managers
Gambling
Gold Standard
Growth Investing
Hedge Funds
Independent Financial Advisers
Index Funds
Inflation
Information for Investors: Lies and Deceits
Investment Trusts and Unit Trusts
Leverage
Liquidity
Luck
Mission Statements
Momentum Investing
Net Asset Value
New Companies
Penny Stocks
Pensions and Retirement
Portfolio Management
Pound Cost Averaging
Price Earnings Ratios
Property
Recession
Regulators
Risk
Safe Investments
Sectors
Selling
Shares
Speculation
Strategic Thinking
Structured Products
Tax
Timing
Trading
Tricksters and Swindlers
Value Investing
Volatility

ACQUISITIONS AND MERGERS

'It is not enough to be busy. The question is: 'What are you busy about?''
HENRY DAVID THOREAU

Directors and senior executives often want to grow a company to justify giving themselves higher salaries and huge bonuses. But, as far as shareholders are concerned, acquisitions can be damaging. There are several reasons for this. Combining two corporate cultures can be difficult (and expensive). Managers of both firms will be distracted (possibly for long periods) when making an acquisition. And, of course, the buyer may pay over the odds for the company it purchases. The real problem, however, is that the people making the acquisition (or allowing their company to be acquired) may well be thinking more of their own interests than the interests of the shareholders. When there is a takeover who do you think the board of directors and the executives are thinking of most? The staff, the shareholders or themselves?

So, remember, company bosses want their companies to be bigger so that they can give themselves bigger salaries and bigger bonuses and more options and more perks. Virtually every manager in a large company gains financially when the company gets bigger. The main losers are shareholders. Companies which get bigger through takeovers do not usually become more efficient or more profitable. If I hold shares in a company which is involved in a takeover I usually sell as soon as I can and regard the takeover premium as a bonus. In my experience the value of the new, larger company will usually fall below the value of the corporate constituents.

When a major report found that 83% of corporate mergers produced no benefits, and half actually made the companies involved poorer – though not, of course, the deal makers – managers tried, and failed, to suppress it. Another study of 124 mergers showed that only 30% produced additional revenue close to that which the acquirer had predicted during the courtship. Executives overpay when buying other companies because they need to expand in order to justify giving themselves bigger salaries, bigger bonuses, bigger expense accounts and bigger aeroplanes. They pay too much because they worry that someone else might steal the deal. And, of course, it isn't their money they are throwing around.

ALTERNATIVE INVESTMENTS (INCLUDING GOLD)

'There is nothing more disastrous than a rational investment policy in an irrational world.'
JOHN MAYNARD KEYNES

If you want to make money out of alternative investments (such as books, paintings, furniture, stamps or coins) then you have to separate your collecting instinct from your investment ambitions. Collecting for fun is an entirely different game to collecting for money, and the methods employed need to be very different.

Your aims as a collector will be quite different to your aims as an investor.

As a collector you are acquiring 'things' to please yourself. As an investor you are acquiring 'things' because you think other people will want them.

Don't mix the two.

I have two book collections.

I buy some books because I want to read them and own them.

But I also buy books because I think they are a good medium and long-term investment. I believe modern authors such as Ian Fleming, Arthur Conan Doyle, Graham Greene and P.G.Wodehouse offer excellent rewards for investors. These authors are still enormously popular and new generations of readers (and cinema viewers) are constantly being introduced to their work. It is difficult to believe that Sherlock Holmes, James Bond or Bertie Wooster will ever go out of fashion. I also collect historically significant authors such as T. E. Lawrence (Lawrence of Arabia). (Most of the books I collect as an investment are first editions of books which I already own.)

* * *

Stamps and books can be a good investment if you buy very carefully. But the mark up and dealers commissions are so great that you have to hold the objects for long periods in order to make money. And you will usually only make money if you buy very rare items – which are worth at least several hundred pounds each. The cost of storage, security and insurance can be high. No one is going to get rich by buying items which cost just a few pounds each.

It's also important to remember that such items can be illiquid. If your wealth is tied up in a Constable painting you are probably going to have to wait a while to get your money. On the other hand you are far more likely to get pleasure out of having a painting hanging on your wall than you are out of putting a share certificate on your wall.

* * *

Pictures that are Great Art often turn to be enormously successful investments. A picture called The Woman In Red, painted by Leger, was bought for 200 francs in Paris in 1921 and was held in the same family until 2005 when it was sold for $22 million. That's a steady return of 19% a year over 84 years. Van Gogh's picture 'Irises' was bought in 1947 for $80,000. It probably seemed a lot at the time. Exactly 40 years later the buyer's son sold the painting for $53.9 million. That's a return of 17.7% for 40 years. And, of course, the families had the joy of having the pictures hanging on their walls.

The problem is that the market for pictures goes up and down. Sometimes artists are in fashion. Sometimes they aren't.

Many investors turned to modern art in the early part of the 21st Century but by 2007 it seemed clear to me that this particular part of the art market had pushed prices up way beyond any sensible levels. Dealers and collectors were, it seemed, conspiring to pay absurd prices in order to keep prices high. If new works of art by a fashionable (if untalented) artist appeared at auction the prices would be kept high because it was in the modern art industry's interests to keep prices high. Dealers and collectors kept bidding up prices of new pieces in order to ensure that the prices of the stuff they'd already bought didn't collapse. It was a classical case of the Emperor's new clothes. Pieces which didn't sell at auction were quietly bought privately, often at discounted prices, by collectors or dealers or even by the artists themselves, determined to keep their prices high.

The absurd boom in modern art prices at the end of the 20th Century, and the start of the 21st Century, is a re-run of something that has happened before. In 1904, a picture by Laurence Alma-Tadema went for £5,240. That was a fairly spectacular price at the time. Half a century later it was knocked down for £252. The world of art is full of similar examples of contemporary art losing its value over the years. So-called art which appeals to one generation of investors is quite likely to leave another generation cold – particular when the 'artists' concerned are far more adept at marketing than at creating.

Writing in the *Financial Times*, one commentator pointed out that 'No part of the market is more vulnerable than contemporary art, much of which will end up in skips, worthless emblems of a period with too much liquidity and not enough cultural judgement.'

* * *

For apocalyptic times, valuable items need to be portable, easily hidden and marketable. Gold coins such as krugerrands are good. Expensive jewellery is good too and many royal families have escaped into exile carrying nothing but the family jewels.

Diamonds are popular with novelists and screenwriters but they are a commodity with a manipulated price and unless you are a diamond expert they are probably best left alone.

* * *

Bullion coins are rare coins which have little value to collectors but which are bought and sold for their bullion content. Coins which have a value to collectors are 'numismatic'. Bullion coins which are rare may have a numismatic value and a bullion value.

* * *

Gold has for centuries been the commodity of choice among investors looking for a safe haven for their savings. Back in the 15th and 16th centuries Spanish and English explorers sailed the world not to build empires but in search of gold. Pirates such as Sir Francis Drake and Sir Walter Raleigh acquired great wealth by stealing the yellow metal from the Spaniards.

Over the years many people have tried to end the idea of using gold as a store of wealth. More than half a century ago John Maynard Keynes, a much admired economist, foolishly described the gold standard (by which Governments were required to back up their currencies with real gold bars sitting in their vaults) as a barbarous relic. Today, however, gold is still a currency rather than a commodity. And it is widely agreed that if governments had kept the gold standard the world's 21st Century economic problems could have been prevented.

As an investment, gold traditionally does well when bonds or stocks or both are doing badly, when there is inflation or deflation or any sort of financial or geopolitical turmoil. When there is a raging bull market for stocks, gold usually slumps.

It is widely believed that the price of gold could soar if any sort of financial, social or political catastrophe hit the world. If you believe, as I do, that the world's oil is running out and the consequences will be more dramatic and far-reaching than most politicians or journalists accept then holding some of your wealth as gold is essential.

Traditionally, experts suggest holding between 5% and 10% of a portfolio in gold. I believe that this is far too low a figure. I am prepared to put up with volatility (the price of gold tends to fluctuate a good deal) for the comforting knowledge that gold is extremely unlikely to become worthless and could, in the not too distant future, become far more valuable than it is at present.

***

Shares in mining companies which dig out gold usually do better than the metal itself when there is a boom in the gold price. This isn't difficult to understand. If the gold price is $400 an ounce a mining company which digs out gold at the cost of $350 an ounce will make $50 dollars an ounce profit. But if the gold price is $1,000 an ounce the price of digging out the gold will probably remain much the same and so the profit for every ounce which is produced will soar. To that has to be added the value of the gold that remains in the mine.

However, this nice and simple equation doesn't always work.

Sometimes, the price of the gold itself can go up while the price of gold mining shares goes down.

This happened to some extent during the 2007-8 bull market in gold. One reason was that some gold mining companies in South Africa couldn't get enough electricity to operate their mines properly. A second reason was that the rise in the cost of oil meant that the cost of extracting gold went up significantly.

Gold mining shares can also suffer when companies hedge their exposure to the gold price by selling their future supplies at the present price.

I think it's a good idea to avoid buying shares in mining and exploration companies that hope to find gold (or oil) on land they've bought. When considering buying shares in a gold mining company it is important to have some evidence that the company actually has some gold and is capable of digging it out.

When the gold price rises many unscrupulous people (sometimes backed by very impressive banks) form gold mining companies which may own nothing more than the right to dig a hole in some far off piece of land. Remember, too, that political upheaval may make life difficult for mines operating in remote parts of the world.

Gold is a controversial, anti-establishment investment. Politicians don't like citizens holding gold. When citizens have a stash of gold coins under their beds they become more independent and less malleable. Some gold-bugs (enthusiastic supporters of gold as an investment) believe that politicians deliberately do everything they can to keep the gold price down – often by selling official reserves of gold and sometimes by announcing that they are going to dump those official reserves on the market.

There are many ways of holding an investment in gold.

1. Buy gold coins and put them somewhere safe (preferably in a safe deposit box and not at home). Make sure that you obtain and keep receipts for gold bought this way. Keep a list of whatever you store in your box. If you store your gold (and other valuables) in a private safe deposit box (rather than a deposit box in a reputable bank) do what you can to make sure that the owners of the deposit box are reputable. There's quite a variety of suitable coins available. South African krugerrands are popular because they sell at very little above the price of gold. Sovereigns are also readily available.

2. Ask a bank to buy coins or bullion bars on your behalf and to put it in their vault. If you do this make sure that the gold is bought and held in your name and cannot be used or accessed by the bank (or any of its creditors if the bank goes bust).

3. Buy shares in gold mining companies.

4. Exchange traded funds are now available, though it is important to be sure that any fund in which you invest is actually holding the gold you've bought in its vault and isn't merely using bits of paper, and contracts with other institutions, to reflect the price of the metal.

5. Some institutions sell certificates 'proving' that you have bought a certain amount of gold and that it is being held in their vaults on your behalf.

Confidence (among investors) has an enormous effect on investment success. If people feel confident about the economy they will buy shares and property (and just about everything else that is for sale). If people feel gloomy about the economy they won't buy anything much except gold. They will want to hoard their cash because they don't know what is coming. Gold, being the oldest currency in the world, is often a good investment at such times.

Gold did badly during the 1980's and 1990's because investors were confident, and were making huge profits from their share portfolios. They didn't need the reassurance of having some of their wealth in gold. Who would bother buying gold when you could get 15% a year by buying stocks you'd chosen by throwing a dart at a newspaper?

* * *

Gordon Brown, when he was the UK's Chancellor of the Exchequer, sold more than half the United Kingdom's gold reserves when the price stood at a 20 year low. By telling the market in advance what he was planning to do Brown managed to get the lowest possible price for the nation's gold reserves.

* * *

Precious metals (gold, silver, platinum, palladium) don't produce dividends or interest. They have value because they always have had a value. And because they are in limited supply. They offer two things. First, they offer some level of security. In recessionary times, when companies are going bust and governments are threatened, gold (and other precious metals) will retain at least some of their value. Your shares in BP might fall to nothing. Your gold coin is probably always going to be worth something. Second, there is an opportunity to make money if prices go up. Note that although gold is used largely as a monetary precious metal (though it does have uses in jewellery), the other precious metals are all used in industrial processes and so also have a commercial value. There are no upper or lower price limits for precious metals.

* * *

It has been alleged (and is fairly widely believed) that it is not unknown for large, famous financial establishments to claim that they are storing precious metals (such as silver and gold) on behalf of their clients and to claim that the metals are safely locked away in their vaults when, in reality, there is nothing stored at all. To add insult to this particular injury, the banks then charge their clients big fees for storing the imaginary metal. One bank, sued by clients for precisely this, defended itself by claiming that everything it did followed 'standard industry practices'.

The answer, if you entrust a bank to buy and store coins or bullion for you, is to ask for a letter, signed by at least one named bank official, confirming that there is real metal stored in your name (not in the bank's name) in the bank's vault.

* * *

Occasionally, things which are offered for sale will have an underlying or intrinsic value which is greater than their apparent commercial value. So, for example, if the price of silver or gold rises a great deal (as happens sometimes) then the price you are asked to pay for a piece of silver tableware or an item of gold jewellery may be less than the price of the metal used to make the item. This does happen from time to time and beautiful and valuable works of art get melted down because they are worth more as bullion than as examples of creative genius.

ANALYSTS AND ECONOMISTS

'Economists forecast not because they know but because they are asked.'
JOHN KENNETH GALBRAITH

The recommendations produced by professional analysts employed by banks and brokers are often treated with great deference by journalists and investors.

This deference is misplaced.

I don't rely on analysts when making investments.

As I write, the Ford motor company has just announced a quarterly loss of 62 cents a share. Analysts covering the Ford motor company forecast an average loss of 25 cents a share. Merrill Lynch bank lost $4.42 per share. Analysts specialising in the bank forecast a loss of $1.94.

Author David Dreman studied 1,500 American shares between 1971 and 1996. He discovered that when analysts picked their top tips they underperformed the market a staggering 75% of the time.

In 2001, three American academics, Brad Barber, Reuven Lehavy and Maureen McNicolls studied the performance of the most and least favoured stocks of analysts in the previous years. They found that the shares with the most strongly positive recommendations subsequently fell by an average of 31.2% while those with the most strongly negative recommendations rose by an average of 48.7%.

Consultants Davis Advisors compared the interest rate forecasts in *The Wall Street Journal Survey of Economists* for the period 1982 to 2008 with actual interest rates. The 'experts' got it wrong 35 times out of 52 – giving them a 67% failure rate.

Writing in his book *A Random Walk Down Wall Street*, which includes the results of his study of analysts, Burton G. Malkiel reports that when confronted with the poor record of their five-year growth estimates, security analysts sheepishly admitted that five years ahead is really too far in advance to make reliable projections. They said they felt that they really ought to be judged on their ability to project earning changes one year ahead. Sadly, for the credibility of the analysts, it turned out that their one-year forecasts were even worse than their five-year projections.

Malkiel also reported that no analysts proved consistently superior to the others. In one year, one analyst would do better. In another year another analyst would shine. 'Analysts who did better than average one year were,' says Malkiel, 'no more likely than the others to make superior forecasts in the next year.'

Other researchers have drawn the same conclusions. A study by David Dreman and M. A. Berry in the *Financial Analysts Journal* concluded that analysts' earnings forecasting errors 'are too large to be reliably used by investors and are increasing over time while analysts' forecasts are too optimistic and the investment community relies too heavily on them'.

Yale professor Robert Shiller says that analysts engage in herd behaviour because they are constantly evaluated against their peers. Younger analysts know that a few failures can destroy their growing reputations – so they stick with the crowd.

Error rates among analysts are embarrassing. 'Financial forecasting,' says Malkiel, 'appears to be a science that makes astrology look respectable.'

There is, Malkiel says, a message. 'Investors who put blind faith in such forecasts in making their investment selections are in for some rude disappointments.'

> *'Be sceptical of macro-economic forecasts. Forecasters have a very bad track record in predicting genuine booms and slumps. They sometimes fail to forecast a recession even when it has actually started.'*
> PAUL ORMEROD

Although this is surprising, given the evidence, professional investors put a lot of faith in the views of analysts. Pension and investment fund managers rely on analysts to tell them what share prices are likely to do in the next three months. And they maintain their faith despite the existence of a good deal of evidence showing that analysts are worse than useless. It is partly because analysts are so useless that investment managers produce such rotten results.

John Maynard Keynes pointed out that for many investors and advisors: 'it is better to fail conventionally than to succeed unconventionally'. Analysts, are frightened of being the lone voice and losing their well-paid jobs if they turn out to be wrong. So analysts tend to keep on promoting the shares that are going up and avoiding the shares that have gone down.

Why are analysts so bad?

There are several reasons.

But the biggest is that analysts rely very heavily on something called the 'discounted cash flow model'. This sounds grand and terribly scientific but it is, in reality, rather dependent on a number of what they call forecasts and what you and I might prefer to call guesses. In order to make their forecasts, analysts have to guess the amount of free cash flow which a firm will generate in the period ahead. In order to do this analysts often rely upon the company's directors. Not surprisingly, company directors are often rather optimistic when it comes to judging their own company's future performance.

> *'All you need in life is ignorance and confidence. Then success is sure.'*
> MARK TWAIN

The vast majority of recommendations made by analysts are 'buys' rather than 'sells'. Buy recommendations issued by analysts often outnumber sell recommendations by 100 to 1. In other words analysts are recommending 100 shares as a 'buy' for every one they are recommending as a 'sell'. This is patent nonsense. The sad truth is that analysts earn millions by disregarding the welfare of their investing clients while promoting the financial interests of their employers.

Can it possibly be true that nearly all companies are worth buying? Of course not. By the time analysts finally issue a 'sell' warning on a stock it is usually far too late for investors to get out with anything other than crumbs.

Analysts sometimes describe shares as 'hold' rather than a 'buy' or a 'sell'. They do this to avoid upsetting people. (Company directors and executives are likely to be unhappy if a bank's analyst describes their shares as a 'sell'.) There are, in reality, only two ways to describe a share. It is either a 'buy' or it is a 'sell'. If you wouldn't buy it then you shouldn't be holding it.

Analysts are supposed to predict. But they usually confine themselves to telling people what they already know. When a share is doing well analysts jump on the bandwagon and say how good it is. They give it a stamp of approval by labelling it with a 'buy' recommendation. Conversely, when a share is doing badly, analysts give it a good kicking and tell investors to avoid it at all costs. It is the work of analysts which at least partly explains why share prices tend to rise far too much and then tend to fall far too much.

Many professional analysts make the mistake of forecasting (or attempting to forecast) what the stock market will do on the basis of current economic information. This is dangerous stuff because the stock market does not follow the economy; the stock market leads the economy and share prices predict the future rather than reflect the past. Current economic information is historic. It relates to the past. And it pays no regard to the future. Economic data is history. The stock market is constantly trying to look into the future. The price of a share today tells you what the market thinks the company will be worth in the future. That is one of the most important things to understand about investing in shares. It's also one of the least known. And, surprisingly, it seems to me that a good many analysts aren't aware of this.

Analysts claim that they use many different tools in order to reach their conclusions. They have lengthy meetings with company managers. They use specially written software to evaluate the companies they write about. They collect (and feed into their computers) endless bits of information. They are paid fortunes. And their expenses are stratospheric. But, in the end, the advice they provide is at best worthless and at worst misleading.

The sad truth is that analysts are self-serving; protecting the interests of the institution for which they work (and, inevitably, their own interests). They have betrayed investors and are best ignored. Their only real value, curiously, is as a guide for contrarians. When all the economists and analysts agree on something they are almost certainly wrong. Whatever they are predicting will almost certainly not happen. There are several reasons for this.

First, analysts and other so-called experts are not as clever as they think they are. Many of them are stupid and incompetent.

Second, many analysts are bent. They are under pressure to produce favourable recommendations. And, too often, they succumb to that pressure. The advice they give is designed to satisfy the needs of their employers (banks and other institutions) and the companies paying their employers to represent them. The Financial Services Authority in the UK found that almost 80% of recommendations from investment banks which also acted as advisers to the companies in question were 'buys'. This was twice as high as the percentage of 'buys' where the investment bank did not work for the company in question. Honest, impartial analysts are about as common as honest politicians. Analysts make second-hand car dealers look ethical. Unless you know the exact nature of the relationship between an analyst writing a research report, the company concerned and the investment bank which pays the analyst's salary, it is very difficult to assess the value of an analyst's report. That level of information is virtually impossible for investors to find and so all analysts' research is worthless and should be ignored. Many so-called experts who promoted Internet stocks with pseudo-scientific hogwash (describing the Internet as a new paradigm) were discredited as dishonest, but far from being banished most are still operating and selling new absurd and shameful nonsenses. Analysts had 19 buy recommendations on Enron at the time it went bust. Between 1996 and 2000 the shares had gone up 350% but earnings per share had gone up 1%.

Enron reported wonderful profits to shareholders and was one of the most admired companies in America. But it told the Internal Revenue Service that it had $3 billion in cumulative losses and the IRS accepted this. Consequently the company paid no taxes. The IRS would have looked at the accounts. They do not allow companies to avoid paying taxes when they are making profits. But the analysts ignored this clear evidence that the company was in trouble. (Companies which are healthy and profitable are usually paying taxes at the normal rate.)

The bottom line is that many analysts are over informed and spend too much time looking at the trees and missing the wood. They are so busy concentrating on minutiae that they miss the strategic moves.

* * *

Macroeconomic forecasting is difficult. Economists invariably fail to forecast recessions and predicting bear markets has proved tricky for them. Most economists agreed that the USA would avoid recessions in 1969-70, 1973-4, 1981-82 and 1990. They were wrong all four times. Generally speaking, economic forecasts are so bad that you're better off believing the opposite, rather than the forecast that the economist has made. It is perhaps not surprising that there aren't many rich economists around. Most of them are academics who make what money they have by teaching, writing and talking about finance.

* * *

Burton G. Malkiel concludes that there are five factors explaining why security analysts have such difficulty in predicting the future. His five factors are:

1. The influence of random events.
2. The production of dubious reported earnings through 'creative' accounting.
3. The basic incompetence of many of the analysts themselves.
4. The loss of the best analysts to the sales desk or to portfolio management.
5. The conflicts of interest facing security analysts at firms with large investment banking operations.

The end result is that when analysts say 'buy' I am inclined to consider selling. When they say 'sell' I am inclined to consider buying. Generally speaking, if all the analysts are praising something you have bought it is probably time to sell, whereas if all the analysts are damning something it is probably time to buy it. Portfolios made up of shares least popular with city analysts have worked well. When Investors Chronicle magazine recommended buying the 10 shares that got the worst press from stockbrokers' analysts they found that a year later the portfolio had risen by 20.4% – a significant 4.6% better than the FTSE All Share's performance during the same period. Research in America has shown the same thing: it is possible to beat the market by buying Wall Street's least favourite stocks.

Finally, here are some concluding thoughts about analysts:

1. Ignore forecasts and predictions which seem unbelievably precise. They may be precise but they are unbelievable. When a forecaster announces that house prices will rise by 8.3% during the next 12 months you can happily ignore everything he or she says.
2. If all analysts scream 'sell' there is a good chance that a share will be pushed down further than is justified. If all analysts scream 'buy' then a share is likely to go up far too much. Analysts inflate bubbles and then ensure that the bubble bursting process is as messy and as expensive as can be.
3. Analysts have a tendency to fall in love with the stocks they cover. This isn't just because they are being paid to promote those stocks. Analysts also seem to get close to the stocks on their 'watch' list. It's a variation on the Stockholm syndrome. They end up believing that the stocks they cover are better than all others and will survive whatever happens.
4. It is wise for investors to assume that everything that analysts (and investment bankers and brokers) say is a lie. Occasionally, analysts may tell the truth (probably because it serves their interest to do so and possibly by accident). But because you will never be able to tell whether they are lying or telling the truth the only safe approach is to assume that everything they say is a lie. There are some analysts who get it right. But you will never know who they are. And so they are all useless.

ASSET ALLOCATION

'As time goes on, I get more and more convinced that the right method in investment is to put fairly large sums into enterprises which one thinks one knows something about and in the management of which one thoroughly believes. It is a mistake to think that one limits one's risk by spreading too much between enterprises about which one knows little and has no reason for special confidence. One's knowledge and experience are definitely limited and there are seldom more than two or three enterprises at any given time in which I personally feel myself entitled to put full confidence.'

JOHN MAYNARD KEYNES

Many investors spend a lot of effort trying to time the market or trying to pick stocks. A study in 1986 by Gary Brinson and colleagues called *The Determinants of Portfolio Performance* involved an analysis of 91 pension funds. The aim was to find out what decided performance most: asset allocation (policy), stock-picking, market timing or costs.

The results showed that asset allocation (between stocks, bonds and cash) decided 94% of performance. Stock picking and market timing had no useful effect. The busiest fund managers seemed to harm their results by too much action (partly because trading involves costs).

The skill, it seems, lies not in choosing particular companies or properties to invest in, but in picking asset classes and investment cycles. If you invest at a time when the stock market is going up then it doesn't terribly much matter which shares you pick – most of them will go up. But if you invest at a time when the market is going down then most of the shares you choose will fall.

More equities mean more risk and volatility but (usually) better returns. With bonds and cash returns tend to be stable but lower.

AVERAGING UP AND DOWN

'Stock prices are anchored to 'fundamentals' but the anchor is easily pulled up and then dropped in another place. Given that expected growth rates and the price the market is willing to pay for growth can change rapidly on the basis of market psychology, the concept of a firm intrinsic value for shares must be an elusive will-o-the-wisp.'
BURTON MALKIEL

If you buy a share and it falls in price for no obvious reason (there has been no change in the company's circumstances or the investing environment) you have three options. You can sell the share. You can hold on and hope it goes back up. Or you can buy more on the grounds that it was worth buying when it was more expensive and so it is now even more worth buying. The third option is called 'averaging down' and the experts say you should never do it. They call it throwing good money after bad.

I'm not sure that the experts are right.

My feeling is that if you thought a share was worth £4 and it falls to £3 (without there being any change in circumstances) then the share must be a bargain at £3. If you buy more shares at the lower price then your average purchase price will be between £3 and £4.

If the share price then falls to £2 and you buy more your average price will be even lower.

Averaging down is a contrarian method of investing. It is contrary to the usually accepted rules.

Many investors claim that they never average losses. They say that if an investment has gone down in price then it means that they made a mistake and that they should be selling not buying more. I can see the sense in the argument but it isn't one that I follow. I believe that I am unlikely to be able to pick the 'bottom' and that, therefore, it is quite possible that an investment I make may fall in price after I have bought it. But if I still believe in my original choice then the investment is now an even better buy than it was when I made my first purchase. For this reason I will, if I am planning to make a new investment, sometimes begin by investing only a proportion of the amount I intend to invest. Then in a week or two's time I will invest some more – whether the price has fallen or risen. And in another week or two's time I will invest a third time. This method enables me to avoid having to try and time an investment – a traditionally impossible task.

I do the same thing when I am selling. When I think a share may be a little expensive, even though the price is still rising, I sell some and then wait a while before selling some more.

The opposite of averaging down is averaging up. This only makes good sense if the argument in favour of the share concerned has improved.

BANK DEPOSITS

'It is amazing that this monster interest has not devoured the whole of humanity. It would have done so long ago had not bankruptcy and revolution acted as counter-poisons.'
NAPOLEON BONAPARTE

There are a few things to consider when putting your money in a bank:

1. How safe is the bank (and, therefore, how safe is your money)? Will the bank look after your money and remain solvent? Will you be able to get your money back when you need it to buy something? Generally speaking, the higher the return the greater the risk. If Honest Albert's International Corner Bank offers you 22% interest and all the High Street banks are offering 3% then you're risking your money if you decide to trust your money to Honest Albert.
2. How much interest are you getting on your money? If you're going to give your money to the bank to look after, you are entitled to receive 'rent' on your money. The bank is looking after your money, it is true, but they won't just stick it in a vault and shut the door on it. They will lend it out and charge interest on it. So it's only fair and decent that you should get a share of the interest.
3. The amount of interest you receive (known as the yield) will depend on the length of time for which you are prepared to loan the bank your money. Banks will often pay a higher rate of interest to depositors who are prepared to abandon access to their money for longer periods. Give your money to a bank and tell them that you don't want it back for a year and

you will probably get a higher rate of interest than if you tell them that you want instant access to your money. But be wary and remember that any institution offering very high interest rates is probably having difficulty attracting money.

> *'A lot of people will also urge you to put some money in a bank, and in fact – within reason – this is very good advice. But don't go overboard. Remember, what you are doing is giving your money to somebody else to hold on to, and I think that it is worth keeping in mind that the businessmen who run banks are so worried about holding on to things that they put little chains on all their pens.'*
> MISS PIGGY

4. The more you save, and the longer you save, the more you will benefit from the wonders of compound interest. Albert Einstein once called compounding the eighth wonder of the world. If you start with £100 and increase your capital by 10% every year then at the end of the first year you have £110. But at the end of the second year you actually have £121 because your 10% rise includes the £10 you have added to your total. Compounding helps your wealth to grow faster and faster. Einstein was right. It is the miracle of compound interest which explains why people who look after their money sometimes become extremely rich. As someone (I forget who) once said to me: 'It is the interest on the interest that made me rich.'

> *'A banker is a man who lends you an umbrella when the weather is fair, and takes it away from you when it rains.'*
> ANON

5. Putting your money into a foreign bank, based abroad somewhere, will sometimes produce a higher rate of interest. But beware, there are potential problems. If you put your money into a foreign bank in a foreign country it will usually be in a foreign currency and you will then be susceptible to the vagaries of the currency markets. When a country lowers its interest rates its currency usually suffers in comparison with those of other countries where interest rates are higher. The reason for this is simple. If an investor can choose between putting his money into a currency with a high interest rate and putting it into a currency with a low interest rate which do you think he will choose? Exactly. As long as the value of the high interest rate currency doesn't go down too much (thereby damaging his capital) he will

put his money into the currency producing the high interest rate. Investors who like to think themselves as terribly sophisticated will borrow money in a country whose currency has low interest rates and then invest that money in a country where the currency carries a high interest rate. Their profit is, of course, the difference between the two interest rates. (Of course, if the currency rates change too much the profit can be wiped out and turned into a loss.) The markets (manned by men in shirt sleeves sitting in front of computer screens) usually try to anticipate all this action, of course. Brokers and banks have a view about whether or not central banks are likely to lower or raise interest rates. And so they mark currencies up or down accordingly. Playing with currencies is really more like gambling than investing. I don't recommend that you do it with your own hard-earned savings.

6. If you remain a passive investor (leaving your savings on deposit at the bank is about as passive as you can get) you will not become rich because those hard-earned savings will, thanks to inflation, probably be shrinking every day you leave them there. In order to flourish and grow money, like seeds, needs nurturing. And that means that it needs to be invested with a little more imagination.
7. One thing is certain: a cash deposit is not a 'risk free' investment. Even if your cash doesn't disappear with the bank in which you put it, its purchasing power will shrink whenever inflation rates are higher than interest rates (which seems to be most of the time these days).
8. For many years Money Market funds were regarded as excellent alternatives to bank deposit accounts. Money Market funds are, as the name suggests, simply funds in which the invested money is spread among a number of banks. The investor in a Money Market fund has the reassurance of knowing that his money is spread around – rather than being deposited in a single bank. But the aura of safety that used to surround Money Market funds has disappeared. During the autumn of 2008 five out of 29 Money Market funds lost money over a single three month period. How did they do that? Simple. They lost money because some of the institutions in which the money was deposited went bust.

> *'Banking was conceived in iniquity and born in sin.'*
> SIR JOSIAH STAMP

9. People expect banks to protect their interests – but why should they? Banks cannot look after the interests of shareholders and customers at the same time since their interests are often diametrically opposed (even though both groups of people may be the same). The shareholder wants the bank to

make huge profits and to pay its depositors a very low rate of interest. The customer wants the bank to do everything for free and to pay high rates of interest on its deposits.

10. And remember: lower interest rates make equities more attractive to most investors. If Gilbert can only get 2.5% interest on bank deposits, but he can get dividends of 5% on investments in Blue Chip companies then he will probably think it makes sense to use his money to buy Blue Chip companies rather than to leave his money on deposit in the bank. Lower interest rates also mean that companies (many of which have borrowed money to expand) will have to pay less interest on their loans. This makes them more profitable – and makes them less likely to default on interest payments. On the other hand, high interest rates make equities less attractive. If Gilbert can get 15% from a bank deposit, dividends paying 5% don't look quite so enchanting. And with interest rates high, companies with a lot of debt are more likely to get into trouble. So, Gilbert sells his shares and puts his money on deposit in the bank and hopes that the bank doesn't go bust and take his money with it.

BEAR AND BULL MARKETS

'Bull markets are born on pessimism, grow on scepticism, mature on optimism and die on euphoria. The time of maximum pessimism is the best time to buy, and the time of maximum optimism is the best time to sell.'
SIR JOHN TEMPLETON

A bull is someone who is optimistic about prospects and thinks a share, or the market as a whole, is going to go up. A bear is someone who is pessimistic about prospects and thinks a share, or the market as a whole, is going to go down. A bull market is one in which shares are soaring ever upwards. A bear market is one in which shares are going down. In a bull market even idiots can make money. In a bear market even geniuses can lose it.

Bear markets can do enormous damage to the wealth of investors and can sometimes be horrendous. In the UK, shares slumped by 74% in real terms in 1973-74. The 1973-74 crash resulted in many big funds disappearing completely. (If you spotted that they were too high beforehand, and you got at least some of your money into cash, this was a buying opportunity of a lifetime.) When there are hard times people spend less. This means that corporate profits must fall. But just as share prices go up too much during a bull market, so they usually go down too much during a bear market. At a bear market bottom shares usually have dividend yields of 5-6%. Bear markets can seem to go on for ever.

The Japanese stock market peaked in the late 1980's. Twenty years later it was still on a downward slide. After two decades of waiting, investors who still held Japanese shares which they had bought in 1987, were sitting on a loss of well over half their original investment.

In a secular bear market, a big bear market where prices seem destined to fall for ever, the decline is likely to be at least 40%. The bear market will probably last for up to five years by which time pessimistic investors will be convinced that the end of the world has come and formerly optimistic investors will be convinced that the bears are right. At the end of the bear market there may well be another five years of nothingness as investors get accustomed to the fact that prices aren't still going down. Cyclical bear markets are much less dramatic and far less destructive.

Bear markets can last longer than most people think and do far more damage than is generally imagined. In a real bear market almost everyone who has money becomes poorer (while, paradoxically, those who have nothing or are in debt may emerge from the chaos much better off since interest rates will be low and inflation may be high.) After the stock market crash of 1929 the American market took 25 years to go higher. In 1957 the Dow Jones index was at 685. In 1970 it was lower than that. In 1966 the Dow Jones was up at 995. By 1981 it was down to 776.

Investors who had merely followed the index over those periods would have lost serious amounts of money when costs and commissions are included.

* * *

Bull and bear markets can last a long time. Here, for example, is a list of major American bull and bear markets in the 20th Century.

1. 1921 to 1929: bull (8 years)
2. 1929 to 1949: bear (20 years)
3. 1949 to 1966: bull (17 years)
4. 1966 to 1982: bear (16 years)
5. 1982 to 2000: bull (18 years)

In a real bear market everything goes down – property, shares, commodities, bonds and sometimes even gold. And, if inflation is higher than interest rates, even cash loses value. Sometimes, as in 2008, nothing remains safe. Shares, commodities, bonds, property were all falling rapidly. Putting money into cash is equally foolish because inflation means that the purchasing value of your money is shrinking. (Plus there is, of course, the risk that the bank holding your cash might go bust and take your cash with it.) Don't believe anyone who tells you that bonds are a safe place to put your money during difficult times. There was a bear market in bonds that lasted from 1947 to 1981. Mark Twain once pointed out that at times like these investors worry about the return *of* their capital, not the return *on* their capital.

Once a bear market develops there is a tendency for analysts, journalists and investors to concentrate on bad news. Every piece of bad news is highlighted and bits and pieces of good news are ignored. The negative is accentuated and the positive is eliminated. Share prices fall more. Investors are terrified. They sell everything they can. (Because they hate taking losses, they sell their best investments first, taking the profits where they can and retaining the shares that have fallen the most.) Eventually, there is usually a 'capitulation' point at which everyone – analysts, brokers, journalists and investors – decide that shares are no good to man or beast and should never, ever be bought again.

In long bear markets there can often be dramatic upsurges in share prices. Shares may go up to four times the level they were at. And then carry on going down again. If you suspect that you are in a bear market you should be very careful. At the least you should try to own things that pay you to own them – stocks that pay decent, well-covered dividends, for example.

In a bear market share prices never seem too low, but in a bull market share prices never seem too high to buy. Profits are easy. In a bear market the slightest bit of bad news will send shares into a tailspin. Exactly the opposite happens in a bull market when shares will often fight a wall of worry. Investors ignore bad news as irrelevant. Slowdowns in profits, rises in input costs, industrial action – all are deemed irrelevant as investors chase prices ever higher, frightened not to buy (and far too frightened to sell) lest they miss out on the chance of huge, apparently no-risk profits. Investors take risks; hope triumphs over fear. But it is vital to remember that when a boom ends the bad years will last just as long as the boom – probably longer. And the fall will be further, as well as lasting for longer, than the rise. When the prices of shares and property have risen to such high levels that experts are explaining that 'it's different this time' and 'it's a new paradigm' then it is time be worried. When the good times end, the bad times will be deeper, and last longer, than seems possible. That is what history teaches us. And it is the way things are.

There is, of course, a third option: the time when share prices are going nowhere in particular. And then, if you have money which you are waiting to invest you must either wait to see if you can see a new direction or else invest in dribs and drabs. The most important thing any investor can do is learn to recognise the onset of a bear market. In a real bear market your primary aim should be to preserve your capital. When you think the market has reached its bottom, or is close to its bottom will be the time to start investing again.

It is sometimes easier to suspect that the whole market has reached a bottom than to decide which particular sectors are most likely to recover fastest and furthest. Following a specific investment strategy and taking a punt on a particular sector will then be more dangerous than simply investing in the whole market by buying a tracker fund or a general investment trust. It is worth remembering that most successful investors claim that the really big money is to be made by being a contrarian in a serious bear market – provided that you can pick a moment to buy when it seems that the end of the world has come and no one else wants to buy. And then buy companies which you believe will survive, which will not need to raise fresh capital (because that would dilute the value of your holding), which will not lose a share of their market because they do not have the money to stay in business through the worst of the economic downturn and which will still be able to take advantage of the boom when it (eventually) comes. Buy too soon as a bear market falls and you could lose a lot of money for bears are dangerous beasts, but get your timing right and you could make the killing of a lifetime.

In contrast, handling a bull market is easy. You buy stuff and it goes up in price. In a real bull market you can buy almost anything and it will go up. Surviving in a bear market is much more difficult than thriving in a bull market. Some people claim they can make money in bear markets by trading aggressively. But such folk always seem to have mislaid the paperwork that proves how they did it.

Towards the end of a long bull market investors tend to be nervous. When there is a correction, and prices start to dip, investors worry that their gains are going to disappear. They are likely to sell their best investments in order to pocket their profits. (Unwisely, they continue to hold their bad investments so that they don't have to face the pain of crystallising their losses.)

But after a day or two they tend to go back into the market. The bull market has given investors false confidence and encouraged them to believe that being fully invested is the best way to make big profits. During the bull market they will have got used to the idea that dips are buying opportunities. And so they buy back the stuff they've sold. If they've done well they might even make a small profit.

But then the bear bites back.

At the end of a bull market shares will become overpriced and the professionals will come up with all sorts of explanations for this. 'The rules have changed,' sneer arrogant, bright young things in silk suits.

The best strategy is to wait for the professionals to panic and start dumping shares.

Eventually shares will become underpriced.

BONDS AND GILTS

'An investor who is seriously eager to make money doesn't have to watch the markets every day. He just has to make, once in a while, a good investment decision on the trends that will last for a number of years.'
MARC FABER

A bond is just a rather fancy IOU issued by someone grand who wants to borrow money but wants to make it sound rather formal and impressive. When companies borrow money they call their IOUs 'bonds'. When governments borrow money they call their bonds something different so that lenders don't get confused (or, perhaps, so that they do). When the British Government borrows money its bonds are called gilts (short for gilt-edged securities). When the American Government borrows money its bonds are called 'Treasuries' (with a capital T to show how important they are).

Theoretically, a gilt is a security which is considered reliable and likely to pay dividends or interest over a long period of time. However, the word is usually kept to describe bonds issued by financially responsible governments or governments which are regarded as financially responsible (which actually isn't the same thing at all).

Bonds and gilts are convenient because they can be bought and sold just like pots of jam, houses and shares. There are two main ways in which bonds vary.

First, there is the amount of interest that is paid. This is known as the 'coupon' because it sounds more impressive and because, at some time in the past, bonds were issued with little coupons attached that you could exchange for money. The word 'coupon' has a number of possible meanings but it is commonly used to describe the nominal rate of interest on a fixed interest security. The word 'coupon' is used by bankers and investment professionals to confuse ordinary mortals. Bankers, like all quasi-professionals, like to think that they are skilled and educated professionals, on a par with doctors and lawyers, and so they try to give themselves an arcane, incomprehensible language just like doctors and lawyers. Incidentally, bankers also often talk about basis points when talking about yields and interest rates. A basis point is one hundredth of one per cent or 0.01%. So, if your bank's interest rate goes up from 7% to 8% it will have risen by 100 basis points.

Second, there is the length of time that the bond lasts before it expires. When it expires the owner of the bond at the time receives a sum of money, the amount of which was usually determined when the bond was issued.

The price of a bond can vary throughout its life. If a bond was issued when interest rates were high its coupon might have been 10%. If interest rates subsequently fall, buyers might be prepared to pay more for such a good rate of interest and so the value of the bond will rise and the original owner (if he still owns it) will make a capital gain.

And, although there are an almost infinite number of complications, that is more or less the way that bonds operate. When interest rates go up (and the rate of interest paid by a bank to a depositor rises) the purchase prices of bonds tend to fall. When interest rates go down (and the interest paid by bonds may seem more attractive) the purchase prices of bonds may rise.

People who buy bonds receive interest payments until their bonds expire or are sold. And when the bonds expire or are sold the owner either makes a capital gain (because the value of the bond is more than the price they paid) or they make a capital loss (because the value of the bond is less than the price they paid).

Bonds are riskier than most people think. Investors buy bonds with the 'safe' part of their portfolio in the belief that bonds are solid investments which produce a steady income and don't move about much. Not much of this is true. Bonds may produce a steady income (unless they go bust) but they are likely to move about far more than you might expect.

Corporate bonds, the ones issued by companies, can be extravagantly volatile. During the financial collapse of 2008 corporate bonds went downhill faster than an alpine skier.

Some bonds, the ones which are considered riskiest, are known as junk bonds. The interest paid by junk bonds may sound very appealing (15% for example, in an era of low interest rates) but I leave junk bonds to the junk bond professionals. Junk bonds are bonds that are risky. And it is because they are risky that they offer a high rate of interest. If you are the sort of person who feels happy to put all your savings on a horse running in the 2 o'clock at Newbury then you will probably be the sort of investor who will be suitable for junk bonds.

The best and safest investments in terms of capital and income are undoubtedly government bonds which are issued by fairly large, stable governments.

There are two main varieties of bonds issued by governments. First, there are the ones which simply pay a small amount of interest. Then there are the ones which are index linked – and which are designed to pay interest at or slightly above the official rate of inflation. These won't keep up with the real rate of inflation (because the level of inflation that index linked bonds protect you against is the variety defined by the government, the sort that doesn't include such 'irrelevant' factors as energy costs, housing costs or food) but government bonds aren't likely to disappear overnight. And the income should keep on coming. Government bonds are liquid (you can get your money back at short notice), the expenses are low and there are sometimes significant tax advantages to be had. You don't have to keep an eye on them and if you purchase long-term bonds the fluctuations in the capital price are irrelevant as long as you are happy with the interest you accepted when you first bought them.

Gilts and bonds are generally thought to be 'safe and stable' investments. But they aren't really as safe or as stable as their reputation sometimes suggests. Their value can rise and fall just as share prices can rise and fall. Many gilts and bonds which were issued years ago are now worth considerably more than they were when they were issued. In times of high inflation gilts and bonds had to be issued with a high coupon in order to attract buyers. As inflation (and general interest rates) have fallen so the price of these gilts has risen. But, on the other hand, there are quite a few gilts around which have gone down in price since they were first issued.

It is widely assumed that governments do not default, and that this makes government bonds totally safe. This is definitely not true. In 2001 the country Argentina defaulted on $100 billion of its loans held by foreigners. In 2005 Argentine generously agreed to repay these loans but said that it could only afford to pay 34 cents on the dollar. This meant that the Argentinian people gained quite a few billion and the investors who had trusted the Argentinian Government lost quite a few billion.

Brokers

'Stockbroking is a trade found in fraud, born of deceit and nourished by trick, cheat, wheedle forgeries, falsehoods and all sorts of delusions.'
Daniel Defoe

There are plenty of ways to trade shares but one of the easiest is probably to do it through your bank. This is easy because you can trade in and out of your current account. If you choose a specialist broker make sure that they are properly registered with all the relevant authorities. Brokers charge more for telephone orders than for Internet orders but I don't trade on line. It may be easy and quick (and cheap) but I fear it also makes life too easy for fraudsters.

Here are some terms you'll hear from (or in relation to) brokers:

1. Execution only dealing

As the name suggests this means that instead of offering you advice the broker simply buys and sells whatever you tell him to buy and sell. I prefer this sort of relationship with my broker.

2. Margin

A loan from a broker to enable the investor to buy shares is called 'margin'. And so investors going into debt are said to buy 'on margin'. If things go badly and the price of the share falls, the broker will call the investor and ask for more money (this is known as a 'margin call'). I never borrow money to buy shares.

3. Market order

If you buy shares 'at the market' or 'at best' your order will be filled as soon as possible and at the best price available at the time. There is no guarantee about the price you will pay but you will get the shares.

And here is something to remember: A brokerage account that can't cope when there isn't any pressure is going to fail completely when the pressure is on. If your broker is slow, or has frequent computer malfunctions when things in the market are peaceful, they will not be able to cope when things in the market are chaotic – at the very time when you need to get in touch with them quickly. So, if your broker is slow, if there are long delays in answering the phone or they are always having unspecified problems dump them and move your money elsewhere. Even cheap dealing becomes expensive when you cannot deal when you want to.

> *'Every man his own broker.'*
> THOMAS MORTIMER
> (THOMAS MORTIMER WROTE THE FIRST INVESTMENT BOOK IN THE 1750'S.)

4. Position

Your position is the number of shares you hold in a security. And so, for example, you might say: 'My position in KuddlyBears Inc is 1,500 shares'.

5. Fundamental Analysis

Analysing a company's prospects by looking at its balance sheet and so on is known as fundamental analysis. Fundamental analysts check all the things that can be found out about the company. The problem is that there are, of course, still many things which remain unknown. And how do you decide how much weight to attach to each piece of information? There's also the problem that although the analyst's interpretation of the facts may be accurate the market may remain stubbornly 'wrong' for years to come. And there is the added problem that fundamental analysis depends totally on things that have happened in the past. And the past, as the authorities insist we be constantly reminded, is no guarantee of the future.

6. Bid-Offer spread

The bid/offer spread is the difference between the price you will pay if you buy and the price you will receive if you sell. This is how the marketmakers (people who buy and sell shares for a living) make part of their profit. (They also charge a commission.) The bid/offer spread will widen when a share or investment is difficult to trade (illiquid) and become narrower when liquidity is good. The spread is, therefore, usually wider for shares in small companies than it is for larger companies. With some shares the spread can be considerable. This is particularly likely to be a problem with a low cost share. If (for example) you have to pay 5p for a share but the selling price is 4p you will lose 20% of your money if you resell immediately. I wouldn't usually buy a share which brought that sort of disadvantage with it.

7. Churning

Trading costs can ruin a portfolio's performance. Add the difference in the buy and sell prices to the commissions that are charged and the taxes that have to be paid and every 'deal' becomes expensive. Some fund managers (and many managers of private portfolios) deliberately buy and sell as often as they can in order to maximise their own commissions and, therefore, their own profits. This is called 'churning' and is a despicable practice.

Investment costs eat away at your capital. Such costs are certain and remorseless. And their effect compounds. Every £1 you pay in costs is £1 you no longer have to invest. Costs tend to destroy investment performance more than anything else. Expenses turn investing into a worse than zero sum game.

> *'A broker is someone who invests your money until it is all gone.'*
> WOODY ALLEN

8. Offshore

Offshore is anywhere that isn't the country where you live. If you are an American, Britain is offshore. To people throughout the world Britain is a major offshore tax haven. London is the money laundering capital of the world for people who aren't British. Governments can sometimes get very greedy. It is not unknown for governments to stop their citizens moving their money out of their country. In bad times governments confiscate money, property and anything they can get their hands on – which means anything that is nailed down and anything that is securely tucked away in a bank. For this reason alone, having some money in an offshore bank might be a good idea.

9. Outperformance and Underperformance

A share or another asset that goes up faster than the market generally is said to be outperforming. Similarly, a share that doesn't go down as fast as the rest of the market is outperforming. A share or another asset that doesn't go up as fast as the rest of the market (or goes down faster than the market) generally is said to be underperforming.

10. Paper profits

Don't confuse real profits with paper profits. A paper profit is a gain which has not yet been realised because the position hasn't been 'closed'. A paper profit isn't something you can spend, because you don't have the money. And, unless you close the position to your advantage, you may never have the money.

11. Ratings agencies

Formidable rating agencies with tremendous international reputations give investment products rating. Traditionally a triple A rating (AAA) suggests that the institution, or its product, is as safe as houses. Well, safer if you're in the middle of a housing crash or live in something built on a flood plain. I ignore such ratings and regard them as worthless. During the crash season of 2008 institutions and products with AAA ratings were disappearing from the scene with a rapidity that would have caused red faces at the ratings agencies had they been capable of embarrassment.

The ratings agencies which hand down these ratings from on high are private companies. They are paid huge fees by the companies which they rate. I no longer pay any attention whatsoever to ratings given to bonds, institutions or anything else. My advice is that all such ratings are worthless. A triple A rating is an AAA rating until the day the rating agency changes it to something less impressive, or the day the company goes bust – which may, indeed, be the same day.

12. Returns

The return is, not surprisingly perhaps, what you get back. Don't be greedy. Bull markets have given many investors an exaggerated idea of what return they can expect from their investments. Anyone who tries to get an endless 15% return on their capital will, outside a roaring bull market, be taking huge risks. And the chances are that they will lose money, rather than make it. In the real world a return of 8% after tax is fantastic. A return of 2% above inflation is perfectly acceptable. In a high inflation world, just beating inflation (and ensuring that your capital preserves its purchasing power) is creditable.

13. The Rule of 72

The Rule of 72 is the one mathematical oddity that is really useful. It enables you to find out how long it will take to double the size of an investment. All you need to know is the annual return you are expecting.

Divide the expected rate of return (the growth rate) into 72 and the number you get is the approximate number of years it will take for the investment to double.

So, if your annual return is 6% it will take 12 years for your investment to double. (72 divided by 6 = 12). If your annual return is a much healthier 9% it will take 8 years for your investment to double. (72 divided by 9 = 8). And if your annual return is a miserable 3% it will take 24 years to double your money. (72 divided by 3 = 24).

Using the Rule of 72 it is possible to see just how dramatic an effect compound interest can have once an investment has started to grow.

So, if you start with an investment of £1,000 and you manage to obtain a 12% return you will have £2,000 in just six years. (72 divided by 12 = 6). And if your money keeps doubling every six years you will have £4,000 in 12 years, £8,000 in 18 years, £16,000 in 24 years and £32,000 in 30 years. Add a nought to a sum of £1,000 to turn it into £10,000 and you can see that at the end of 30 years you'll have a pension pot worth around a third of a million pounds.

If your money is growing at 10% per year then it will double in around seven years. If it is growing at 5% per year then it will double in around 14 years. If it is growing at 1% per year (and in high inflationary times you may be lucky if your after tax gain is that high) then it will double in around 70 years.

If you are feeling more ambitious, you can divide 115 by the interest rate (or rate of growth you are getting) to find how long it will take for your money to triple.

14. Stop-loss orders

Investment journalists often tell their readers to put stop-loss orders on shares they recommend. The idea is that the broker sells the share once the price falls to the stop-loss price that the customer has designated. The aim is to minimise losses. Journalists and investment advisers recommend stop-loss orders because they enable them to claim that their advice is more successful than it often is. So, for example, if they recommend that their readers buy shares at £1.50 and put a stop-loss order of £1.20 on the holding, the investor can (theoretically) lose only 30 pence per share.

There are, however, several problems. First, not all brokers will provide a stop-loss selling service. If your broker won't (and in my experience most won't) you have to sit there all day watching share prices to see if any of your holdings totters down through your stop-loss level. Life is too short for that. I have better things to do with my time and I'm sure you have too. Second, if a share is falling rapidly it may not be possible to sell it at the stop-loss price. The price obtained may be much lower than the £1.20 requested. Third, shares which are volatile may wander through the stop-loss price and trigger an unwanted sale before going back up again. You might want to hold onto the share, but your holding will be sold and you will have made a loss.

Many investors who favour stop-losses raise their stop-loss price as the share price rises. They do this to ensure that if a share goes up 50% and then down, say 10%, they can sell without losing the rest of their profit. The problem here is that prices rarely go up in a straight line and it is perfectly possible that if the share hadn't been sold it might have gone up another 50%. Or 500%. Who knows?

My view is that stop-losses are impractical and a waste of time.

If you have done your research and you believe in the share you have bought, and have great expectations, why sell it just because the price goes down? You should, of course, sell if the fundamentals have changed. But if the fundamentals don't change, and your expectations are still the same, and the share becomes cheaper that could just mean that the share is even more of a 'buy'. Shares often go up and down for no very good reason. A geopolitical shock might have affected your shares temporarily. There might have been an item of news which scared the whole market and produced a general overreaction. A stop loss might mean that you sell shares that might have made you a lot of money.

The bottom line is that I believe that stop-losses are for sissies who can't trust themselves to make decent decisions.

15. Short selling

Short selling is selling shares you don't own in the hope that the price will fall. If this happens you will be able to buy the shares you have sold but don't own. You will pay less for them than the buyer who bought from you paid and so you will make a profit. The snag (and it's a big one) is that you can lose everything (and more) by short selling. The maximum profit you can make when shorting is 100% (if you can buy the share you have shorted back for nothing) but the maximum loss is everything you have and then more (if you have to pay a much higher price for the share because it has risen enormously since you sold it). If you buy a share at £1 and it falls to £0 you have lost only what you invested. But if you are short selling and you sell a share for £1, hoping to be able to buy it cheaper, you will be in a tricky position if the share price goes up to £50 or £100. When you buy long you can only lose what you have invested. When you short sell the sky is the limit.

Bottom line? Going short is for gamblers who want to lose their money so that they can feel aggrieved with society and bad about themselves.

Here are three basic terms all investors should know:

Long: You are 'long' in a share or an asset class if you invested in it, or have an interest in it, or in some other way will benefit if the price goes up and lose if the price goes down.

Short: You are short in a sector or share if you will profit if the value of the sector or share goes down. You can 'short' shares by selling them when you don't own any or by using complex financial instruments known as derivatives.

Flat: If you are neither 'long' nor 'short' then you are flat. If you don't have a financial interest in pork bellies (you don't stand to make money whatever happens to their price) then you are 'flat pork bellies' and you probably sleep better at night than the bloke who isn't.

16. Top Down and Top Up Investing

Top Down investing means selecting and buying shares according to sector or geographical area. The investor picks a sector (or a country or region) and then picks shares within that sector, country or region. The antonym is Bottom Up Investing which means buying individual shares for their own special appeal and ignoring wider criteria – such as the stability of the sector or the currency involved.

17. Underweight and Overweight

You are underweight if you don't have as much money invested in an individual share (or sector) as you would if you were trying to match a specified benchmark such as, for example, the FTSE 100 or the FTSE All Share Index. In contrast (and I bet you didn't see this coming) you are overweight if you have more money invested in an individual share or sector than you would have if you were trying to match a specified benchmark such as, for example, the FTSE All Share Index or the FTSE 100.

18. Trackers

When you are buying a tracker to follow the market there are several options because the market is subdivided. If you are investing in the UK you can buy a tracker following the FTSE 100, the FTSE 250 or the FTSE All Share. You will probably not be surprised to learn that the first of these follows the fortunes of shares in the FTSE 100, the second follows the fortunes of shares in the FTSE 250 and the third follows all the shares quoted on the stock exchange.

Funds which aim to match the rise and fall of a particular index are known as trackers. Since the dealing for tracker funds is usually done by computer the costs should be considerably lower than for funds where the dealing is done by absurdly overpaid fund managers. A very large number of allegedly actively managed funds are, in reality, simple tracker funds. The fund manager pretends to be making decisions based on extensive research and experience when, in fact, he is buying and selling shares simply to match what is happening in an index. Investors are paying for a service they aren't getting: they are paying huge annual fees for something that can be purchased for a fraction of the cost by investing in a tracker fund. Most actively managed equity funds have, for many years, underperformed index tracker funds.

BUBBLES

'When the rest of the world is mad, we must imitate them in some measure.'

JOHN MARTIN (JOHN MARTIN WAS A BANKER IN THE 18TH CENTURY, ACTIVE DURING THE SOUTH SEA BUBBLE OF 1720. THE THEORY HE WAS EXPRESSING WAS THAT IT IS POSSIBLE TO BUY OVERPRICED SHARES AND MAKE A PROFIT BY SELLING THEM ON TO THE NEXT SUCKER. THIS IS ALSO KNOWN AS 'MOMENTUM INVESTING' AND IS THE FINANCIAL EQUIVALENT OF THE CHAIN LETTER. INCIDENTALLY, MR MARTIN LOST ALL HIS MONEY WHEN THE SOUTH SEA BUBBLE COLLAPSED.)

A bubble exists when an asset price rises to absurd levels.

Every now and again investment experts talk of a new era. They say stuff like 'things are different now' and they talk about 'gardens of prosperity', 'perfect economic climates' and 'Camelot'. This sort of talk usually leads to the top of a bull market top and, shortly afterwards, a great bear market. Experts talked of a new era in the late 1920's, the late 1960's and the late 1990's. Talk of a new era in the 1920's led to a massive bear market. Talk of a new era in the 1960's led to a massive bear market. And talk of a new era in the late 1990's led to a massive bear market. In each case the bull turned into a bubble which turned into a bear.

There have been many bubbles in history but gullibility and greed ensure they keep coming. Shares in Internet companies were in a bubble at the end of the 20th Century and houses were a bubble of their own at the beginning of the 21st Century. There have always been bubbles, financed by greedy, stupid people. But modern bubbles do more harm because bankers have worked out ways to make them more explosive. And there will, doubtless, be many more bubbles in the future.

When a bubble has grown and grown and grown enthusiasts will always be able to find good reasons why the price of the underlying asset(s) should continue to rise. Bubbles always go on longer than seems possible. The fuel that keeps bubbles growing is money. If there is plenty of money available then it tends to be invested. And when large amounts of money are being invested then the price of something tends to go up.

In a bubble, prices never look silly (however silly they make look in retrospect) and investors who are involved in the bubble believe that prices will continue to rise. The words 'this time it's different' and 'you don't understand the new paradigm' are heard and read often. Finally, everyone has bought into the dream.

The bubble has become a dream. Everyone is calm and happy. But there is a problem. There is no one left to buy. And so when one or two people start to sell (maybe to take a profit or maybe just because they need their money to fund a house purchase, a divorce or another investment) the price must inevitably fall. The fall in price wakes people up. The bubble may not continue to grow indefinitely after all. More people want to sell to preserve their profits. But there is no one buying. And so the price crashes. When a bubble bursts the damage is done quickly and fiercely.

CASHFLOW

'That's the way the money goes, pop goes the weasel.'
W. R. MANDALE

The dot.com companies went bust long before they made a penny in profits. Many had no income at all. Some had never even worked out how they were going to make a profit. It wasn't surprising that when they had burnt through all the cash they'd started with they went bankrupt.

But even small companies which are profitable can go bust.

There are a number of potential downfalls. Cash is the lifeblood of any company and if the cash doesn't flow properly the company will die. Surprisingly, a company that grows too quickly can sometimes get into serious trouble. Look at what could happen to a small publishing company. The publisher does well and sells £1,000,000 worth of books in a month. The opening stock (at the start of the month) cost £100,000 and the extra books it purchases during the month cost another £500,000. At the end of the month the publisher has £150,000 worth of books left unsold in its warehouse. The cost of selling £1,000,000 worth of books is therefore £100,000 plus £500,000 minus £150,000. We will assume that the £150,000 worth of books left will be sold in due course and we will, for the purpose of this exercise, ignore other costs such as employing staff and finding somewhere for them to work. Assuming that other costs are under control the business seems to be doing well. The cost of selling £1,000,000 worth of books is £450,000. So that means that the gross profit for the month is £550,000. The company is doing well.

But it is unlikely that the money for the books which have been sold will be received straight away. Many bookshops take 60 to 90 days credit. Let us assume that only 25% of the books were paid for by the end of that successful month. That means that the cash flow into the company is 25% of £1,000,000 which is £250,000.

On the other hand the suppliers, the people who printed the books, may want to be paid up front. The company is small and new and the printer has lost money before on new publishers. So, in order to get the books it sold, the publisher had to pay out £600,000 during that first month.

The cash flow does not now look so good.

The company has £250,000 in cash but it has spent £600,000. It is short of £350,000 and unless the company has an understanding bank manager and a large overdraft it will go bust. It is, surprisingly easy for an enormously successful company to go bankrupt.

CHARTS (TECHNICAL ANALYSIS)

'History doesn't repeat itself, but it rhymes.'
MARK TWAIN

Some investors believe in charts and historical patterns. They believe that things that happened to shares in the past will happen again in the future. Charts of historic prices are created, and conclusions are drawn. There are many different varieties of chart produced and there are many different ways to interpret charts.

Technical analysts use charts to predict the future path of share prices. They plot their charts using historic prices and details of the number of shares traded. They also create charts showing relative strengths (the way one share performs compared to another, or compared to the index as a whole). They then look for patterns in their charts. The technical analyst believes he can use the past to tell him which way prices will go in the future. I have known many technical analysts but I have to admit that the only ones who genuinely got rich did so not by buying and selling shares but by buying and selling charts.

I steadfastly ignore the claims of those who believe in charts (sometimes also known as technical analysis) just as I ignore the claims made by those who believe that share prices are influenced by the movements of the planets. If prices could be predicted by using charts then all chartists would be rich and we would all be chartists.

Charts are useful only if you use them to tell you what has happened in the past – and not because you expect them to tell you what will happen in the future. A chart showing a company's share price over the last five years may show a steady decline. This does not necessarily mean that the share price will continue to decline.

However, it is true that knowing what has happened in the past can sometimes provide hints as to what will happen in the future. So, for example, you may notice that a company's share price always goes down in the summer and up in the winter. Maybe the company sells skis or umbrellas. There is no guarantee that the company share price will follow the same pattern in the future. But there's a chance. Making decisions on the basis of this information alone is, however, gambling and not investing.

And, despite my general scepticism (and my fear that many chartists put far too much faith in their bits of paper or, rather, their computer screens) I do admit that I often look at charts. I don't make decisions on the basis of the information available in charts but I do use charts to help me get a general view of how a share has performed in the past. Charts are a good way to display basic information about a company or a market. And it's true that patterns do emerge. It is, for example, often possible to see on a chart that a particular share price usually bounces upwards when it reaches a certain low point. This doesn't mean that the share will always bounce up when it goes that low, but it does suggest that there is a certain level of support.

Put very simply, a chart is the easiest way to look at the history of a share's price performance over a period of time. Charts are usually available for quite short periods (a day or a week for example) but I find charts which show the performance of a share over two, three or five years to be most useful.

COMMODITIES

'A mine is a hole in the ground with a liar standing over it.'
MARK TWAIN

There are several types of commodity. There are base metals such as aluminium, copper, lead, nickel, tin and zinc. There are precious metals such as gold, silver, palladium and platinum. There are energy commodities, such as oil (of various kinds), natural gas and uranium. And there are the soft commodities such as sugar, corn, wheat, soya beans, cotton, coffee, cocoa, palm oil, live cattle, lean hogs, frozen pork bellies and orange juice. There are variations on these individual themes, of course, and so different varieties of coffee are traded at different prices.

Throughout the early years of the 21st Century there was growing talk of a super-cycle in commodities. The theory was that the price of commodities (such as oil, metals and soft commodities such as wheat and corn) would all rise to great new heights as China, India and other emerging nations began to drag themselves through the Industrial Revolution. The theory was that China and India would grow as fast in a few years as Europe and America had grown in centuries. There would be a huge and unprecedented demand for concrete and steel (for building things) and because the vast populations of these rapidly developing countries would demand a Western type of diet there would be a huge demand for wheat, soya, corn, meat and other 'soft' commodities. There was, said those who believed in the super cycle, another reason why commodity prices would go up higher and for longer than ever before: many of the commodities the developing countries would need were in short supply. The world's oil supplies are hardly enough to satisfy the needs of the West. Add the needs of the East and there will be a crisis.

I explained this problem in detail in my book *Oil Apocalypse*. It is, to me, an utterly compelling argument, one that we ignore at our peril, and, almost certainly the most significant problem faced by mankind.

Sceptics dismissed the boom in commodities as nothing more than another bubble; little different to the dot.com bubble that had marked the end of the 20th Century and which had done so much damage to the portfolios of so many investors. During the dot.com bubble the enthusiasts claimed that the Internet would change everything. Nothing, they said, would ever be the same again. It was, of course, pure rubbish. The Internet was never anything much more than a new way of selling stuff by mail order. The commodities super-cycle, said the sceptics, was no different. The argument put forward by those who didn't believe it was that human beings have always found a way of coping and that things will never be as bad as seems possible.

In the long-term I don't see how energy companies are suddenly going to find enough new supplies of oil and gas to cope with the world's exploding demand. The amount that was previously available was hardly enough to satisfy the demands of America and Europe. China and India are both huge countries. How, can oil and mining companies suddenly find stuff that they hadn't been able to find before? Those dismissing the idea of a commodity super-cycle claimed that mining companies would look harder when prices rose high enough. But I don't find that argument convincing either. And if prices rise high enough to make it worthwhile for companies to spend even more money on exploration then the effect on our society will be devastating.

There have been modest commodity super-cycles before. There was one towards the end of the 19th Century and another in the 20th Century. The first was a result of the emergence of the United States of America as a superpower. The second was a result of Japan becoming a superpower.

> *'Clients should note the following: Trading physical commodities is highly speculative and very risky; the vast majority of investors have lost money trading commodities.'*
>
> FROM AN ADVERTISEMENT FOR A METALS TRADING BROKER.

I believe that, in the long-term, commodity prices are likely to keep rising.

But (and there is always a 'but' and if you are planning to invest and haven't spotted the 'but' then you are probably always heading for trouble) even in commodity super-cycles prices don't move upwards smoothly.

The prices of all commodities (whether they be oil, copper, wheat or whatever) will go up and down. There will be moments of panic when prices will seemingly collapse. But the trend will, I believe, be upwards.

One enduring problem is, of course, that it is extremely difficult to put a precise value on a barrel of oil or a sack of wheat. There are a large number of weird and wonderful mathematical formulae around which enable investors to assess the value of companies making cars, toothpaste and sewing machines. These formulae aren't always as useful as their inventors and supporters would have us believe but at least they are there. With commodities there are no ways of assessing value. How much is an ounce of gold really worth? How much is a barrel of oil really worth? You can't measure their value by the dividends they produce because they don't pay any dividends. You can't decide to buy because the directors are buying. You can't assess the value of a pound of uranium by looking at its balance sheet because there isn't a balance sheet. Commodities are worth what people will pay for them. It's as simple and as complicated as that.

COMPANY ACCOUNTS

'Business must be run at a profit, else it will die. But when anyone tries to run a business solely for profit...then also the business must die, for it no longer has a reason for existence.'
HENRY FORD

There is very little point in reading published accounts and expecting to find much worthwhile information. If a company has a problem it will probably find a way to hide the problem and to disguise the truth. Published accounts are worth a glance but they aren't worth a lot of your time. Company accounts are difficult to read because there are so many tricks that can be used to manipulate the way the accounts appear. For example, over how many years do you depreciate assets? Do you depreciate at all? Simple decisions like this can make a huge difference to a company's profits. The company accountant who wants to hide something has an easy time of it even today. For example, all he has to do is change the way the company's pension commitments are included in the accounts, or the value of the company's inventories, in order to alter the accounts completely. Company employees have learned a lot from politicians over the years. Rather than studying the accounts, I prefer to see if the directors have a large personal investment in the company. Or are they just paying themselves huge salaries and giving themselves lot of bonuses and free shares?

Company accounts are out-of-date the day they are sent to the printers. And, of course, people sometimes lie. All you can get from the annual accounts is the stuff the writers want to tell you about what the company does, and how enthusiastic the directors are. Company accounts are a snapshot of the company's financial situation and are, therefore, not much more use than a single bank statement. Finally, of course, knowing about the past tells you very little about the future. And although company directors may be good at running their company they are not often good at predicting the future.

COMPANY REPORTS

'Annual reports are now far less useful to private investors than they were 20 years ago. Their volume and opacity is bamboozling.'
ROBIN ANGUS

When I look at company annual reports I look for several things. First, I want to check out the company's five (or, preferably, ten) year performance. This is difficult to fake. Even though past performance is no guarantee of future performance I want to know that the company has continued to grow over a decent period of time. Second, I want to see that the directors have invested their own money in the company. They should have at least a year's salary invested. Third, I want to check that the directors aren't paying themselves too much. Fourth, I want to be able to understand what the company does to make money. Fifth, I need to check the company's fixed assets. I'm not much interested in intangible assets (brand names, copyrights, patents, etc.). I am interested in buildings and land. It is sometimes still possible to find companies which are selling for less than the value of the real assets they own. And sometimes it is possible to find a company which hasn't revalued its real assets since 1959.

> *'It's not the figures. It's the tale you tell.'*
> COMPANY REPORT AUTHOR.

Two final thoughts on company reports:

First, I tend not to buy shares in companies which produce hugely expensive glossy annual reports which are full of colour photographs of the directors and their offices.

Second, if a company's results seem too good to be true, assume that the executives are lying. It is more likely that the executives are lying than that the results really are too good to be true.

COMPLEX INVESTMENTS

'Your goal as an investor should simply be to purchase, at a rational price, a part interest in an easily-understandable business whose earnings are virtually certain to be materially higher five, 10 and 20 years from now. Over time you will find only a few companies that meet these standards – so when you see one that qualifies, you should buy a meaningful amount of stock. You must resist the temptation to stray from your guidelines: if you aren't willing to own a stock for 10 years, don't even think about owning it for 10 minutes.'
WARREN BUFFETT

The investment professionals are constantly coming up with new ways to part investors from their money. Some of the complex investments available have been around for a long time and can, on occasion, be an excellent choice for the careful investor. Preference shares, convertibles, corporate bonds and permanent interest bearing shares can all be a great source of profit. So can warrants and capital shares. They all have advantages and disadvantages. But if you are going to invest in them you have to do more work and learn more things. And, in my experience, the risk-time-reward relationship is not convincing. I've invested in all these things, and have generally made money out of them, but these days I prefer to keep my investments simple.

CONTRARIAN INVESTORS

'If you can find unanimity and do the opposite you can be certain to be successful.'
JAMES GOLDSMITH

A contrarian is someone who believes that the crowd is usually wrong. When most people are bulls, contrarians may well be bears. Most investors regard themselves as contrarians because they don't want to think of themselves as just part of the general herd but they aren't, of course, because only a minority can ever truly be contrarians. The world is full of investors who think they are contrarians. Ask 20 investors if any of them are contrarians and they will probably all say 'yes, me'.

Contrarians understand that you cannot make good investment or policy decisions based on projecting past trends forwards. And they are aware that sooner or later every investment theory will be hyped up too far and will, therefore, fall. Contrarianism is based on a healthy scepticism about uncritical political or market manias, a realisation that you cannot make good investment or policy decisions based on projecting past trends forwards and an awareness that sooner or later everything that is hyped will fall to earth.

To be a successful contrarian investor you need to understand and play on the psychological weaknesses of other investors.

Conventional wisdom results in conventional returns. Running with the crowd is fine as long as you don't want to get anywhere quickly. And running with the crowd can be dangerous. Being a contrarian during the final stages of the dot.com bubble would have saved you a lot of money.

You should not, of course, be a contrarian for the sake of it. That would be potty and counterproductive. You should only be a contrarian because you believe that the fundamentals support your stance. Don't oppose the herd just to be contrary.

> *'If everybody agrees that you should increase capacity in ball bearings you can be absolutely sure that there's going to be a glut of ball bearings, and you'll end up losing money.'*
>
> JAMES GOLDSMITH

Here are some things you should know about contrarians and contrarian investing.

1. Contrarians are often 'value investors' (see page 243).
2. The contrarian should not find it too difficult to spot the top of a market – and the setting for a crash-to-be. When hairdressers, taxi drivers and shop assistants are investing (whether in shares or property) and are talking (and boasting) about their successes then the time has come for the cautious investor to think about selling up. When people in general are optimistic and self indulgent then a crash is not far ahead. When people are borrowing heavily and accumulating huge personal debts then dark days are not far away. When newspapers and television programmes are full of advertisements for smart cars and expensive holidays, a collapse is coming. When fashions become more daring and extravagant and moral standards drop, the end is undoubtedly nigh. When obesity becomes a major problem and thousands turn to drugs and alcohol for excitement it's usually fair to say that there are problems ahead. When people stop saving (because they have no fears about the future) it is time to tighten your belt. Markets that foster excesses are usually the product of a permissive attitude. A consensus of the best and brightest brains is so likely to be wrong that it acts as a useful contrarian indicator. When a group of Nobel prize winning scientists say something about finance or economics they are almost certain to be wrong and if you want to be right you should do the opposite to what they recommend. Looking at magazine covers has always seemed to me to be a good way to spot trends at a very early stage.

When magazine covers shout loudly about some new investment trend it is probably time to sell not buy. *The Economist* has always worked well for me as a contrary indicator. If they run a story on the cover promoting oil or diamonds then the bottom is probably about to fall out of the market for oil or diamonds and so you should do the opposite. I don't know why this works so well, but it does. Magazine editors are, perhaps, slow to spot trends but rather sensationalist. They certainly seem poor at spotting trends but very good at jumping on bandwagons that are running out of power. The more emphatic and emotional a story, the more you can trust it to be wrong. On the other hand when the experts are predicting the permanent end of banks (housebuilders, commercial property or whatever) that will be the time to buy.

3. Doctors, lawyers and other sensible people usually do badly on the stock market, and tend to underperform, because they always like to do the logical, sensible thing that everyone else is doing. If you do what everyone else is doing you will never make money as an investor because you will never beat the 'averages'. (Costs of one sort or another will ensure that you do worse than 'average'). The investment winners are more likely to be those who always seem to be doing the 'wrong' thing.
4. When hunting for an investment a contrarian will look for shares that have fallen in the last six months. He will, for example, look for a sector that is down at least 50% on its recent highs.
5. When newspapers or magazines think they have spotted a contrarian theme worth following, they are almost certainly wrong. When you see a headline that reads 'A Brave Bet For Bold Contrarians' you can safely ignore the recommended investment; it is almost certainly a sure way to lose money.

Corporate Pay

'The salary of the chief executive of a large corporation is not a market award for achievement. It is frequently in the nature of a warm personal gesture by the individual to himself.'
John Kenneth Galbraith

Today, corporate bosses are paying themselves obscene salaries. The average chief executive officer (CEO) of the average listed firm is paid more than three hundred times as much as the average worker. These huge salaries are often dwarfed by even larger bonus payments, expense accounts and share options. The schemes devised to reward successful directors and executives with bonuses are invariably woefully undemanding. In 2008, it was revealed that, despite the fact that many companies were making losses, 95% of British company executives would receive bonuses. One study of 1,500 companies found that two thirds claimed to be outperforming their peer groups. Naturally, they used this outperformance to justify their high salaries. It was also revealed that, in view of the fact that operating conditions were difficult and corporate profits likely to be low, many remuneration committees were looking at ways to alter the way in which bonuses were awarded. One of the biggest absurdities about corporate pay is that bosses invariably receive huge bonuses when a company does well (and the criteria are usually arranged so that most companies do well most of the time) but never have to give anything back when the company does badly. Because of this, the interests of bosses are divorced from the interests of shareholders.

Chief executive officers frequently claim that they have to be paid these huge salaries in order to stop them leaving to do something else. No one ever seems to bother asking them what else they are likely to do. This is the same empty argument used by council leaders and senior hospital administrators, who justify their six figure salaries by arguing that they are merely receiving what they would be paid in the private sector. This, of course, is nonsense. Most council leaders and senior hospital administrators wouldn't last five minutes in an enterprise which had to make a profit. (And, of course, the public service employees receive vast pensions, long holidays, endless time off work when they are suffering from mild backache or 'stress' and a working week that probably doesn't match the number of hours put in at the weekend by the average industry boss.)

As a result of obscene greed, executive pay has rocketed unreasonably in recent years. In the 1970's company bosses usually earned between 30 and 40 times the income of ordinary workers. In 1984 the average executive earned 45 times the shopfloor pay (so if the guy working on the shopfloor earned £10,000 a year the boss would earn £450,000). In 2007 the ratio was between 175 to 1 and 400 to 1 (so if the average worker was taking home £20,000 the boss would be earning £8,000,000). The bosses receiving these enormous salaries weren't people who had created companies. They were people hired to do a job. They were people hired to attend meetings and shout at the people who did the work. It is true that in the same period share prices went up but this was a result of rising global prosperity, technological advancement, the fall of communism and the opening up of new markets – and not the skills of company bosses.

It is staggering and appalling to realise that in 2007 the CEOs of large public companies averaged 344 times the average pay of workers. In 2008, the combined revenue of 1,130 of the world's leading Chief Executive Officers was 2.224 trillion dollars. Would they do the work for less? Of course they would. (Would footballers kick a ball around for less than £150,000 a week? Of course they would, if anyone had the guts to offer them less. What else are they going to do for a living? Wash cars? Cut lawns?) The problem is that the boards of public companies are largely occupied by the bosses of other public companies.

And they are all too busy scratching one another's backs, and feathering one another's nests, to worry too much about shareholders.

Too often these days directors, executives and employees get rich but the investors don't. An increasing number of companies now exist to make their key employees – rather than their shareholders – wealthy. An official investigation in the USA showed that almost two thirds of American firms avoid corporate income taxes altogether most years. They do this by recording high expenses. And expenses are kept high by paying employees (particularly executives and directors) huge salaries, huge bonuses and vast expenses. Very little is left over for the taxman but, more importantly, very little is left over for shareholders.

And, finally, many companies give out stock options to directors and other favoured employees. These options give the right to purchase shares at absurdly low levels. It is, of course, just another way of taking money away from shareholders and giving it to employees. Be aware that is not unknown for company directors and executives to manipulate their company share price (either by buying back shares or fiddling the accounts to boost the company's apparent earnings) so that they can push up the share price and sell their share options for a huge profit. The methods they use to achieve this selfish aim rarely lead to any lasting increase in the company's value.

CORPORATE POWER

'It is a strange desire to seek power and to lose liberty.'
FRANCIS BACON

The people who run companies think they have the power. But in an increasing number of companies the people with the big offices and the chauffeur driven cars have remarkably little authority. Today, companies have lost control over their staff who demand a bigger and bigger share of the profits. (Think of footballers demanding such huge salaries that their football clubs can only survive if billionaires subsidise them and think of investment banks paying out multi-million pound bonuses to their employees.) Companies have lost control of their customers who demand better and better prices (because the Internet has given consumers the information they need to be able to compare prices quickly). Consumers think that this has given them more power. But, although it has given them cheaper prices, it has also ensured that they receive poorer service. And companies have lost control of their own environment, and the way they do business, because of the thousands of new laws which have been brought in by various regulatory authorities.

The people who run large companies may think that they are in control but in reality they aren't. The directors have to do what is in their company's best interests. If they don't then their company will falter and that can't be allowed to happen. The company, the unimaginably powerful corporate demon, must come first. Every multinational company has a constant thirst for cash. In order to satisfy bankers and brokers, companies need to produce quarterly figures which show a nice profit on the bottom line.

So, for example, consider what happens if the directors of a drug company find that one of their products causes lethal side effects. They may, as human beings, feel ashamed about this. Individually the directors may want to withdraw the drug immediately and to apologise to the people who have been injured by their product. But this course of action would not be in the company's best short-term interests. Withdrawing the drug would doubtless cost the company money. Research and development costs would have to be written off. And apologising would expose the company to lawsuits. So the directors, acting in the company's best interests, must keep the drug on the market and deny that there are any problems. In these circumstances the company (a non-human entity which only exists on paper) is in control. The decisions are made not in the interests of people (whether they be customers or directors) but in the interests of the corporate 'being'.

The problem is compounded by the fact that, big as they are, multinational companies have no souls and no sense of responsibility. Moreover they never think beyond the next set of profit figures; they are ultimately ruthless and (since they are inanimate and bloodless) utterly 'cold blooded', but they are also ultimately short sighted. Big institutions, like computers, are inherently, irretrievably, stupid. They do not realise that their behaviour will, in the long run, lead to their total destruction – partly because it will annoy and alienate their customers and partly because in some circumstances it may even result in the deaths of many of their customers!

By and large, the men and women who run large drug companies, arms companies, food companies and genetic engineering companies don't really want to destroy the world in which we all live. They know that their families have to breathe the same air as you and I. They know that they too need good food, clean drinking water and a healthy environment.

However, despite the evidence being to the contrary the people who run these companies probably think that they are doing good and useful work. They have denied the truth to themselves in order to avoid coming face to face with a reality which would probably drive them insane if they accepted it. It is only through denial and self-deceit that most of the men and women who work for tobacco companies can continue to sell a product which causes so much misery and so much death. Adolf Hitler killed fewer people than the big tobacco companies have killed. But I doubt if many of the people running big tobacco companies think of themselves as evil.

Occasionally, this constant denial and self-deceit breaks down and absurdities appear. For example, British Members of Parliament have, as members of an institution, consistently voted to allow multinational corporations to pollute our drinking water and to tamper with and pollute our food. And yet MPs themselves, as individuals, are so conscious of the value of pure food and clean drinking water that in the House of Commons they have arranged to be given spring water to drink and to be fed on organic food which has not been genetically modified. The men and women who vote to allow our water to be polluted and our food to be genetically modified are voting as representatives of institutions rather than as representatives of people. They know that they are creating a world in which the food is unfit to eat and the water unfit to drink. But they can't stop it happening because they are operating for the benefit of institutions rather than people.

The huge organisations which now run the world have developed identities, strengths, purposes and needs of their own. And in order to continue to grow in size and in strength those organisations need to ignore or suppress as much of the truth as they can – and to ignore the truths which they cannot suppress. Obviously, the people who work for those institutions must also ignore and suppress the unpalatable truths (and they must find ways to hide from the reality of what they are doing).

Some years ago, Dr Albert Schweizer saw the first signs of what has happened. 'Another hindrance to civilisation today,' he wrote, 'is the over-organisation of our public life. While it is certain that a properly ordered environment is the condition and, at the same time, the result of civilisation, it is also undeniable that, after a certain point has been reached, external organisation is developed at the expense of spiritual life. Personality and ideas are often subordinated to institutions, when it is really these which ought to influence the latter and keep them inwardly alive.'

CORRELATION

'Charlie and I let our marketable equities tell us by their operating results – not by their daily or even yearly price quotations – whether our investments are successful. The market may ignore business success for a while, but eventually will confirm it.'
WARREN BUFFETT

Investing experts with pointy heads like to measure the extent that the prices of different types of asset (they are known as different asset 'classes') move in line with each other. They call this the 'correlation' and measure it from 0 to 1. The idea is that by having a portfolio in which the various ingredients have a low correlation you will be able to protect yourself against a fall in any particular market. So, the experts claim that gold and property both have a low degree of correlation with shares. In recent years it has become clear that correlation measurements really aren't as useful as the pointy-headed people once thought they were.

The 'alpha' is an individual share's ability to outperform the average return from the stock market. The average return from the stock market is known as the 'beta'.

I regard this sort of information as being of very little value – mainly because the figures involved are entirely retrospective. The sort of people who spend hours fiddling with computer software may find alpha and beta of interest but in the real world I don't regard either as being of much practical significance.

COSTS

'Beware of small expenses. A little leak will sink a great ship.'
BENJAMIN FRANKLIN

Every time you trade you incur costs. These add up rapidly. They eat away at your investment and are a major reason why investors lose money. Expenses include: spreads (the difference between the buying and selling price), stamp duty (a tax on each transaction), commissions (a fee on each transaction), custody fees (a fee for holding whatever you've bought and which, since it is probably only held electronically, is a bit of a cheek), management fees (which can range from modest – in the case of an index fund – to outrageous – in the case of a hedge fund), taxes on income, taxes on gains. The spread alone can often be 3% to 6% and may be considerably more in the case of a stock which isn't traded very often.

If you have a financial adviser you are paying money to him and to the manager of the fund in which you invest. If your financial adviser suggests that you buy a fund of funds hedge fund you will be paying a fee to the financial adviser, a fee to the manager of the fund of funds fund and fees to each of the managers of the funds your fund of funds is invested in. Management costs add up rapidly when one manager invests in a fund run by a second manager. There is very little left over when everyone has taken their cut and all this, remember, is before the directors of the companies in which you invest have taken their bonuses and cheap shares.

The more advisers, consultants, financial planners and self-styled experts you employ the less profit there will be for you and the more risk you will have to take to stand a chance of keeping up with inflation.

The moral is simple: trade as little as you possibly can and try to ensure that your trading costs are kept to a minimum.

DIRECTORS

'I am their leader; I must follow them.'
BERTOLT BRECHT

Company directors often pay themselves too much and give themselves too many perks. They also often fail to do things in the shareholders' best interests. (It is frequently forgotten these days but the sole reason for the existence of the company is to make money for the shareholders. Companies don't exist to make the world a better place or to provide employment. In theory, companies exist to make money for shareholders). Directors get away with all sorts of naughtiness because most shares are not held by individuals but by funds whose managers also have a vested interest in allowing directors a good deal of leeway – and maintaining the status quo. Neither company directors nor fund managers do jobs which merit the sort of money they are paid. So both do little to rock the boat. In some companies directors continue to bleed the company dry – and to pay themselves huge salaries and huge, undeserved bonuses – while fund managers stand by and pay themselves huge salaries and huge, undeserved bonuses for buying shares in those companies. Directors and fund managers like to maintain the fiction that running a company and investing are difficult tasks that deserve much more money than running the country, making movies or performing brain surgery. The truth is that company directors and fund managers are members of a privileged group whose exceptional and utterly undeserved prosperity depends upon their maintaining the status quo and covering up the truth.

I feel more comfortable about directors when:

1. They have a good chunk of their own money tied up in the company. Share options don't count.
2. Directors don't pay themselves too much compared with other companies of the same size.
3. There is a well balanced board, with strong non-executive directors on board to keep the executive directors under control.
4. The directors have a good track record. I don't like investing money in companies when the directors have presided over a series of companies which went bust.
5. The directors don't have advantages over other shareholders. This can happen when the company has 'special' links to other companies or organisations owned or controlled by the directors or their wives.
6. The directors don't own too many of the shares.

I don't invest in companies where the chairman and the chief executive share the same brain. The most important duty of the chairman of a company is to get rid of the chief executive if he is failing. The chairman is unlikely to sack the chief executive if he is the chief executive. Research has shown that companies in which these two posts are combined have a more than 50% greater chance of going bust than other listed companies. That's a huge risk.

* * *

It has become popular in recent years for investors to take note of when directors buy and sell shares in their own company. Theoretically, this is a good idea. You might imagine that directors would know their own company's prospects better than anyone else. This is one of the few ways that it is possible for investors to check whether their interests are aligned with those of the directors. In practice, however, there are two problems. First, directors are not allowed to trade in their own company's shares when they are in possession of sensitive, privileged information. If they do so they can get into terrible trouble. (It's called insider trading.) The second problem is that, when they're not in possession of special information, directors aren't terribly good at deciding when to buy or sell their own shares.

Here are some facts you should know:

1. If you are watching to see when directors buy or sell shares in their company, look at the number of shares they have bought or sold. Directors will sometimes buy less than £10,000 worth of shares in an attempt to encourage investors to pile in. If the director is being paid £500,000 a year in salary and another £500,000 in bonuses and options, a £10,000 investment is of no positive significance. It is in fact of negative significance because it suggests to me that the director is so concerned about the company's share price that he is prepared to try and trick investors into buying shares.
2. How many directors are dealing? If two or more directors are buying (or selling) then their actions are more significant than if one director is dealing. If the whole board is busy buying huge amounts of shares then it's possibly worth getting involved. If one director is selling it may be because he's getting divorced. Directors of small companies who buy in clusters often know what they are doing.
3. Share sales which relate to share options don't count. Share purchases and sales only count when real money is involved.
4. Remember that company directors are not investment experts – and although they may know their own company very well they probably don't know the general market terribly well. Bank directors bought lots of shares in a variety of banks early in 2008. They lost a ton of money when their shares continued to plunge. It quickly became clear that their confidence had been entirely misplaced. The directors lost money and anyone who followed their example lost money too. Even as a director of a company it is difficult to get your timing right when conditions are volatile and economic

conditions are deteriorating rapidly. The fact that directors often time their sales and purchases badly shows just how difficult it is to time the market. If company directors can't tell when to buy a share how can anyone outside the company? This rather confirms that it is usually a good thing to bet the field (and to buy shares in a whole sector) rather than on a particular horse. However, if you are following directors' share dealings, it is probably more significant (and a bad sign) if directors sell shares when the price is falling. This suggests that the price will go down further and the directors know it. If directors sell when the share price is rising they could just be taking profits.

5. The overall ratio of director buying to selling is useful. If more directors are selling than buying this suggests that the overall future for the market may be bleak. If most directors who are trading are buying then there is probably a mood of optimism in boardrooms. That isn't usually a bad thing for share prices.
6. It is a good sign when directors make purchases in the period just before the company's results are declared.
7. The size of a purchase relative to the director's holding is important. If a director is doubling an already sizeable stake in a company, he probably believes that the price is too low.
8. Are the directors who are buying executive or non-executive directors? Non executive directors often buy shares when they are appointed and know nothing about the company. They do this because it looks good. But they often time their purchase badly. However, I think it is a good sign if outside directors (who aren't being paid a huge fortune as executives) have a big investment in a company. It's nice to know that people who attend board meetings are prepared to put their own money into the company.
9. When executive directors buy shares in their company even though the shares are generally thought to be expensive their purchase usually does well. On the other hand when executive directors buy shares in companies regarded as cheap, they may be about to lose at least some of their money.
10. Watch out that a director isn't building a controlling stake. Don't buy or hold shares in companies where less than 25% of the stock is in public hands. A number of small companies, which are quoted on the stock market, are controlled by one or two directors who hold the majority of the shares. It is always good to have the directors interests allied with those of the shareholders but when the directors have too much control there is a danger that the interests of small shareholders may be forgotten or ignored.
11. I am not terribly interested in how much money a director invests. I am far more interested in what percentage of his personal wealth he has invested in the company.

12. Be wary of investing in any company which puts the sons or daughters of the boss or a former director onto the board. The original boss might have been a genius but that doesn't mean that the child will be. How many wonderful pieces of music were written by Elgar Junior? How many great plays were written by Shakespeare's grandson? Similarly, don't invest in a company which puts celebrities or former politicians on the board of directors. The celebrities or former politicians can be hired for a fee if they have some special knowledge that will be of help to the company. Celebrity endorsements are just as likely to damage a company's reputation as they are to help it. And politicians are all self-serving, grasping crooks. Why would any company want a known self-serving, grasping crook on its board?

DIVERSIFICATION

'To carry one's eggs in a great number of baskets without having the time or opportunity to discover how many have holes in the bottom, is the surest way of increasing risk and loss.'
JOHN MAYNARD KEYNES

Investors are usually advised to reduce their risk by investing in a variety of investments. A well-diversified portfolio might include shares, bonds, money market accounts, currencies, precious metals, property and collectibles (such as books, stamps and art). Within some sections there will be investments in different countries, though hopes that national stock markets will eventually decouple have proved fruitless and shares in most markets round the world tend to go up and down together. Investors diversify in order to reduce their risk. The idea is that if one investment does badly another will do well (or, at least, not do badly).

Diversification is the key to investment survival. But most people are confused about what it means. I have known people describe their investment portfolio as diversified because it contains a dozen different UK shares. When examined carefully, however, it was clear that the shares were likely to go up and down together.

There are four main investment classes: cash, bonds, property and shares. You should aim to have your money spread among these four groups. And within each group you should diversify again. You need to make a decision about how much of your money you want to put into each category of investment. And, if you are going to diversify properly, when you're selecting shares, you should choose companies in different sectors and different parts of the world. And diversify through time too. When making investments do so over a period of time. So, if you have £100,000 and want to invest it in equities do so at the rate of £10,000 a month. If shares rocket after two months you will kick yourself. But you'll probably kick yourself more if they collapse after two months.

Some experts say that you need around 30 stocks for a properly diversified portfolio but that involves a lot of work, not just in choosing and buying shares but also in watching them all and in dealing with dividends, sales, and tax consequences. You can reduce your holding to a more manageable number by putting at least some of your money in investment trusts which specialise in specific sectors. For example, one investment trust could cover all emerging countries and another could provide you with exposure to mining or property companies.

Diversification is truly vital for the preservation of your money. And it's a good idea not to have too much of your wealth in any particular investment. As a general rule it's wise not to have more than 5% of your total wealth in a single position. Your investments should be diversified to a degree that you will never have to worry too much about any one investment.

However, although diversification is vital for preservation, if you want to make money you need to be a little more daring; you need to specialise in something. If you diversify too much you will always fail to beat the market, and you might as well just put your money into a collection of cheap tracker funds. Diversification may reduce risk (depending on the way you are diversified – if you just buy shares in ten banks you aren't diversified at all) but the more you diversify the more you are likely to end up just matching everyone else. Diversification can be numbing. If you have a truly diversified share portfolio you will only ever match the average return produced by the market. Your overall portfolio should be diversified. But if you want to beat the market you may have to put part of your money into a range of shares which aren't really diversified. In other words, if you want to make big money you need to back your instincts and put a larger proportion of your wealth into one sector than might be generally considered wise. If you have a sound view of the future then perhaps you should take your chances.

DIVIDENDS

'Well managed industrial companies do not, as a rule, distribute to the shareholders the whole of their earned profits. In good years, if not in all years, they retain a part of their profits and put them back in the business. Thus there is an element of compound interest operating in favour of a sound industrial investment.'

JOHN MAYNARD KEYNES

Companies don't pay interest. They pay dividends. Dividends are important. I look for shares paying a real, decent, worthwhile dividend of at least three to four percent. And I want to find companies which have a long, stable history of paying a dividend and which make sufficient profit to keep paying the dividend even when the economy or the company or both are going through difficult times.

Here's what I think you need to know about dividends:

1. The dividend yield may be measured as a historic figure (what investors used to get) or a prospective figure (what they hope to get). It is obtained by dividing the gross annual dividend into the share price. Companies which are growing quickly may have low dividend yields because investors are hoping to make money through capital growth. Some companies (such as utilities) are bought and sold largely for their dividend yield (because there is only limited room for capital growth).
2. The dividend cover is the amount by which the net amount paid to shareholders is covered by the earnings generated by the capital they have invested in the business. The dividend cover is obtained by dividing the net dividend per share into the earnings per share.
3. If you buy a share ex-dividend you will not receive the recently declared dividend. The previous owner of the share will get the money. Share prices are usually adjusted when they become ex-dividend. Newspapers which list share prices usually put 'xd' by the side of share prices so that investors can see when a share goes ex-dividend.
4. If you spend your dividends you will have a good time but your money will only increase through capital growth. If you reinvest your dividends in shares your money will grow much more rapidly and you will become seriously wealthy much more speedily. If you had invested £100 in UK shares in 1899 your money would, if you'd spent all your dividends, have grown to an inflation adjusted £279 by the end of 2007. On the other hand, if you had reinvested all your dividends, and taken full advantage of the miracle of compound interest, your money would have grown to £4,061 in the same time. An alternative bank, working out the same figures, came to the conclusion that a pound invested in British shares in 1900 would have grown to £161 (ignoring inflation) by the end of 2006 but £21,174 with dividends reinvested. A third set of investment gurus worked out that £1 invested in 1900 would have produced £16,160 by the end of the 20th Century if all the dividends had been reinvested but would have turned into just £149 if they had not. I quote these three different pieces of research not because they are different (they relate to slightly different time periods) but because the conclusions are, effectively, the same. Dividend income, particularly if reinvested and therefore compounded, plays an extremely significant role in investment return.
5. Some companies offer investors automatic reinvestment programmes. Instead of receiving dividends investors who sign up for one of these

schemes get extra shares. It's a nice idea but it is one which has, over the years, caused me considerable annoyance. The problem is that this sort of scheme is likely to leave you owning small amounts of shares which you forget about when you sell your holding. Sometimes, I have received notification of extra shares being allocated to me after I've sold my main holding. When this has happened I have been left with a handful of shares. And small quantities of shares aren't economical to sell or to hold. The accounting and tax problems can be horrendous.

6. Companies that pay big dividends usually increase their earnings faster than those that don't. It's worth remembering that growth stocks often don't pay dividends. That's bad. Value shares (see page 243) usually do. That's good.
7. Dividends drive value. Without dividends a company has no value to shareholders. Many investors put their money into a company hoping for a capital gain. But it is companies which produce steady dividends which produce the most significant capital gains. In the long term, investors will pay for income. And by paying for income they also produce capital gain. At the end of the 20th Century investors who only put their money into companies paying a dividend avoided the dot.com stocks and saved their shirts. In order to pay a dividend a company needs to produce cash, and to produce real profits (rather than the sort of profits produced by creative accounting).
8. Small, long-standing companies often pay regular dividends, especially when many of the shares are held by a family whose members need the income. Such companies are often reluctant to reduce the dividend, even when times are hard. The directors will use whatever cash the company has in the bank to continue paying dividends.
9. Buying shares because they pay a high dividend is unfashionable. But I know one successful investor who buys shares when dividends are increased and sells them when dividends are reduced. It's a good way to pick companies which are thriving and to avoid companies which are struggling.
10. Be wary, and suspicious, if a company seems to be paying a very high dividend – above the rate of dividends paid by companies in the same sector. This might be because the company concerned is in trouble and is about to cut its dividend. The share price may have fallen (and pushed up the apparent dividend yield) because investors know that the next dividend will be lower than the last one.
11. The fundamental reason for buying shares is income. (Expecting constant capital gains is a triumph of innocence and hope over experience.) And income comes through dividends. A share price is a measure of the expected future dividends. If a share price rises dramatically it is because investors

believe that the company is growing quickly and that the dividends available will also grow. During the dot.com boom of the 1990's investors forgot this. 'This time it's different,' they cried. Investors bought shares in companies that paid no dividends and had no chance of ever paying any dividends. Many dot.com companies had no profits and didn't even have any plans for making profits. Without profits it's difficult to find any money with which to pay dividends.

12. Traditionally (i.e. for a long time) investors have accepted a lower dividend from shares than the yield they would receive from holding gilts. The reasoning behind this is that shares are more likely to produce capital gains than gilts – and that the dividend should grow over time. However, when shares are unwanted (usually because investors are frightened that something terrible is happening) the dividend yield on shares may rise above the yield on gilts or other bonds. This may happen because companies are in trouble and their yield may be about to fall. Or it may be because shares are cheaper than they are traditionally. And this may mean that brave investors can make money by buying shares.

EFFICIENT MARKETS HYPOTHESIS

'Markets can remain irrational longer than you can remain solvent.'
JOHN MAYNARD KEYNES

In addition to being a great economist, Keynes, was also a well-known speculator who is reputed to have made four fortunes and lost three of them. Keynes was pointing out that your logic might well be correct, but that the market may take a long time to catch up with logic. The dot.com bubble, in which the shares of Internet companies were blown up to absurd levels, lasted for just under five years. That's a lot of irrationality.

Academics claim that all known information is already priced into the market. This is the theory behind the philosophy that markets are generally efficient and it is known as the Efficient Markets Hypothesis (EMH). First developed by Eugene Fama at the University of Chicago the hypothesis suggests that you can't beat the market – whatever method you use – without taking on extra risk. Academics who believe this assume that all human beings are rational and argue that the few investors who do beat the market are just lucky and that the wisest move is simply to put your money into index funds and go away and do something else.

> *'Madness is rare among individuals but common among crowds.'*
> FREDERICH NIETZSCHE

Here's a story which illustrates the Efficient Market Hypothesis quite nicely.

Two economists are walking down the street. One sees a £10 note lying on the pavement. He stoops to pick it up. The other economist, who believes in the efficient market hypothesis, stops him. 'If it were a real £10 note, someone would have already picked it up,' says the second economist.

The Efficient Market Hypothesis means that the prices of shares are governed by the available information. Changes in share prices (whether up or down) are, by definition, unpredictable because they occur as a result of information that wasn't previously available becoming available.

It is true, of course, that most of the business and investment news that you hear on television or the radio, or read in newspapers or magazines or on the Internet has already been discounted by the stock market before you can pick up the telephone to deal. Much of the geopolitical news will have already been discounted too (though not necessarily the inferences likely to have been made by strategic thinkers). In that respect the Efficient Market Hypothesis does work and you are wasting your time if you think that you can beat other investors simply by keeping up with the news. In order to be successful you need to be able to predict and to anticipate. Indeed, if someone tells you that the shares of company A are going to rise because (for example) they have a new product ready to hit the market, you should ask yourself why the information isn't already reflected in the price. (If you are receiving information which is not generally available then you need to be aware that insider trading is a serious crime.) There may be a genuine and honest reason why the information isn't widely available and has not pushed up the price. But before you invest you should know what it is.

It is also true, of course, that investors can get too excited and too depressed. And the information produced by analysts and provided by the media is often inaccurate. And markets get it wrong. The dot.com bubble at the end of the 20th Century was an obvious example of irrational exuberance.

Academics argue that bubbles are only recognised in hindsight. This is rubbish. I believe now (and believed then) that the dot.com bubble was pretty obvious. And the housing bubble of the early 21st Century was pretty obvious to anyone who wasn't earning a living as an estate agent or a mortgage broker.

Another problem the EMH supporters have to face is the fact that stock prices show momentum – in other words they keep going up (or down) without there being any logical reason for their doing so. They move because they have moved. Some experts argue that momentum exists because investors sometimes over-react to news and sometimes under-react to news. A company which is doing well issues a warning but no one takes it seriously and so the price continues to rise. Another company which is doing badly issues a warning which results in a huge crash.

The bottom line is that you and I can safely let all the clever people do all their clever stuff with company reports and figures and statistics in the comforting knowledge that they are wasting their time. They are wasting their time for two reasons. First, all their efforts cancel out the value of the information they have. (They will all buy or sell at the same time). Second, you cannot trust the figures obtained from politicians or company directors. The wise investor assumes that all politicians and company spokesmen are lying. Everyone who has made decisions according to the available information is making a mistake. (They are all making the same mistake.)

EMERGING MARKETS

'A man should know something of his own country, too, before he goes abroad.'
LAURENCE STERN

Emerging markets are markets in countries that are not well-established but which are probably growing rapidly and developing. It is possible to make a lot of money by investing in emerging markets. This is because it is easier for a small country to grow quickly than it is for a big country to grow quickly. (This is the same philosophy which explains why it may be more profitable to invest in small companies than in big ones. A small company can easily double in size. A big company is unlikely to double in size.) Unfortunately, a lot of other people know that emerging markets can be enormously profitable (either because they have worked it out for themselves or because they have read about it in a magazine) and so share prices may have already been pushed up to quite high levels. When the world economy does badly emerging markets may go down even faster than established markets. It is possible to benefit from the growth in emerging markets by investing in commodities rather than in the emerging markets themselves. (If emerging markets are going to grow, and build roads and factories, they will need steel, concrete and copper and so the prices of these things will probably go up.)

ETHICAL INVESTING

'A man must believe in himself and his judgement if he expects to make a living at this game. Nobody can make big money on what someone else tells him to do. That is why I don't believe in tips.'
JESSE LIVERMORE

In recent years ethical investing has become extremely popular. The funds that claim to invest money ethically tend not to do terribly well, but well-meaning investors really don't seem to mind this as long as they can claim that their money is invested 'ethically'. The warm glow they receive from knowing that their money is behaving itself presumably overwhelms the cold shiver they feel when they open their quarterly or half yearly statement and see just how badly their investment has done.

I'm afraid I don't have much faith in, or respect for, the ethical investment funds which exist. The problem is that some of the funds may call themselves 'ethical' but, nevertheless, invest in companies which I don't regard as the slightest bit 'ethical'.

So, for example, it is not unknown for ethical funds to eschew tobacco companies, companies which make their money out of betting and publishers which produce books or magazines which are not considered 'acceptable' in what the fund manager imagines to be polite society, but to invest enthusiastically in drug companies, banks, breweries and even arms companies.

When you consider the damage banks have done to modern society over recent years it is laughable to realise that fund managers who claim to be running ethical investment funds have been merrily putting huge chunks of their investors' money into bank shares.

I prefer to make up my own rules about what I will and will not invest in. I have never invested in companies of which I disapprove. I don't approve of animal experiments and so I refuse to invest in pharmaceutical companies. I am vegetarian so I won't invest in food companies or farms which deal in animals or meat. I know that there have been times when I could have made a lot of money by ignoring my principles. But I don't want money if that's the price. I will not invest in companies making or dealing in arms or tobacco. I won't buy shares in companies which do anything with, for or to animals (either as food or fashion). I won't buy shares in companies which use genetic engineering for anything. I have stuck to these simple rules for many years without any obvious hardship.

If you want to be an ethical investor then I think you really have to make up your own mind about what you consider to be 'ethical' and 'unethical'. I don't allow other people to make moral judgements for me so I don't allow strangers to make judgements about which investments are moral. Handing over money to a so-called ethical fund manager seems to me to be chickening out. It's not necessarily ethical and it's morally invalid. The joke is that it's probably also a bad move financially since such funds rarely do as well as other investments.

You don't have to do anything dishonest, disreputable or immoral to make money. You can retain all your principles and still make money. I wouldn't want money if in order to get it I had to rip people off, take advantage of people or do wicked things.

(Incidentally, there are now funds which specialise in investing in non-ethical companies. Such funds, which put their money into gambling, alcohol, tobacco and pornography tend to do much better than average.)

Of course, some investors take a different view, claiming that they can separate their personal sense of right and wrong from the way they invest their money. Legendary investor George Soros has said that he sees 'nothing wrong with investing in companies with whose activities you disagree'. He argues that buying a stock has no impact on the fortunes of a company 'because you are one in a crowd'.

However, even Soros admitted that he had sold shares in a company that manufactured landmines while he was involved in a campaign to ban the mines. He said he did that to avoid public pillory for double standards. 'It was hypocritical,' he said,' because if I had followed my beliefs I wouldn't have sold the stock. It was a good investment and I lost money by selling.'

EXCHANGE TRADED FUNDS (ETFS)

'Never is there just one cockroach in the kitchen.'
WARREN BUFFETT

ETFs are single shares, which track an underlying index or sector. ETFs follow all sorts of indices in the UK and the rest of the world and can also be used to track the price of commodities, either in bundles (groups of agricultural commodities for example) or as individuals (as cotton, sugar etc.). Fees are low. Theoretically, it is possible to create a balanced portfolio using just a handful of Exchange Traded Funds.

There are several kinds of ETFs. First, there are the ETFs which broadly hold the underlying securities of the index they track. If the fund provider fails, the investor has recourse to the fund's ring-fenced assets. For example, physical ETFs hold between 90% and 100% of the stuff they are selling. So, a gold ETF of this type which tracks the gold price must be backed by at least 90% gold. Then there are 'swap based' ETFs which invest in derivatives contracts, offered by banks and brokers, and designed to provide exposure to a particular index. If the fund issuer collapses the investors can claim the basket of securities. If the banks and brokers offering the contracts go bust then the investor will probably be left whistling. ETNs are exchange traded notes and investors are exposed to the counterparty going bust. Exchange Traded Commodities (ETCs) are ETNs which are linked specifically to commodities or to commodity indices. Some are backed by physical assets. Others are backed by guarantees and promises.

The bottom line is that although physical ETFs should be pretty safe, other varieties of these products can be riskier than some investors realise. The investor may think that his only risk is that the price of wheat, orange juice or copper will go the wrong way and that he will lose money. In reality, he may also lose some or all of his money if counterparties are involved and they go bust.

When ETFs first became available I (like many investors) regarded them as an excellent, hassle-free and competitively priced way to invest. And fees are certainly low (they are sometimes less than 0.5% though they do vary).

But, in addition to the counterparty risks, which can be scary, you do need to check exactly what an ETF is tracking before you buy.

For example, there are several ETFs which track BRIC economies (shares in Brazil, Russia, India and China) but the constituents of the available ETFs vary enormously. As I write, one such ETF currently offers 5% exposure to the Russian market, with the other 95% invested in the other three markets. The other two ETFs have a much higher percentage of their shares in Russian shares. One has 30% and the other has 29% in Russia. (These will have doubtless changed by the time you read this. But the principle remains the same.)

Then there is the problem of very small ETFs which deal with very specialised markets. Very small ETFs, which are not heavily traded, may develop price anomalies – with the price of the ETF not being the same as its net asset value.

For some investors, the beauty of ETFs is that they give an opportunity to invest in sectors easily, quickly and cheaply. If you think that shares in oil companies are likely to rise, but you are not sure which oil companies to select, you can, by purchasing a relevant ETF, invest in the whole sector.

And there are many investors who feel that Exchange Traded Commodities are the best way to deal in commodities. Before the invention of ETCs it was difficult and expensive for private investors to put money into commodities. Now, it's remarkably simple.

Exchange Traded Funds which deal with commodities track the performance of indices – usually based in the USA – and are traded on ordinary stock exchanges so that investors can buy and sell them just as easily as they can buy and sell shares in Marks and Spencer or British Telecom.

Today you can buy almost anything as an ETF. You can buy single metals or soft commodities (such as cotton or sugar) and you can buy baskets of commodities. There is, for example, a precious metal basket which contains gold, silver, platinum and palladium. If the value of these four commodities goes up then the price of the ETF goes up. And there are baskets which contain a bit of every sort of commodity – oil, precious metals, non precious metals and soft commodities such as farm products.

There are variations in the types of ETF available. Some deal with spot prices (the price that a buyer would pay today if he bought and had delivered a barrel of oil, an ounce of gold or a bushel of corn), but many are based on a commodity index where the price varies with futures prices – the price the buyer would pay if he took delivery at some time in the future. If you hold one of these ETCs for some time the contracts to buy in the future will be automatically sold and rolled over into new ones as time goes buy. If the new futures contract costs more then you lose out. If the new futures contract costs less then you gain.

And, as I explained at the start of this chapter, you can buy physical ETCs too. These track the real physical commodity price. When you buy into one of these ETCs you are buying an allocated bit of the commodity named. These funds can be a good way to buy precious metals such as gold and silver. The underlying metal, the gold or the silver, is (or should be) held in trust by a custodian.

You can even buy geared Exchange Traded Commodities which enable you to double your risk. If the index on which the ETC is based goes up by a factor of one your investment goes up by two. On the other hand if the index goes down then your investment goes down twice as much. And you can buy ETCs which enable you to short commodities (to profit if they go down in price and to lose if they go up in price.) It is even possible to invest in different currencies by using Exchange Traded Funds.

I used to be a great fan of ETFs.

However, as I've already explained, my enthusiasm diminished during September 2008 when trading in many varieties was suspended because of the problems traced back to AIG the huge American insurance company. I had been under the mistaken impression that these investments were secure and independent and depended for their viability solely on the financial strength of the company issuing them. But it then became clear that investors in some commodity indices did not own hard assets but (in the words of the *Financial Times*) 'a swap on an index of commodity futures with counterparty risk'. Thousands of investors had put money into ETFs believing that the low charges and apparently simple structures were an attractive alternative to other forms of investment. But nothing tests out a new investment scheme better than a crisis.

The problem with ETFs and ETCs was that the counterparty risk (the hazard that the firm on the other side of the trade would not be able to meet its contractual commitments) suddenly increased dramatically.

Over 100 exchange traded commodity products from ETF Securities were backed by AIG, the American insurer which had to be bailed out by American taxpayers. Dealing in the commodity products was suspended when no one knew what was happening with AIG. In the end AIG honoured its contracts and everything ended happily. ETF Securities took commendable steps to reassure investors. These products are potentially complex and explosive and in a world where strange things seem to happen with unusual frequency I decided that most ETFs were a risk too far for me.

With considerable regret I sold the majority of my commodity investments in Exchange Traded Funds (most of which had made a profit). I kept only the ETFs which were backed by something real, rather than by paper promises. Some providers of ETFs have now made great efforts to remove (or minimise) this risk but I remain cautious.

Incidentally, there are many other risky ways to invest. Contracts for difference, futures, spread betting, warrants, capital shares and turbo derivatives are just a few of the ones I have considered or tried over the years. I have now resolved not to touch any of these products again. (Nor, incidentally, will I ever put money into an insurance company with profits fund. These are, in my view, one of the most efficient ways to get rid of money known to man. And unlike other ways of getting rid of money there is no pleasure to be obtained from investing in with profit funds promoted by insurance companies.)

Financial engineering, and clever financial products, make money for bankers and brokers. They do not make money for ordinary investors. Fund managers, investment banks, brokers and so on are not altruistic. They do not exist to help private investors make money. Their aim and purpose and ambition is to make money out of us. They do not care what happens to us. If we lose all our money they will dump us, like empty banana skins, and find richer replacements.

If I am tempted to succumb to any of their promotional material in the future I will wander into the nearest betting shop and put a fiver on any horse with a name containing the same number of letters as his jockey. If the horse wins I will repeat the exercise until a horse loses. I will then stop, feel better, and go back to rational investing; buying only solid investments which are based on 'real' things, rather than on promises exchanged between bankers.

FASHION

'The fashion of this world passeth away.'
THE BIBLE

Don't ever invest in stuff just because it's fashionable. I have a friend who is a keen investor. His problem is that he always insists on making fashionable investments. He assumes that because something is new, and being talked about on the feature pages, then it must be successful. This, of course, is a nonsense. By and large the books that get all the reviews aren't the ones that sell the most copies. And similarly the companies that get all the publicity aren't necessarily the ones that make the profits. If you are buying shares in order to make money then you shouldn't just buy shares in companies that are fashionable and getting a lot of publicity. Remember, at the end of the 20th Century the companies that were getting all the column inches in the broadsheet newspapers were the dot.coms. Nothing has ever been more fashionable. And the people who put their savings into the dot.coms are now working at McDonalds flipping burgers. Incidentally, when you read news about a company in a newspaper or magazine, or hear it on television or radio, it is worth remembering that the news story was almost certainly manufactured by a public relations agency. Most investment news isn't news at all. It is propaganda.

> *'If all economists were laid end to end, they would not reach a conclusion.'*
> GEORGE BERNARD SHAW

I steer clear of most technology companies for two reasons. The first is that most are over-hyped by enthusiasts who believe they've found something to replace the wheel. The result of their exaggerated enthusiasm is that the share price is usually pushed up far too high. The second reason I avoid technology companies is that many of them do stuff that I don't understand. And I'm not prepared to spend the time I would need to spend so that I did understand.

And, despite the fact that I am convinced that the oil is running out, I am also reluctant to invest in alternative forms of energy and alternative forms of transport. There are, for example, now many so-called experts who claim that electric cars are the future. Plug in your car and you can whizz around without having to worry about oil prices (or, indeed, oil running out). That, at least, is the theory. In practice there is, of course, a rather large problem: electric cars operate with batteries and capacitors which do not, themselves, produce any energy. For every kilowatt hour available to the driver of an electric car, two kilowatt hours are lost in generating the original energy and transmitting it to the car battery. Electric vehicles are not an energy-saving alternative. They consume electricity which, in the absence of large supplies of electricity derived from renewable sources, is often derived from oil, gas or coal. The other fib sometimes told is that electric cars reduce carbon emissions. They don't and until the electricity they use comes from wind farms (or other renewables) they won't.

FOREIGN INVESTMENTS

'I do the opposite to what I feel I should do. When I'm sick in my stomach, it's time to buy. When I feel great, it's time to sell.'
ELAINE GAZARELLI

If you are investing in companies based outside the country where you live then I recommend using an investment trust specialising in the country you are interested in. Indeed, investment trusts are perhaps at their most useful when you want to invest in a foreign country. Buying shares in Chinese companies can be expensive and difficult. But it is easy to buy shares in an investment trust which holds shares in Chinese companies.

Occasionally, I have invested in foreign companies when no suitable investment trust was available. At the start of the boom in the price of uranium I believed that uranium mining company stocks would rise in price as the world's energy crisis became more apparent and so I purchased a number of foreign uranium mining stocks – such as Cameco in Canada. I sold all of these investments, and took substantial profits, when it seemed to me that the price of uranium had gone up too far, too soon. (I do believe, however, that in the medium and long term the price of uranium and, therefore, the price of successful uranium mining companies will rise and rise again simply because the problems created by 'peak oil' mean that a number of countries are now building nuclear power stations and the demand for uranium must therefore increase.)

When investing abroad, remember that you may also be exposed to currency changes. This is just as true of investment trusts unless the managers have decided to hedge their fund to protect it against currency losses. By and large I prefer to take the currency risk, and so tend to choose investments which are not hedged against a currency loss. I do this because if I am investing in a country then I believe that the country concerned has a strong future. And if a country has a strong future then its currency will probably do well.

Some experts claim that you can gain exposure to emerging markets by buying shares in large multinationals which trade around the world. But multinationals tend to behave much as their home stock market behaves.

To diversify effectively I feel it is necessary to invest in emerging countries directly. Since I don't have the time to investigate and buy specific shares on foreign stock exchanges I get around this by buying shares in investment trusts which do this for me.

FUND MANAGERS

'Be sceptical of track records. There are so many funds and forecasts that at any point in time, someone has to have been right. With enough monkeys in the room, one of them will type Hamlet. But it doesn't mean the same monkey will then go on to write Macbeth.'
PAUL ORMEROD

A well-known fund manager speaking on television said: 'It is not possible for private investors, sitting at home in an easy chair, to work out where the market is going. They are much better off investing in a professionally managed fund.' This seemed to me to be arrogant, stupid and wrong. Most people who invest with funds run by managers like this one do worse than if they'd just dumped their money in an index fund (see page 133).

The truth is that the investment professionals are nearly always wrong. They are certainly worse at making investment decisions than the ordinary investor who is handling only his or her own portfolio. Under-performance is the norm, rather than the exception, among investment professionals. The world of investment is one of the few areas of life where the amateurs are frequently more successful than the professionals.

The stock market discounts all known information. Everyone has some information about investments, shares, companies, interest rates and so on but market professionals have access to far more information than people who don't work in the investment business. This is the basis of the efficient market hypothesis.

So, why do amateurs do better than professionals?

The first reason is that the professionals have too much information. Most of them are so busy examining the branches and the twigs that they cannot see the tree – let alone the forest. As investment amateurs, we should limit the information we seek out. The amateur investor who has too much information at his fingertips will be in the same boat as the professional – suffering from information overload.

The second reason that fund managers do badly is because in order to avoid holding too large a stake in the companies they like (a problem which might push them into having to declare their holding and suggest they are planning a takeover which they have no interest in making) they have loads of holdings in companies which they don't really like. Investment fund managers frequently end up with a huge list of investments in their funds.

The third problem fund managers have is that they cannot invest in really small companies because there simply aren't enough shares available for them to make a worthwhile investment. If you are running a fund which is measured in hundreds of millions then a half a million pound investment in a small, exciting company will make little or no difference to the success or failure of your fund. And managers know that if they try to buy large stakes in small companies they will move the price up so that they will end up paying more than they should have done.

The fourth reason amateurs beat professionals is that because fund managers are judged on their performance over very short periods (quarterly assessments are usual) they don't have the time to invest and wait for a recovery. This is a huge disadvantage for them. They must take a short-term view.

The fifth reason is that professional managers compare their results with a benchmark. They (and their bosses) are obsessed with benchmarks because doing this enables them to compare their results with the results of their competitors. The trouble is that when the competitors are doing badly a fund manager can easily match his benchmark simply by doing badly. The other problem is that fund managers have to be exposed to certain sectors in order to benchmark their progress. They have to do this whether or not it makes any sense. The result is that many funds are invested in terrible companies (or, even, good companies in terrible circumstances) simply because all other funds are invested in them. Incidentally, if a fund manager fails to beat or match one benchmark he can always find another one he can beat. Managers can always find a benchmark that proves they have done well. Unlike football club managers, whose results are out in the open for everyone to see, investment managers can switch leagues with impunity if they fail to do well in one league. Every investment fund manager will be able to produce charts and tables showing that his fund is better than all the others. How can they all do this? Simple. They pick their parameters carefully when creating their tables and their charts. Look at the small print and you'll probably find that their fund was, for example, enormously successful between March 1997 and June 1998. Take a look at the fund's record since then and you may well find that it has been far less successful. In the long run most investment companies do not do as well as the market. When their costs and expenses are taken into account the vast majority of investment funds do worse than average. Many fund managers are so desperate not to come last that they run closet tracker funds and accept that they will never beat the market.

The sixth reason is that fund managers feel they always have to be doing things. They are always buying and selling so that they look busy. Being overactive is bad. Overtrading results in more mistakes and higher costs. Doing nothing is often the best strategy but it's a strategy that the professionals eschew.

The seventh reason is that if a fund manager is running a North American equity fund then he will probably have to stay invested in North American equities. Even if everyone in the world knows that North American equities are about to fall off a cliff he will stay invested. It is what he is paid to do. You can, of course, always sell the fund. But if you stay invested in the fund you will probably do badly. The fund manager does not have the choice of moving into cash when he thinks it might be safer to do so.

The eighth reason is that as a lone investor you have one additional advantage over the professionals. Many investment funds are run by teams or committees. And most committees seem to have a collective IQ slightly lower than the IQ of the most stupid person on the committee. The more compatible the people on a committee are, and the more they respect and admire one another, the less likely they each are to say things which might question the others. The bigger the committee, and the more people like being on it (and the money and authority they get) the more likely they are to make bad decisions. Respect and politeness mean people don't say what they feel. The truth gets suppressed.

The next problem is that because all the professionals have the same information they all tend to behave in much the same way. And that means that they will do the same things. Fund managers tend to stop buying stocks when they are cheaper. At the beginning of a bear market (before the carnage starts) investment experts tell investors to buy shares. As the bear market develops they tell investors to buy because these prices are cheap. And then when prices fall through the floor they tell investors not to buy. It's the same companies, doing the same things, making the same profits. And they are a lot cheaper. When shares go down and you can get more for your money people stop buying them and won't have them in the house at any price. The professionals behave like this because it's what their peers do and they're scared of being left behind. Fund managers are unlikely to be fired for sticking with the herd, even if the herd does badly. On the other hand if you say and do the opposite to the herd, and you do badly, then your career is over. An investor who picked a bundle of stocks at random would have a better than evens chance of beating most fund managers. Remember, fund managers aim not to make money for you but to avoid doing a lot worse than their peers and, therefore, losing their jobs. The reward for outperforming is smaller than the penalty for under performing (which is probably unemployment and the need to find future employment outside the absurdly overpaid confines of the fund management industry).

Institutional investors tend to be momentum investors. They know that they will be measured not by their real success but by how they do compared to their peers. And so if stuff is going up, and being bought by other fund managers, then they will buy it too. Even pension fund managers who should have long-term horizons do this. Fund managers are terrified of being beaten by their peers. And so they usually do the same things that their peers are doing. If their peers are buying oil shares then they buy oil shares. If their peers are selling oil shares then they sell oil shares. By making the same investment decisions as their peers they ensure that they do not do worse than their peers. Of course, they don't do any better either. Inevitably, this means that when expenses and costs are taken into account most of the funds they manage will fail to beat the market.

What all this means is that if you can work out what the professionals believe is going to happen you can be pretty sure that it won't happen.

If, using all the information available to them, the professionals say that Vodafone shares are worth £1.50 each then the chances are that in the near future they are going to be worth more or less than that. If the professionals all believe that current information shows that the price of oil is going to rise then the chances are that it won't.

Knowing this is the essence of a contrarian viewpoint.

If the investment professionals all believe that the available information shows that the price of oil is destined to rise then the professionals will all buy oil. And they will push the price of oil up.

What will happen next?

No one can tell you that.

But whatever happens next will not be what the professionals expect because whatever happens next will, by definition, be triggered by something the professionals don't expect.

* * *

I have always recommended that patients take control of their own health (and their own illnesses) and use doctors as technical advisers. I believe that the same approach is the sensible one to take when dealing with money. When an expert controls your money you have lost control. And although there are a lot of so-called experts around most of them are no better than you are at managing financial matters, and none of them will be as good as managing your affairs as you can be. Certainly, none of them will care as much about your money as you do. The people selling financial products have a completely different aim to you. They want to sell a product and make a sale. You are looking for a profitable investment or a safe place to put your money. These two aims have nothing in common.

* * *

Your first advantage is that you know all this. The professionals, overcome by hubris, don't. They think they know best because they have the biggest and most powerful computers.

Your second advantage is that you do not have to do what the professionals do. You don't have to buy oil when they're all buying oil. You don't have to buy Vodafone shares when they are all buying Vodafone shares. They are frightened to do anything different to their colleagues in case they get it wrong. If they get things wrong they will be fired. You don't have that concern. Your only aim is to make your capital grow.

Your third advantage is that you don't have to waste your life studying the minute detail of annual reports and press statements. The market professionals will do all that boring stuff for you. They will study every branch and every twig.

You can use your time trying to work out what is likely to happen in the future. Because that's your edge.

You know what isn't likely to happen in the future because whatever the market professionals expect to happen according to all the available information has already been discounted and so is unlikely to happen.

Let me give a practical example.

The professional investors may, for example, think that building company shares are going to crash because all the available evidence suggests that there is going to be a housing price crash. The professionals will, therefore, sell shares in building company shares and the price of those shares will fall. They will probably crash. The share prices will fall to the level that they would fall if there was a housing price crash. The share prices of building companies have responded to what the professionals believe is going to happen according to all the information they have available. The professionals, remember, are reacting to everything that is known. They will sell building company shares as fast as they can. There will be very few (if any) professionals buying building company shares. Everyone knows that there's going to be a crash. So everyone sells the shares. And down they go.

All you've got to do next is to work out what you think really will happen next.

And the best way to do that is to keep your eye on the forest as a whole.

If, to continue with the example I've given, you believe that the housing price crash is going to be much worse than the available information suggests then building company shares will have further to fall.

But if you believe that there will be a recovery in house prices then it is probably worthwhile looking at building company shares as a possible investment. After all, the fall in the price has already allowed for a housing price crash. And, as you know markets always go down too far (just as they always go up too far).

The investment professionals are very good at looking at the past.

But it is what hasn't happened yet (or even been contemplated) which decides what happens to prices in the medium and long-term future.

Here are some more advantages you have over the professionals:

1. You're not going to upset important people by buying or selling 'inappropriate' shares.
2. You don't have to worry about short-term performance. No one is going to measure how well you've done this week.
3. You can buy shares in small companies (which are far too small for large investment funds to bother with).

4. Your performance isn't reported every day in the papers. No one but you need ever know if you make a mistake.
5. No directors (or angry shareholders) are going to question your every move.
6. You can ignore the blatherings of analysts.
7. You have no benchmarks to match.
8. You can buy and sell shares without moving the market.
9. You don't have to worry about regulators watching your every move.
10. You also have an advantage because you don't speak to company directors or managers. Investment fund managers often claim that they have an edge over private investors because they are allowed to speak to company managers. This is nonsense. Talking to company directors and executives doesn't help. On the contrary, I suspect that being too close to these people – and listening to their lies – is a huge disadvantage. All company employees are (if they are doing their jobs properly) going to say good things about their company. But how could you possibly know whether or not their views are reliable and whether or not they are telling the truth? You can't. And nor can fund managers. You're much better off not wasting your time talking to such people.

* * *

It is important to remember that the aim of bankers, brokers and investment managers is not to make their clients rich but to make themselves rich. Investors are farmed by investment managers in the same way that farmers keep sheep and cows for profit. The aim of the men in expensive suits is to make themselves rich. You can't blame them for that. Just don't misunderstand the relationship, believe all the fine words and expect them to care about your financial wellbeing.

Investment fund managers love bandwagons. If Bolivia is doing well they will launch a seemingly endless series of funds specialising in Bolivian shares. Naturally, by the time their funds are being advertised Bolivia will have peaked. But they don't care. They just want your money. If the price of copper is rising they will produce funds investing in copper mining companies. They don't care whether the mines will ever produce any copper. They don't care that the price of copper is at an all time high. They don't want to know whether it will keep going up. All they care about is spinning the facts so that they can persuade us to buy their products so that they can make money out of us. The we're-so-smart-boys on the inside intend to carry on eating caviare and foie gras and drinking Cristal champagne. We, in raggedy trousers, are supposed to stand outside and watch, sharing only insofar as we are allowed to pay the bill for their joyful extravagances. Fund managers (and their marketing and promotional staff in particular) are greedy, ruthless, unscrupulous bastards; they are a danger to our wealth and our health.

Or they were.

Now that you know how dangerous they are you will never again be as vulnerable. And you can take advantage of the best available funds in ways that suit you.

* * *

Some of America's largest pension funds have given up putting their money into active funds. Instead, they invest their money in passive investments such as index funds. Their rationale is simple: investment fund managers lose money just as often as they make it, and the fees they charge for the poor service they provide means that putting money into a plain index fund works better in the long run. Fund managers are, quite literally, often worse than useless.

Remember that everyone in the investment community makes money out of investors like us. Many of these people are very rich. The highest paid people in the country are people managing investments. Remember that their interests and ours are not allied. When they get up in the morning and go to work their aim is not to make us rich (or even to protect our capital) but to make themselves rich (and to increase their capital). Don't trust any investment professional unless you sleep with them or are closely related. Money managers want to look after themselves and their chums. It's a club to which you and I do not belong. Their interests are not just not aligned to our interests; they are diametrically opposed to our interests. Their aim is to make money out of us not for us.

Most fund managers, brokers and money managers know very little about finance or investing. So why are they so rich? They are super-salesmen (and saleswomen). They are very, very good at marketing themselves and their products. And they work in an area where it is terribly easy to pull the wool over the punters' eyes.

During the American bull market that ended in the year 2000 the S&P 500 compounded at 16% a year. The average American equity mutual fund compounded at 13.8% a year. Most of the idiots running funds couldn't even manage to be as good as 'average'. In 2007 only 25% of funds in the UK All companies sector beat the FTSE All Share. Astonishingly, 99% of all active fund managers fail to outperform the market in the long-term. What this means is that if you simply put your money into a cheap index tracker (with very low expenses) you will probably have a better return than if you put money into an actively managed fund. (The costs for tracker funds are about a quarter of the costs of actively managed funds.)

Most UK actively managed funds now have charges of between 1.5% and 1.7% and this compares badly with funds in other countries. In the USA funds charge an average of 0.67% for the same service. This difference may not sound a lot but over a period of time these charges can eat huge holes in an investment – particularly in times when returns are low. (When returns are 15% a year a 1.7% charge doesn't make too much difference to the end result.

When returns are 5% a year or less such a charge can be crippling.) Costs really are enormously important.

If you pick a fund or an investment that costs you a total of 2.5% a year, the chances are that you will not beat the market. To beat the market with that sort of inbuilt handicap your investment manager's ability to choose investments will have to be 2.5% better than all other managers. And that is a burden that is simply too great for any manager to carry.

If you invest £100 and get an 8% capital gain each year, and you leave your money for 65 years you might expect your £100 to grow to £14,880 by the end of the 65 years. But if your costs are 2.5% (average gross costs) you will get £3,250. You get 5.5% (8% – 2.5%) but that eventually yields just 17/80ths of the potential final pot – that's compound interest at work for you. By taking under half of your income the money managers end up with nearly four times as much of the potential final pot as you get. The reason is simple: the money managers get a regular infusion of capital – the 2.5% every year that you pay in costs – and that builds up steadily.

The expenses charged by investment managers may not sound much. But they can have a dramatic effect on your investment success. If your expenses are 2% you might be inclined to dismiss their potential effect. But consider: if your investments produce a return of 10% and are allowed to sit and compound for 50 years you will turn £10,000 into £1,170,000. However, if you take 2% expenses from your 10% return your 8% compounded will, after 50 years, result in a fund of £469,000. It is this effect which helps ensure that simple, low cost investments do considerably better than fancy, but expensive investments.

Fees are an enormous drain because they are constant. The drip drip drip of expenses can destroy even the best managed fund. Even 2 per cent a year will badly damage your growth prospects. In a study of 15,000 funds offered to the public over the last 20 years, only 10 managed to outperform the market index by an average of 2.4% a year for 20 years. And that is before costs.

I remember one major bank had a money market fund in sterling. There was, consequently, no currency risk. This was during a period of high interest rates. The fund actually lost money during a twelve month period. I did write and ask the bank how their fund managers succeeded in doing this but they either couldn't tell me or they didn't want to share their secret.

Some money market funds charge more than 1% in fees for putting the customers' money on deposit. Put £10,000 into one of these funds and you are paying a £100 fee to have your money split up and deposited in a few banks. Add on the fees paid to brokers and advisers, the vast expenses involved in putting money on deposit, the backroom staff required to make a note of where the money is, the taxes paid and all the other incidental costs and fees and I suppose it isn't difficult to see how even money market funds can lose money.

* * *

I beat most of the professionals by a huge margin. And you can too. Here's a summary of our advantages over fund managers:

1. We don't have to worry about what other people think about our performance. Most analysts and fund managers run together. They buy together and sell together. They are frightened to do anything different in case they fail and lose their jobs. We don't have to worry about losing our jobs.
2. We can deal in small quantities. This means that our trades won't move the share price. And we can buy shares in small companies. A professional handling a multi-billion pound fund isn't going to bother investing in a £10 million company because unless he wants to take over the company (which he won't) he can't invest enough to affect his overall performance. Even if the share price rises 1000% his holding will not show up in his overall fund. We can research, and invest in, small stocks that the big city professions won't be interested in.
3. We have tax breaks we can use to help us. We can invest in a pension fund. We can make some profits each year without paying capital gains tax.
4. We can invest for the long term. Money managers have to do well each quarter. We can buy shares that may not go up for a year. A fund manager who has two or three bad quarters will be under tremendous pressure. His time horizon is very short.
5. Professional fund managers are usually constrained by the rules of their fund. We can invest anywhere we like and in anything we fancy. And if we feel that it's better to be in cash we can be in cash. We can invest in their funds when it suits us.
6. Our overheads are smaller. Fund managers have posh offices filled with expensive staff – traders, analysts, compliance officers, corporate lawyers, public relations experts, marketing teams, human resource specialists and so on.
7. We don't need to justify our decisions to anyone.
8. We care more because it is our money.
9. We know our own appetite for risk.

> *'People of the same trade seldom meet together even for merriment and diversion, but the conversation ends in a conspiracy against the public or some contrivance to raise prices.'*
>
> ADAM SMITH

Finally, here are a few more things you should know about investment fund managers:

1. There are two basic types of fund manager: active managers and passive managers. A passive manager is a manager who tries to match the benchmark. For example, if he is investing in FTSE 100 shares his benchmark will be a chart of the ups and downs of the FTSE 100. The best way to match a benchmark is to buy an index tracker. An active manager is one who tries to beat his benchmark by using his skills. Unfortunately, the extra costs of hiring active managers (and the extra trading costs they incur) mean that the vast majority of active managers fail miserably.
2. Whenever a fund manager or professional investor has one or two good years he becomes an 'investment guru'. Journalists flock around, asking him for his secrets and his advice. The new guru doesn't really know why he's done well, of course. He's just been doing the same thing for decades. He just struck lucky. But he can't possibly admit that. So he looks at the shares which did best for him, works out a secret and shares it with the world. The chances of him having another successful year are slim and so next year there will be a new investment guru for us all to admire. Most of what passes for brilliance among fund managers is in fact simple luck. The fund manager who has been told to manage a fund specialising in a country or sector which rises will look good.
3. Experience matters enormously. A study of stock managers published by *Fortune* magazine showed that fund managers who had been managing investments for more than four years were much better than ones who had been doing it for less. Those who'd been doing it for ten years were better still and those who had been fund managing for more than 20 years were comparatively brilliant. Older investors usually do better than young ones. There are two reasons for this. First, older investors are usually more patient than young ones. They don't expect their investment decisions to produce a result in days. Second, older investors have lived through bear markets. They know how dangerous and unforgiving the markets can be. There is nothing more dangerous than an investment adviser, or a fund manager, who has not lived through a bear market. There are two provisos: the successful older investor must not be too confident of his ability and he must retain the ability to adapt to new circumstances. The problem, of course, is that you won't know if a professional investor is any good until he has been doing it 30 years by which time he will either be retiring or his fund will be at a huge premium to its net asset value. There aren't all that many elderly professional fund managers around. Successful, older fund managers, who have usually become enormously rich out of other people's money, tend to retire early to tend to their roses and sail their yachts. Unsuccessful, older

fund managers, who have usually become just ordinarily rich out of other people's money, tend to be fired and given the opportunity to spend more time tending to their roses and sailing their yachts.

4. When buying an investment fund you should check to see if the fund manager has his own money in it. Invest in funds where the managers have invested a significant portion of their own assets. This is a new variation on the old saying: 'Eat in restaurants where the chef eats his own food'.
5. Advertisements for funds are often cleverly designed to confuse potential customers. The advertisers look at periods when the fund manager did well. So, for example, they will say: 'In a twelve month period the fund showed a 36% increase.' This looks good. What the advertisement doesn't tell you is that the twelve month period was from April 1st 1996 to March 31st 1997. And all other twelve month periods you might look at were disastrous.
6. Fund managers and investment analysts don't share your aims. Your aim is probably to preserve your capital, receive some income and, hopefully, see your capital grow. Their aim is to find a way to take some of your money from you. Fund managers and investment analysts are selling their 'skills' and their 'knowledge'. But they aren't very skilful or very knowledgeable. In the end what they are selling you is marketing sizzle.
7. Most professional investors do precisely the wrong thing at precisely the wrong time. They buy high and sell low because they look back at what has been profitable, long after the reasons for it being profitable have gone. It's like publishers bringing out new variations on last year's hit books. Pension fund managers put 91% of their cash into equities in 1971 – just before a major bear market. Three years later, when stocks were cheap, they allocated just 13% of their cash to equities. And the same managers (or their descendants) bought stocks with gay enthusiasm between 1998 to 2001 when buying shares was a disastrously dangerous thing to do.
8. Never before in the history of the world have so many untrained, talentless, unskilled 20 somethings made so much money as they now make at banks and investment houses and hedge funds. Footballers are wildly overpaid but at least they provide some entertainment and have some rudimentary skills. Bankers and brokers and fund managers provide no entertainment and, apart from being able to add up the money they are taking from hard working citizens, don't even have any rudimentary skills. The people who work in the financial services industry are the most highly paid people in any country. They earn more than footballers for heavens sake! These people earn their money through creating and selling investments. They have no great skills or great knowledge. They have no talents or charm. They earn huge sums of money (and obscenely large bonuses) for flogging

financial products and moving money about. Many of them are, quite simply, crooks.

9. Some investment managers (and this is particularly true of hedge fund managers) claim to have a secret system. I would no more give these people money to look after than I would entrust my health to a man or woman with a magic black box in the consulting room.
10. You cannot expect an equity fund manager to put all his fund's money into cash when shares are too expensive. He won't do this for two reasons. First, he will be frightened that if shares go up he will be left behind by his colleagues managing other funds. Second, his job is to invest in equities. If you feel uncomfortable with having money in equities it is up to you to sell your investment in his fund and reinvest later.
11. Fund managers vote on behalf of shareholders but not for them. They vote to re-elect directors, they pass remuneration proposals, they say 'yes' when new auditors are selected. They support the gravy train because it is their chums who are benefiting (and they themselves may well be on one or two boards and benefiting too). Fund managers aren't in the business of making trouble. Incidentally, whenever I am offered a vote on any company matters I always vote against everything supported by the board. I do this to support anyone who is trying to question the way the company is managed. It seems wise to question the way companies are managed.
12. In my view the investment funds most worth buying are specialist funds which make a good range of investments in a specific area. So, for example, if you want to invest in commercial property I think it makes sense to look for an investment trust which has a decent, long-term record of investing in commercial property companies and which holds shares in most of the largest and most successful companies in that area. Similarly, if you want to invest in Russian shares then the easiest way to do this is by buying shares in an investment trust which specialises in Russian shares.
13. In the 1990's it was found that monkeys throwing darts at lists of shares did as well as professional fund managers.
14. The sharks who run investment companies, and the advisers who offer to invest your money for you, do not have your interests at heart. They just want your money. They will take as much of it as they dare. Never forget this.
15. Fund managers and analysts like to hide in the crowd. They know that if they invest conventionally, and follow the herd, they will be unlikely to look bad when compared with their peers. The fact that they do not stand a chance of beating the crowd is of no concern to them.
16. The people who run investment funds sometimes include photographs of their fund managers in their advertisements. The photographs often

show young, handsome people smiling prettily for the cameras. These advertisements do not persuade me to hand over my money. I do not want a handsome fund manager. If I am to entrust my money to someone else I want a manager who is old enough to have experienced many crises and I want someone who is so darned gnarled and ugly that he could not possibly get a job doing anything else other than sit in an office working hard. Young, handsome managers (whatever their sex) are far too likely to be distracted by life.

17. Q. 'What's the difference between a fund manager and a carp?' A. 'One's a scum sucking bottom feeder, and the other is a species of fish.'

GAMBLING

'Investment is like a game of musical chairs. What matters is not the intrinsic value of the stock but whether you are left standing when the music stops.'
JOHN MAYNARD KEYNES

Anything you do with money that doesn't involve spending it is gambling. I don't believe any investment is totally safe. In a way, all investment is gambling. There is no such thing as an entirely safe investment. If you save money then you are a gambler. You are gambling that crooks in the financial industry won't take it away. You are gambling that your government won't find a way to take it from you. Coming to terms with this is the first priority for all savers. It is possible to argue that the word investor should be banished and replaced with the word gambler since this is far more honest.

Anyone who offers you a completely safe investment, something which will always go up, which can never lose and which will protect you eternally against the ravages of inflation, is either a fool or a liar. Or both. If you put your money in a biscuit tin and hide it under the bed you are gambling. If you put money in a sock under the bed burglars might get it. If they don't get it your house might burn down. If your house doesn't burn down the currency might be changed – leaving you with the problem of taking your bank notes to the bank and changing it into new notes. And, finally, however honestly your savings may have been earned you will, if you hold a lot of money in cash, end up having to explain how you came by your wealth (and having to produce all the paperwork to prove that it was come by honestly) and then having to explain why you kept it all in cash.

All investing is gambling. So improve the odds by making sure that you only invest in things you understand and can believe in.

GOLD STANDARD

'You have to choose (as a voter) between trusting the natural stability of gold and the honest and intelligence of members of government. And with due respect to those gentlemen, I advise you, as long as the capitalist system lasts, to vote for gold.'
GEORGE BERNARD SHAW

The gold standard was the scheme under which a piece of paper (a bank note) could be exchanged for a specified amount of gold. The gold standard prevented governments building up huge deficits and it gave citizens a currency that maintained its value. When countries kept to the gold standard inflation was never much of a problem because the amount of available gold is strictly limited and so governments couldn't keep printing currency. Politicians didn't like (and still don't like) the gold standard because it forced them to balance their budgets and it put power in the hands of the people.

Most, if not all, governments used to back their currencies with gold. But these days they don't. New money is just produced as quickly as the printing presses can run. Governments no longer try to back what they print with stores of gold bullion. (One of the first things the Labour Government did in Britain when they took power in 1997 was sell off much of the nation's gold.)

When currencies become weak people tend to buy gold, in preference to holding paper money. When this happens governments tend to get twitchy. Back in 1934 the American Government confiscated gold from all Americans to stop them dumping their currency and buying gold coins.

* * *

Most people think of Isaac Newton as being the bloke who sat under a tree being bombarded with apples. But Sir Isaac wasn't just the man who thought up gravity, calculus, mechanics, the laws of motion and just about everything else worth thinking up or inventing, he was also the Master of the Mint and, therefore, the man in charge of England's currency. He was given the job partly because he was the most famous scientist in the world at the time and partly because he knew all the right people. When he was given the job it was one of those posts like the Poet Laureate – more of an honour than anything with great responsibilities.

But when Newton took over as Master of the Mint he really got into the job and one of the things he did was say that a guinea (twenty one shillings) would be made of gold and would hold its value. He tied the nation's currency (which came to be known as sterling) into the metal of which it was made, and ensured that sterling had a real value. He even ensured that the guinea could not be clipped. Up until Newton, crooks had often clipped bits from the circumference of metal coins. But Newton ensured that the guinea could not be clipped. It was solid, it rang if you dropped it and it was worth its weight in gold. Thanks to Newton the English currency was regarded as 'pure, noble and of quality' (the modern definition of sterling). It was 1717 when Newton tied the currency to gold.

Only twice, between 1717 and 1931 did the British suspend the link between sterling and gold. On each occasion it was because they needed to print more money than the available supplies of gold would allow. They suspended the convertibility of sterling to gold in order to fight Napoleon and the Kaiser. On each occasion much paper money was printed and on each occasion inflation resulted. (Wars nearly always produce more currency and, therefore, a rise in inflation.)

After Waterloo the English managed to maintain sterling as a key currency. The Government was stable and the nation's institutions were respected worldwide. The Royal Navy controlled the high seas and trading vessels followed in their wake. The industrial revolution originated in England and England's manufactured goods spread throughout the world. The words 'Made in England' were, for decades, more ubiquitous than the words 'Made in China' are today.

Whenever there was a flicker of worry about the pound the English Government would raise interest rates. This attracted foreign investors and kept the pound strong. High interest rates caused temporary hardship at home but maintained the nation's position as holder of the world's most important currency. English ships brought in raw materials from its colonies around the world. English factories then 'added value' by turning the commodities into manufactured goods. The English pound was the one currency everyone in the world wanted to hold.

And then came the Great War, the First World War.

Wars are incredibly expensive in terms of men, industrial production and assets.

After the War attempts were made to keep the pound strong. Interest rates were pushed up to bring in foreign investment. But the effect on the domestic economy was devastating. The Wall Street crash of 1929 inspired a credit collapse in England and in 1931 the pound was allowed to 'float'. It was no longer pegged to gold. On any given date the amount of gold you could get for an English pound varied according to the needs of buyers and sellers. The English pound, for so long as good as gold, became another tradeable item, like potatoes or cotton.

Suddenly, there was no key currency. Trade died because countries no longer trusted one another. Before 1931 countries could trade in pounds sterling because everyone knew what a pound was worth in terms of gold. After 1931 no one really knew what anything was worth; there was no 'safe' currency.

During World War II the dollar became the world's key currency. There was no fighting on American territory, and gold was moved to the USA because it was the safest place to keep it.

In 1944 finance ministers from 44 countries met at a place in America called Bretton Woods in New Hampshire. The currencies for those 44 countries were fixed against one another. An ounce of gold was worth $35 on every day of the week. All other countries were pegged to the American dollar. Pegging a currency to a precious metal such as gold restricts the printing of paper money because the amount of a precious metal is, by definition, finite. Restricting the amount of paper money means that everyone can trust that currency. When a currency is backed by gold the bits of paper actually mean something.

In the decades immediately after the Second World War the Americans ruled the world through the dollar. The dollar was better than gold. It could be converted into gold if you wanted the metal, but in the meantime you could use it to buy any other currency you wanted and if you left it in the bank you received interest on it.

But the Americans quickly got greedy. They found their monetary power intoxicating. And they used their dollars to buy raw materials, and all sorts of businesses and property around the world.

Quite soon more dollars were leaving America than were returning. The American balance of payments had a deficit. There were too many dollars abroad.

And then, in the 1960's, after a scant two decades of ruling the world through the dollar, things started to go sour for America.

The world started buying its oil from places other than Texas (which didn't have enough of the stuff) and car manufacturers in Germany, France and Britain started to sell cars in serious competition with the big American companies.

Central bankers could still exchange their dollars for gold, at $35 an ounce, and lots of them started to do just this. During the 1960's, the dollar started to look a bit iffy.

And then in August 1971, US President Richard Nixon stopped pretending that the US dollar had gold backing and the United States Treasury stopped handing out gold in return for dollars. There were too many dollars and not enough gold and the Americans realised that since other countries (especially France) were exchanging their dollars for gold there would eventually be an embarrassing moment when the American Government would run out of gold and have to say 'No' and refuse exchanging their currency for the lovely yellow metal. The dollar was no longer a key currency that had any backing. The American dollar was, quite suddenly, just a piece of paper.

But the dollar was still useful. It was still the world's only super currency.

And gradually the dollar split into two.

There were dollars which were available within America and which were under the control of the American Government (which could tell banks when they could or could not send dollars abroad).

And there were the vast number of dollars which were already outside America and which the American Government could no longer control. These dollars were exiles. They lived abroad, outside the American banking system and outside the control of the American Government. They became known as eurodollars.

And gradually the Americans realised something else. They did not have to make things or sell things or dig things out of the ground to become wealthy.

Since so many people around the world relied on dollars, the Americans could buy whatever they wanted to buy simply by printing more dollars. America as a nation got rich simply by running the printing presses. Getting rich had never been easier. Dollars that came off the presses were just as much dollars as dollars earned by selling Texan oil to Britons or by selling Cadillacs to Germans. Naturally, printing so many dollars meant that inflation became a real and consistent problem in America.

Inflation also became a problem in other countries, too. As American dollars flooded the world's markets so other countries had to print more money to keep up. When an American tourist went into a bank in England or Japan and exchanged his dollars for local currency he was given bits of paper printed by the British or the Japanese Governments. When an American company wanted to buy a Swedish company or an Australian company they did so by handing over dollars. All over the world, governments had to print more of their own currencies in order to keep up with all the dollars on the market.

After the Americans abandoned the link between the dollar and gold other central banks abandoned the fixed-rate relationships which had been agreed in 1944. A franc, a mark, a pound and a dollar all bounced up and down in value; each was worth what buyers and sellers decided they were worth. Central banks spent much of the 1990's trying to sell off their gold reserves. Not surprisingly the price of gold fell dramatically and stayed down. Now, although there is still some gold in the vaults of the world's governments, there is far less than most people imagine. No modern paper currency is backed by gold.

* * *

Since the gold standard was abandoned the USA has benefited from having the world's major 'base' currency. The USA gets free money from the rest of the world because it can issue dollars to be used as cash in other countries. America is successful because it made the money rules to suit itself – and the rest of the world has had to live (or die) by those rules.

At the end of World War II (and the real beginning of America's modern prosperity) the USA devised the Bretton Woods Agreement which gave the USA the right to have its dollars considered the same as gold in Central Banks throughout the world. In 1971 president Nixon refused to continue exchanging dollars for gold. At this point America gave itself the right to print as much money as it wanted. For the last thirty years the Americans have had the right to create their own wealth – at the expense of the rest of the world. The world is controlled by American currency policy. This is what has given Americans the wealth and power which they believe makes them superior to the rest of the world.

The Americans have bought companies, land and so on and paid for everything in dollars – which their Government has printed. Trillions of dollars have left the USA and been used to buy property in other countries. America has, inevitably, got richer and richer. And the rest of the world has got poorer and poorer. This is a sort of American tax on everyone else. The Americans have no intention of ever bringing those dollars back to their shore. And they have no intention of replacing the dollars with real goods and services. Other countries have to 'buy' imports by exporting goods or services. This is not true for America. America's annual trade deficit is simply a massive tax on the rest of the world. America has 'stolen' the world and has left other countries impoverished as a result. America cannot lose. For decades America has been buying 'things' without paying for them.

* * *

Finally, here are some facts you might like to know about money. These facts won't help you invest more wisely, but they will, perhaps, induce a certain healthy scepticism about money and the way governments create it.

1. The biggest, unanswered question in the world is: 'Where does money come from?' Currencies issued by governments used to be based on the gold each government had stored in its vaults. If you went along to the Bank of England, for example, you could exchange your five pound note for five pounds worth of gold. Since governments decided that they needed more money than they could get from the gold they had stored they have been 'creating money'. The money in circulation isn't real. It's just numbers. Today the total value of notes and coins produced by the Royal Mint, and issued by the Bank of England, is around 3% of the money in circulation. The rest is created electronically by banks. In other words, they just pretend that it exists so that they can lend it to people.
2. The money produced by the Royal Mint doesn't have much real value, of course. The notes are worthless and the coins are made of a mixture of metals. They are nowhere near worth their face value. (Occasionally, countries will produce coins which are made of pure metal and are worth more than their face value. When this happens people often start buying up the coins and melting them down. This is usually frowned upon very firmly.)
3. America is creating new paper money 24 times as fast as gold is being

mined. America produces about a quarter of the world's currency every year so since 4 x 24 = 96 the world is producing 96 dollars of paper for every new dollar of gold.

4. In June 2007 the Bank for International Settlements reported that the total value of global derivatives in existence was $415.2 trillion. This was just under 800% of global GDP. Which means that in 2007 bankers, pension companies and investment companies (the guys buying the £10 million London houses) were playing Monopoly with eight times the value of everything made and every service on the planet.
5. In 2008 the US money supply was growing at approximately 10% a month. That's the effective rate at which the American Government was printing new money. The value of the American dollar was decreasing by that amount every month.
6. When computers were very young, programmers saved storage space by putting only the last two digits of the year into the clocks in computers. As the year 2000 approached thousands became worried that the world's computer controlled infrastructure would stop working at the turn of the millennium. This prompted central banks to pour cheap money into the market (just in case things went wrong). It was this cheap money which fuelled the boom in dot.com and other technology stocks and which gave birth to the new theory that profits didn't matter because everything was now different. Actually, it wasn't only profits that were missing. Many of the newly launched dot.com companies didn't ever have any hope of making profits. They had no potential income source but blithely claimed that they could sort this detail out later if necessary. Eventually, of course, the absence of profits led to the dot.com bust and the destruction of billions of pounds of investors' money. The American Government solved this problem by making really cheap money available in truckloads. And that made the credit market grow at an absurd rate. Everything was done with borrowed money.
7. The creation of giant mortgage lenders (Fannie Mae and Freddie Mac), which were protected by an implicit government guarantee, meant that the bosses of these two lenders could take big risks since they knew the American Government would bail them out if things went wrong. This forced other mortgage lenders, not fortunate enough to have the same protection and therefore unable to compete, to become even wilder. It was this which led to the creation of ultra risky subprime lending. And to the 'credit-crunch' of 2008. None of this would have happened if governments had kept to the gold standard.

GROWTH INVESTING

'Our equity-investing strategy remains little changed from what it was fifteen years ago, when we said in the 1977 annual report: 'We select our marketable equity securities in much the way we would evaluate a business for acquisition in its entirety. We want the business to be one a) that we can understand; b) with favourable long-term prospects; c) operated by honest and competent people; and d) available at a very attractive price.' We have seen cause to make only one change in this creed: Because of both market conditions and our size, we now substitute 'an attractive price' for a 'very attractive price'.'

WARREN BUFFETT

Growth investors look for companies which are destined to get bigger. They look for companies with good management and a unique, proprietary position in a potentially profitable business area. They want companies which are highly profitable and getting more so. They want companies growing fast enough to beat the cost of living and inflation.

You are a growth investor if you buy shares (or a sector) because you think the price will rise in the long term. It was, for example, growth investors who bought dot.com shares at the end of the 20th Century, believing that their price would keep going up and up and up for ever.

There are many specific ways to identify growth companies but the problem is that although there aren't many companies which are genuinely growing there are lots of investors searching for such opportunities. All want to buy companies which are cheap but starting to grow and all want to sell out right at the top. The result is that the share prices at which growth companies sell often roar way ahead of reality. It is difficult to pick out good growth shares. Most investors find that by the time they have identified a company which is genuinely growing the price will be too high – driven upwards by journalists, analysts, tipsters and enthusiastic investors.

If you are keen to invest in companies which are growing then you should look for companies in a market which is growing. The company you seek should have, or be creating, products or services which will enable it to increase its market share in that growing market and in new markets.

One of the best ways to identify growing companies is, of course, to keep your eyes and ears open. For example, I bought my first batch of Psion shares when I flew to Paris in the 1980's. On the flight over a man came up to me and asked me where I'd bought my Psion handheld computer. A couple of hours later I sat down in Deux Magots cafe in St Germain. A Frenchman came up to me and asked me the same question. I immediately used my mobile phone (quite a novelty in those days) to ring my broker and buy shares in the (then comparatively young) company. Two or three years later, after the shares had risen dramatically, I needed to call Psion with a minor technical query. Getting through to speak to someone was a nightmare. In the end I gave up. And two minutes after I'd decided to give up I sold the shares. It was a good call. They duly plummeted.

There are many dangers which befall growth companies. One is that the company grows too fast, runs into a cash flow problem and explodes in a tsunami of debt. Another common problem is that the company stops growing and the investors who had pushed up the price all bail at once. The share price then collapses. Growth companies invariably mature and become no-growth companies. This happens simply because as a company grows bigger its ability to grow shrinks. If you are a burgeoning retailer with one store you can double your number of stores by opening a second store. When you have opened shops in every major town and city it's difficult to find new places to open stores. It is not uncommon for companies to grow and grow and then slowly turn into utilities. For example, a telecom or software company might grow at a dramatic rate for a few years and then slow down when it has sold its products to so many customers that there really isn't anywhere else left for expansion. At that point the company may become more like a utility, producing good regular dividends, than a growth company.

Investors sometimes buy growth stocks because they are exciting. Growth stocks offer technological change and a chance to be in at the ground floor when a new world-changing company emerges. I think this is a huge mistake. Don't ever invest for excitement. And don't invest because you want to be part of new, exciting changes. You will probably lose money if you do. If you want excitement use your investment profits to pay for scuba diving lessons. Or go bungee jumping.

HEDGE FUNDS

"It's different this time' are the four most expensive words in English.'
SIR JOHN TEMPLETON

Theoretically, a hedge fund is designed to protect investors' money. And in theory hedge funds sound like a good idea. When they were invented, hedge funds were supposed to protect the customers' money by making sure that if one investment in the fund went down another one would go up. The idea was to create a fund that beat the market by 'hedging' against all possible downturns. So, the fund manager would put some of the fund's money into things that were likely to go up when other investments in the fund went down. Simple.

That's what hedge funds are supposed to do.

However, most hedge funds aren't hedge funds at all and if there were effective laws which regulated honest advertising the majority of hedge fund managers would be sewing mailbags for a living and worrying about the calluses on their fingers rather than the weed on the hulls of their yachts. Today a hedge fund is little more than a method of transferring wealth from private individuals to rich, egotistical, confidence tricksters. As an individual private investor I expect to be able to do better than most (if not all) hedge funds on a regular basis.

Most modern hedge funds are designed with one purpose only: making money for the people who manage them. Setting up and running a hedge fund is one of the great cons of our time. People who invest in hedge funds (however astute they may think themselves) are the marks in a very modern version of the "find the lady" three card scam.

And that's the first thing that is really bad about hedge funds: the interests of the investors and the managers are not aligned – in fact they are very precisely misaligned. Modern fee structures enable poor investment managers to become extremely rich not by making money out of the market (by being clever) but by using their investors' money to make bets and then taking profits when the bets win and losing nothing when the bets lose.

Here is how it works.

If you're setting up a hedge fund and you charge the normal sort of rates you will take 2% of the total sum in the fund as a management fee (to make sure that whatever happens you make a small profit) and then give yourself 20% to 50% of any return above, say, the first 5% of the profits.

As far as the hedge fund manager is concerned, the beauty of this arrangement is that although hedge fund managers take a big chunk of the profits they don't share in the losses. They can't lose money. The hedge fund managers use their investors' money to help themselves get rich but if the fund loses money they themselves don't lose a penny (unless they've put some of their own money into the fund to convince investors to get involved).

The system that has been operating now for some time actually rewards hedge fund operators for taking huge risks with other people's money. It's difficult to blame the hedge fund operators. Offer £10 million to the man on the top of the Clapham Omnibus and tell him that he will get 20% of any profit he makes, but that there will be no loss to him if he loses it all, and see what happens. He will either rush to the nearest race track and put the lot on an outsider at 100 to one or he will totter along to his local casino and put everything on his favourite number. If he is feeling really greedy he will use your money to raise some more (leveraging up the bet). He will then put your money, and the money he has borrowed on your behalf, onto a horse or lucky number. If the money is lost he will walk away.

Amazingly, that is exactly how hedge funds operate.

When the fund fails, because a bet has failed, the hedge fund manager walks away and starts another fund. In some instances the manager walks away with a 20% profit after one year's life span of a, say, 10 year investment, when there was no guarantee that by the end of the investment's life the investor would have any genuine profit at all.

The loser is always the investor (or the pension fund which has foolishly chosen to invest in the hedge fund.)

Hedge fund managers have found a way to take the financial benefits of entrepreneurship without taking any of the risks or skills traditionally required. To a certain extent the same thing is true of some private equity fund managers who also help themselves to a big chunk of the loot made by investing other people's money.

Running a hedge fund is, without a doubt, the great confidence trick of all time. It makes the guy who sold the Eiffel Tower three times look amateurish. It's no coincidence that some of the richest men in the world are hedge fund managers. These guys make hundreds of millions a year (in whatever currency you can think of) but most of them do it by gambling with other people's money rather than by beating the market.

If the fund goes bust they have to close it, of course, but they also close the fund if they lose money. From their point of view (and with hedge funds everything is done from their point of view) there is a good reason for this. If the fund loses money the manager won't get an incentive fee the following year until the losses are recouped and the 'high water mark' is reached. So it makes more sense to close down and start another fund. The investors lose money but who cares about them?

The managers of hedge funds are usually very secretive about what they do with their investors' money. As you might expect they think up all sorts of rubbishy (and sometimes very complicated) reasons for not telling people what has happened to their money. But the truth is very simple. Hedge fund managers don't like telling the customers what they are doing with their money because if they did, most of the customers would have twenty kinds of fit and demand their money back immediately. Most hedge fund managers seem adept at avoiding legislation which forces other investment managers to publish pretty precise details about what they do with the customers' money. In truth, many hedge fund managers seem to me to be little more than gamblers. They put all their investors' money on red and then cross their fingers.

The next really bad thing about hedge funds is that they tend to be very illiquid. When you put your money into a hedge fund you have to wave goodbye to it because you don't know when, or if, you will see it again. If you put in money you may have to agree to leave it there and to redeem your investment only at quarterly intervals (assuming there is any left). If times are really bad the managers may simply refuse to let you have your money back at all. Hedge funds are very illiquid.

One of the worst things hedge funds have done has been to spread their philosophy of greed throughout the wider banking system. Employees of big banks gave themselves a similarly one-sided bonus system which encouraged them to take big risks because although they could benefit enormously if they 'won' there was no downside for them personally if they 'lost'. They were gambling with the bank's money and for them there was no downside. If the gamble worked they made a ton of money. If the gamble failed they just received a huge salary and a smaller bonus. (They nearly always managed to find a reason to give themselves a bonus.) Employees of investment banks took home a huge share of their firms' revenue in the good years. They took home an average of 60% of revenue in 2007. The prospect of making big bonuses encouraged the investment bankers to goose profits by excessive borrowing. In 2008 around 4,000 British bankers received bonuses of more than £1,000,000 a year each.

* * *

If you think I'm being unfair about hedge funds, consider these facts:

1. The average life of a hedge fund is four years.
2. Every year the number of hedge funds closing down (through failure) is matched pretty closely by the number opening up (with big promises). The new funds are often run by the same people who ran the funds which failed.
3. Hedge fund managers have a duty to themselves to take big risks with their investors' money. They can always start again when they go bust.
4. Because of the enormous risks involved with hedge fund investments many financial advisers now recommend investing in a hedge fund fund of funds. These are, as you might expect, funds which invest money in a number of different hedge funds. The aim is to reduce the risk of making a loss by investing in a poorly run hedge fund. Hedge funds are rubbish but fund of fund hedge funds are terrible rubbish. You are paying huge amounts in expenses to be part of this con. The manager of the hedge fund fund of funds takes another huge bite at any profits you make (but takes on none of the losses, of course). The result is that even if the funds in the super fund do well the profits left over for investors are likely to be pretty mingy.
5. Some hedge fund investors undoubtedly do make a profit. Just as a few people who bet on horses occasionally make a profit. The hedge fund investors will, like the horse racing aficionados, probably quickly lose their winnings and their original stake if they don't get out when they are ahead.
6. The tricksters who manage hedge funds have a number of techniques for

parting their marks and patsies from their money and for making huge amounts of money for themselves.

Here's one simple method of making money as a hedge fund manager by using lots of gearing to boost your returns (even though it puts your investors at greater risk).

First, you collect £100 million from gullible investors.

Second, you use the £100 million to buy something (anything) you think might go up. For the sake of this example, let's say you decide to put the money into snowdrop bulbs. You do not, however, merely invest the £100 million in snowdrop bulbs. Instead, you boost your possible returns by buying warrants or options or some other fancy folderols. You leverage your investment as highly as you can. If you leverage by ten times you will then have used your clients' £100,000,000 to enable you to put £1,000,000,000 into the market.

If things go well and the price of snowdrop bulbs doubles you now have £2,000,000,000. (I'll ignore the fund's expenses for simplicity.) You have made huge amounts of money for your clients (who are undoubtedly very happy) and you get 20% of the profit (£2,000,000,000 minus £100,000,000) at no risk to yourself.

If things go badly, and your bet doesn't come off, the price of snowdrop bulbs might halve. You have now lost half of the £1,000,000,000 you invested. That means that you have lost £500,000,000. That, of course, is five times the amount of money you raised from your investors. So your fund has gone bust and your investors are wiped out.

At this point you simply close down and start a new hedge fund. Even among the very best hedge funds around 40% close within five years (not surprisingly, hedge funds are very secretive about this).

7. Here's another little trick the hedge fund tricksters try.

Hedge fund A begins by making an investment in Buttonhooks and Shoehorns Limited. This is a start up company which is not yet quoted on any stock exchange. At the end of the first year hedge fund A sells its investment in Buttonhooks and Shoehorns Limited to hedge fund B and takes a 100% profit. The managers of hedge fund A take 20% of this profit and the investors in hedge fund A get the rest and are very happy. However, this is definitely a zero sum game (for every winner there is a loser) and the investors in hedge fund B are now left with an overpriced investment on their books. The investment is, however, kept on the books at the price that has been paid for it. The managers of hedge fund B aren't as stupid as they look and so they sell their investment in a second unquoted company called Homburg Hats Limited to the managers of hedge fund A. Naturally, the managers of hedge fund B sell their investment at a price that will give them and their investors a 100% profit. They then give themselves 20% of the profit as their share of the loot. The shares in the dead duck that is Homburg Hats Limited are left on the books of hedge fund A, but they sit there at the price that has been paid for them so the managers of hedge fund A are not affected. When the two hedge funds are eventually wound up both will be carrying worthless investments on their books. But since the managers of hedge funds don't share in the losses only the investors will lose money.

8. Hedge fund managers claim that they can protect investors' money in a downturn. But during the investment carnage of 2008 the average hedge fund lost more than 13% in nine months and the industry as a whole lost nearly £200 billion of investors' money. By October 2008 the average listed fund of hedge funds open to UK private investors had managed to lose 32% of their clients' money in the previous twelve months. Naturally, many funds of hedge funds had done considerably worse than this. And these figures suffer from 'survivor bias' because they don't take account of all the funds that shut down or went broke. If these funds were taken into account the final figures would be considerably worse. For this disastrous record the hedge funds charged their hapless investors vast sums – after promising security and positive results, with their clever long-short plays, whatever the market might do. By October 2008 it was estimated that at least half of hedge funds, which had at last turned out to be little more than a complex and highly profitable fee structure in search of an investment rationale and a population of willing and naive suckers, would disappear completely. In addition to all this financial carnage it seems likely that the indiscriminate selling of shares and other holdings by hedge funds (which were being forced to sell both as they deleveraged and as their investors demanded their money back) contributed to the collapse of the stock market in the autumn of 2008.
9. I always avoid companies where the directors are encouraged to take huge risks with my money so that they can make themselves rich – at virtually no risk to themselves. Since this is what hedge funds do I never invest in hedge funds. Hedge fund costs are so high that, with a few exceptions, most do badly for their investors.
10. If you are determined to put money into a hedge fund then perhaps you should use your own money to set one up. Once you have set up your hedge fund all you have to do is to print a smart looking brochure and persuade some rich and stupid people to invest in your fund. This is, I believe, the best way to get rich out of a hedge fund.

INDEPENDENT FINANCIAL ADVISORS

'Everyone's got a plan till they get punched in the mouth.'
MIKE TYSON

There are two types of independent financial advisor.

First, there are the ones who earn their living by receiving a commission from the investment company whose products they are selling. These advisers are worse than useless. They will often flog their clients the products which carry the highest level of commission – whether they are suitable, or any good, or not. They will, for example, suggest that their investors put money into unit trusts (which do pay a fee) but they will ignore investment trusts (which don't pay a fee). If you take advice from someone on commission then the chances are high that you will end up investing in the funds which pay your adviser the biggest commissions – rather than in the funds which are best for you. Make sure that your advisor carries indemnity insurance so that if he or she does sell you something entirely inappropriate you will stand a chance of getting serious amounts of money in damages if you need to sue him or her later. And remember that the executive saloon car outside the adviser's office has probably been paid for by the fees he or she has charged people like you rather than by the profits he or she has made through his investment skills. (The advisor might like you to think that the car was paid for out of successful investments. It was almost certainly paid for out of commission paid by rubbishy investment groups.) Big banks, brokers and advisers will all sell you what is good for them to sell and not what is good for you to buy. They are, after all, in the business of making money and not in the business of helping you make money.

Second, there are the rare advisors who charge a fee for their advice. These advisors charge the same sort of fees as the most expensive solicitors or doctors though I doubt if even they would claim to have spent as long being trained.

I suspect that most independent financial advisors are 'independent' in the same way that car salesmen are independent. The financial advisors I have spoken to have known far, far less about investing than you will know when you have finished this book.

I'm afraid I don't have much faith in investment advisors. Actually, scratch that. I don't have any faith in them. I've never found one who knew what he (or she) was talking about, though I've met quite a number who managed to sound good and to make some impressive sounding promises. Bankers, insurance salesmen and independent financial advisors are no different to second hand car salesmen or estate agents. They are no more interested in your financial welfare than the car dealer selling you an old banger might be and no more interested in your financial stability than an estate agent flogging you a house is anxious to ensure that you buy just the right property. All these people see you as the 'mark'. They want the commission. No one cares about you and your needs as much as you.

* * *

Financial advisors make a living because there is a myth that looking after money is terribly confusing and requires a professional.

'You wouldn't try and remove your own appendix so why would you try to manage your money yourself?' demanded one advisor.

There are two flaws in this argument.

The first is that looking after money is as complex as removing an appendix or, even, doing the conveyancing on a house. It isn't. Looking after money is something you and I can do quite well for ourselves. And the more we learn the better we will become at it.

The second flaw is the suggestion that investment advisors are professionals who know what they are doing. The truth is that even the ones who are fully 'trained' have often only acquired quite modest academic qualifications.

The bottom line is simple: don't bother hiring an independent financial advisor. Keep your investments as simple as possible. The more layers of management there are between you and your money, the more chances there are of someone screwing up or ripping you off.

Nor do I have much faith in private wealth managers. Private wealth management sells itself well. Well-spoken men and women in beautifully tailored suits will sit you down in expensively panelled rooms and serve you delicious coffee in delicate bone china cups. They will give you a leather portfolio statement book and a smart, expensive pen. But most don't have a good record of keeping, let alone growing, their clients' money.

Oh, and one other thing: you should be aware that if you consult an accountant, a financial advisor, a banker or a solicitor about your finances there is a good chance that every secret you share will be passed onto the authorities. New laws forcing advisors to contact the authorities about the slightest suggestion of a suspicion mean that honesty no longer offers adequate protection against this sort of rough intrusion. Advisors (and this counts for their staff too) are fined heavily if they do not pass on anything they think could possibly be of interest to the authorities. And don't rely on your adviser warning you: it is an offence for advisers (of any variety) to tell their clients what they are doing.

INDEX FUNDS

'Though the stock market functions as a voting machine in the short run, it acts as a weighing machine in the long run.'
BEN GRAHAM.

If you want to match the market (and, therefore, beat most of the investment professionals) you can do so by investing in index funds (also known as tracker funds). These funds merely track indices by buying a few of all the shares in whichever index you choose. You can, for example, pick an index representing the top 100 companies in the UK, an index representing the top 250 companies or an index representing all the shares which are quoted on the London Stock Exchange. Index funds charge investors less because a computer (instead of an overpriced fund manager) can do the buying and selling. And because they spend less on advertising (and pay little or no commission to middlemen or 'investment advisors' as they so pompously call themselves) they will do better for you than most of the actively managed investment funds you are likely to come across. By definition, trackers will never outperform the market. But a portfolio of trackers will, over the medium to long-term, outperform the majority of active managers – particularly because of the additional cost of fees charged by the active managers. It costs around 2.5% a year to have your money managed in an ordinary, active investment fund. So, to earn his or her keep the manager has to make 2.5% a year more than you could get from a tracker. In practice, virtually none do that. Naturally, this means that the majority of active managers – who are, individually, paid huge fees to manage people's money – underperform the market. There are thousands of professional investment managers in Britain. Over the last few decades just six of them have beaten the index. (And the chances of those six beating it over the next few decades are incredibly slim. Most will, in any case, have retired by then.) Investment managers should be embarrassed by this but few seem to be.

If you find investing too scary or too time consuming or you find that you fail to beat the index, give up and buy a tracker fund. Smart investors can over years beat the indices but if you can't make 2% more than an index fund then it isn't worth the effort. With an index fund or a tracker you will more or less match the market (even though index funds are supposed to match the market precisely there are usually some slight differences) and that will enable you to beat the vast majority of active investors.

If you are choosing an index fund buy the one with the smallest expenses on the grounds that if all horses are equal the one with the lightest jockey wins the race. Investing in index funds is the best way to match the market and to beat the investment professionals. And since you're buying a basket of shares there isn't much need to keep too close an eye on things. A 'buy and hold' philosophy is fine for index trackers and for good investment trusts. The less you buy and sell the less your trading costs will be. The miracle of compounding should do the hard work.

INFLATION

'Invest in inflation. It's the only thing going up.'
WILL ROGERS

Governments lie about inflation.

First, they claim that inflation is a rise in prices which is outside their control, and which they are struggling to hold back. This is the first lie. Inflation is caused by governments printing more money, and devaluing the stuff that is already in existence. If the government doubles the amount of currency in circulation then it halves the value of the money that's already out there. And that pushes up prices. So governments cause inflation.

The second lie is the size of the problem. Inflation is usually much higher than they say it is. This is because the official figures exclude luxuries such as housing, energy and food. Education, pensions and healthcare are also routinely omitted – even though these are, for many people, the biggest costs in their budget. It is for this reason that people whose income is inflation-linked (people with inflation-linked pensions or private pensions depending on index linked gilts) find life difficult. In order to retain your spending power (and your quality of life) you need to make much more than official inflation levels from your investments – otherwise your capital is shrinking. So if you don't take risks you are going to become poorer.

When the official level of inflation is 5% the real level of inflation will be at least double that. This means that if you are earning less than 10% a year on your investments you are losing money. With a lower official level of 2.5%, and an unofficial level of 5%, any increase in your capital of less than 5% means that you are losing money.

All this means that unless you are very rich, or are prepared to accept a deteriorating standard of living, you have to take some chances with your capital. Government policy means that you really don't have much choice.

* * *

It is vital to understand that inflation figures are now crooked and that the inflation figures governments talk about bear no relationship to the real inflation figures.

> *'Inflation is like sin: every government denounces it and every government practises it.'*
> SIR FREDERICK LEITH-ROSS

The official inflation figures in the UK and the USA in 2008 were both over 5% – excluding non-essential fripperies such as food and energy. So, if you didn't spend money on food or energy you only needed to grow your money by 5-6% a year to ensure that your capital remained the same. Of course if you did feel the need to spend money on food or energy then you would need to increase your capital by 10-15% a year or more in order to stand still. (Gas prices went up by 35-40% in the UK in the autumn of 2008 alone.) Unfortunately, most people's investments actually fell in value during the first years of the 21st Century. Indeed, many investment funds were, in 2008, at more or less the same level that they had been in the mid 1990's. It is hardly surprising that many people felt that there was really little point in saving.

Inflation has a powerful effect on investments. Rising inflation is toxic for shares and for bonds. When inflation goes up interest rates also rise and governments tighten up monetary policy. When inflation falls share prices and bond prices tend to go up, and sometimes soar. The huge bull markets of the 1980's and 1990's were a consequence of the fact that inflation was falling from the high levels of the 1970's. Many investors who did well during the 1980's and 1990's still believe that their success was 'normal' and to be expected. Some actually believe that they are entitled to gain 15% returns from their portfolios for ever more.

Here are some things you should know about inflation:

1. Inflation was kept down at the end of the 20th Century because we were importing cheap stuff from China. Cheap television sets, cheap bras and cheap shoes. This helped enormously in the 1980's and 1990's. It meant that we could buy more stuff with the money we had in our pockets and our bank accounts. But the Chinese workers now want higher wages. They want motor cars and they want television sets of their own. So our inflation rate will rise.

2. The rate of inflation has a vital influence on the economy. Rising inflation means that interest rates have to go up (or must, at the very least, be kept at their current level). Rising inflation also means that monetary policy must be tightened. Falling inflation, on the other hand, results in lower interest rates and a booming economy. If inflation is not considered a threat central bankers can, if they think it is necessary, reduce interest rates in order to stimulate a stagnant economy. But if inflation is considered a threat central bankers will usually keep interest rates fairly high because

they will be worried that if they lower interest rates too much they will over-stimulate the economy and produce more inflation. (Governments constantly claim to have found the way to conquer the 'boom and bust' economy. They are lying, of course.) The bull market of the late 1980's and 1990's followed the high inflation rates and big bear of the 1970's. It was the falling inflation rates that drove the powerful bull markets of the 1980's and 1990's. I remember locking in loans at 11-12% for property investments in the 1980's because the rate seemed absurdly low (to me and to everyone else). As inflation fell and productivity went up (as a result of new technology and as China and India started manufacturing things) so we did better and better. Cheapish oil made everything very easy. Those were the days when investors got, and learned to expect as normal, returns of 15% a year on their equity investments. If you wanted your money to grow there was no other game in town. Just buy shares and sit back and wait. And you didn't have to wait long.

3. In the middle of the 20th Century governments undermined the value of our money (and discouraged savings) by printing too many banknotes. The more money in circulation, the less the money is worth. (Because there is a finite number of things that can be bought with the money in existence). Today, the amount of money in circulation (in the form of real notes) is only a tiny amount of the money available. Banks are now creating money by lending it as a debt (with interest attached, of course) and it is that practice which has really pushed up inflation. The whole problem started when bankers and politicians got rid of gold as a basis for our currencies. When governments could only print as much currency as they had gold, the politicians were restrained. When the link with gold was abolished governments were free to print as much money as they wanted. Then they made things even worse by using computers to create seemingly endless supplies of 'imaginary' money. It's hardly surprising that house prices have been rising (with occasional slumps) for decades. I bought a birthday card for my wife yesterday. It cost more than my first car. That's inflation. Inflation really does eat away at savings. If you had put £1,000,000 in a box under your bed 40 years ago it would now have a purchasing power of £77,000. (Yes, I know the notes would be out of date and useless even if they hadn't been eaten by mice.)
4. Paradoxically, politicians and central bankers love some inflation. The reason is simple. When the value of money goes down a little bit (which is what happens in inflation – you can buy less for your unit of currency) debts get washed away. If you are a government with huge debts then inflation is a wonderful thing. It helps diminish the value of your debts as time goes by. (By the same principle, inflation helps reduce the value of debt for everyone else, too.)

5. Rising commodity prices usually result in a rise in inflation in countries which have to import commodities. Countries which produce the commodities which are rising in value usually do well. I am very long-term bullish about the price of oil and other commodities (commodities of all sorts are running out and the demand for them is rising inexorably). I therefore believe that high inflation is likely to be a consistent problem in countries such as Britain (which rely on importing commodities such as oil). I also believe that countries such as Canada and Australia (which produce huge quantities of essential commodities) are likely to have a relatively strong future.
6. Inflation hit nearly 15% in the USA in 1980. (It was much higher in the UK.) This was a direct result of America's 1971 decision to abandon the link between the dollar and gold. Freed from the need to back up their dollars with gold the American Government printed more and more dollars. And the dollar became increasingly worthless. Will inflation ever get back to those now seemingly absurd levels? Why not? Governments are still printing vast quantities of currency and backing up their banknotes with nothing but hot air. It seems inevitable that the value of currencies just about everywhere should continue to shrink. And that, after all, is all that inflation is.
7. Inflation means that for most people their salaries and wages have failed to rise for many years. People think they are better off than they were twenty years ago. But when inflation soars it enables workers to have pay rises without the pay rises actually costing anything. People aren't really better off because costs have risen faster than pay.
8. Real inflation is around 10% (maybe more) so if money isn't invested and growing then your purchasing power is diminishing and you will get poorer. If you are reliant on an allegedly inflation-proof pension you can rely on the fact that your pension will not keep up with inflation. Falsifying the inflation figures means that inflation-proofed salaries and pensions paid by the government can be increased by a much smaller figure than would be necessary if they were being increased by the real level of inflation.
9. Officially, inflation in the UK for the last 30 years has averaged 5.3% a year. That means that if you had money invested for that period and your after tax income was less than 5.3%, you were losing money. If you are a 40% taxpayer it's quite difficult to get an after tax income of 5.3% without taking considerable risks.
10. Governments don't just ignore rising costs in food and energy when they are assessing inflation figures. (They fiddle the figures in this grotesquely dishonest way because it is easier to keep the official inflation figures down – and to convince everyone that they are doing a good job – if they don't count the things that are going up most.) They also use astonishing little

tricks such as including hedonic adjustments and rental-equivalent home pricing and using geometric averaging when working out different varieties of inflation.

Geometric averaging means that if the basket of goodies measured to find the inflation figure contains one item which goes up 10% and another which goes down 10% the effect on the basket isn't 0% (as you might imagine) but a 1% fall. Governments produce this miracle of accounting by multiplying 110 (the figure obtained because of the 10% rise) by 90 (the figure obtained because of the 10% fall). This gives a total of 99. And, lo, a fall in inflation (and the cost of living) of 1%. Only politicians and economists can do this.

Hedonic adjustments enable politicians to take advantage of progress to keep inflation low. If you bought a computer a year ago for £1,000 and you replace it with a computer which costs £1,500 but is 10 times as fast then the computer is registered by the government as costing less even though it really cost more.

And rental-equivalent home pricing? That's a trick they use to minimise the effect of rising house prices (when they include them). If your home is now worth twice as much as it was a few years ago but the rent you would have to pay has only gone up by half then the inflation figure is deemed to be a half. The real rise in the cost of the home is ignored.

All these utterly, deplorably, dishonest inventions were designed to enable politicians to lie and cheat the voters. There are more tricks: for example, when they measure gross domestic product they tend to ignore the fact that the population has grown and that the per capita GDP – the figure that really matters – is probably going in the other direction but I'm getting weary and I suspect you are too. Unravelling the lies they tell can be tiresome work. The lies have worked very well on both sides of the Atlantic. Politicians and civil servants are concerned only with what they can get away with. They ignore the moral and ethical dimensions.

In the summer of 2008 the official US inflation figure was between 2% and 2.5% but, if the American Government hadn't changed the way it measured inflation back in 1992, the official inflation figure would, during that summer, have been close to 9%. The real, practical inflation figure would have been even higher.

Businessmen and women who lie usually fail eventually (though they may get exceedingly rich before they fail). Investing in companies run by crooks can damage an investment portfolio. But politicians who lie (and lie well) usually do well. The electors consistently choose the politicians who lie most convincingly.

11. Inflation is an invisible tax. Although it is a boon for borrowers (the

£250,000 borrowed to buy a house shrinks as a result of inflation) it is a curse for savers (the £250,000 pension fund shrinks in value and purchasing power as a result of inflation). Pensioners and others on a fixed income lose out because their buying power is constantly being eroded. Earners whose income doesn't match inflation (the real figure, rather than the false 'official' figure) also lose out. They may seem to be getting richer, as their income grows, but in reality they will be getting poorer. And everyone who pays tax will lose out. Tax thresholds do not usually rise with inflation. So stamp duty on house purchases affects an increasing number of people as house prices rise and the stamp duty thresholds remain the same. And since the point at which taxpayers find themselves liable for higher rates of tax tends to stay the same (or to rise nowhere near as much as inflation) the number of people paying higher tax rates is rising rapidly. You will probably not be surprised to learn that governments don't usually take inflation into account when helping itself to a share of your income. So, if you have a 6% income on your investments and tax rates are 40% you will pay 40% of your 6% to the government. That leaves you with a 3.6% return. But if the official level of inflation is running at 5% then you are losing 1.4% a year. If real inflation is 10% you are losing 6.4% a year. You may think you are getting richer but in reality you are getting poorer.

12. In August 2008 Zimbabwe issued a Z$100 billion note to keep up with inflation (then running at 2.2 million %). That was not, however, the highest denomination banknote produced in the last 100 years. In the 1920's Germany had a 100 trillion Papiermark note. And in 1946 Hungary printed notes with a face value of 1,000,000,000,000,000,000 pengos (that's one followed by 18 zeros and it is known to its friends, if it has any, as a quintillion). One German I know recently pointed out to me that his father had taken out an insurance policy in 1903. Every month he made payments. The policy was for a 20 year term and when it matured he cashed it and took out the proceeds. He used the entire proceeds to buy a single loaf of bread. A Berlin publisher reported that an American visitor tipped their cook one dollar. The family met and it was decided that a trust fund should be set up in a Berlin bank with the cook as beneficiary. They asked the bank to administer and invest the dollar. The price rises in inflation-crazy Germany became dizzy. A student at Freiberg University ordered a cup of coffee in a cafe. The price on the menu was 5,000 marks. He had two cups. When the bill came the price for the second cup of coffee had risen to 9,000 marks. He was told that if he had wanted to save money he should have ordered both cups of coffee at the same time. The printing presses at the Reichsbank could not keep up. Factory workers were paid daily at 11.00 a.m. A siren would sound and everybody gathered in the factory forecourt where a five ton lorry waited. The lorry was full of paper money. The chief

cashier and his assistants would climb up onto the lorry, call out names and throw down bundles of notes. People rushed to the shops as soon as they had caught their bundle. Doctors and dentists stopped accepting currency and instead demanded butter and eggs. When the Germans introduced a note for one thousand billion marks hardly anyone bothered to collect their change. It wasn't worth picking up. By November 1923 a single dollar was worth a trillion marks.People living on their pensions found that their monthly cheque would not buy a cup of coffee. People dependent on insurance payments were destitute.

When traced back it is clear that hyperinflation in Germany started when Germany abandoned the gold backing of its currency in 1914. The Government borrowed to finance the war.

Half a century later the Americans borrowed to finance the Vietnam war (their philosophy was identical: the war will be over quickly). And since America left the gold standard and started borrowing big time inflation has been a constant and serious problem. (Though the extent of it has been ignored and suppressed.)

13. It is partly because of their unspoken fear of inflation that ordinary people throughout the world have unwisely (but understandably) relied on buying property as a defence and a way of preserving wealth.
14. In spring 2007 the Japanese Government sold a two year bond which promised to pay interest of 1% a year. This was the highest bond the Japanese Government had issued in ten years. When Governments flood their countries with money that doesn't cost much to borrow (because interest rates are kept low) they are deliberately creating inflation. When money is 'cheap' people buy more houses. Between 1985 and 1991 houses in Japan rose by 51% before the bubble burst. Similar things have happened in America and the UK. In America, where interest rates were kept low, house prices rose 90% between 2000 and 2006. And then the bubble burst. In the United Kingdom, where interest rates were also kept low, house prices rose 118% between 2001 and 2007. Many so-called experts dismissed thoughts that this was a bubble and claimed that house prices could, and would, continue to rise indefinitely.

'Last year if you didn't eat, didn't drive to work, didn't heat your home, didn't visit a doctor, didn't buy a house, didn't buy insurance of any kind, didn't have a child in college and didn't pay...taxes, your cost of living agrees with the Government's cost of living index.'

CLYDE HARRISON

Printing lots of new bonds (and ultimately lots of new currency notes) is an easy way to improve your exports. It was started in earnest by the Americans in the 1990's. It works because when you print more currency you lower the value of the stuff already in existence. And when the value of your currency falls when compared with the currencies of other countries your exports become cheaper. All the world's major powers are now increasing their money supply by over 10 per cent a year. The Americans are now increasing theirs by around 14% a year. It is hardly surprising that the American dollar has been on a downward slide for years. This is not an accident. It is the American Government's deliberate policy. The dollar has lost more than seven eighths of its purchasing power over the last 60 years.

Of course, it isn't only the American dollar which has been destroyed by Governments deliberately printing more money. The British Government is printing new money at around 13% a year. The European Bank is printing money at 9% a year. And so on. The British Pound, the Euro and even the once powerful Swiss Franc have all lost value in recent years. Today there is $40 trillion worth of paper money in the world and $50 trillion worth of bonds. A trillion is a million million or a thousand billion.

Information for Investors: Lies and Deceits

'Where is the wisdom we have lost in knowledge?
Where is the knowledge we have lost in information?'
T. S. ELIOT

The truth is the rarest and most valuable commodity of them all. If truth were a tradeable commodity it would cost more than gold or platinum.

When I first started out as an investor I assumed that everything I read would be accurate and that everything I was told (by brokers, bankers and company directors) would be honest and well meant. Sadly, I now realise that this was woefully optimistic of me. Over the years I have come to realise that the world of finance is rich with liars, fraudsters and crooks. And my early hopes that my interests would be protected by politicians and civil servants employed as regulators have been dashed by the realisation that neither group care a jot about private investors. For example, the British Government dismissed investors who had lost money in the blue chip Railtrack and the insurer and pension company Equitable Life as 'grannies' or 'middle class' and therefore irrelevant and unimportant.

Sometimes the lies told are blatant. Many company directors will, it seems, do almost anything to keep their jobs, their bonuses and their share options. Sometimes investors are misled by deceits rather than direct lies. Relevant facts are buried deep in an annual report or are conveniently forgotten. Honour and integrity are rare beasts in the investing jungle. It is sometimes difficult to tell where negligence ends and dishonesty starts.

Having been an investor for nearly half a century I have become cautious about who and what I believe. I suspect that any investor who has been around a while will have acquired a similarly cynical view of human nature. Either that or they will have lost all their money. When you've been ripped off by large companies and deceived by governments it becomes difficult (and financially dangerous) to accept anything at face value.

It seems to me that these days things are worse than ever. The Internet, widely regarded as a useful research tool, is now of very little value to those looking for facts. It is, on the contrary, a splendid medium for rumour mongers, gossips, liars, cheats, confidence tricksters and others with self-serving ambitions. In the world of finance the driving force is, of course, usually greed. People want to get rich or stay rich and in order to do so they lie.

But, although it is the lies and deceits of the investment professionals, the journalists, the politicians and the people employed to police the markets, which cause most damage to the ordinary investor, it is important to remember that, in recent years, much of the damage to our financial environment has been done by ordinary people.

Many of those who lied about their income when applying for mortgages will claim that they were encouraged to do so by mortgage brokers and bankers. Many will regard themselves as ordinarily honest individuals who succumbed to temptation; purchasing property they couldn't afford to pay for in the naive belief that they would be able to make money because property prices always rise.

But the people applying for loans they couldn't afford to repay were driven by the same greed as the mortgage brokers. People who lied about their income in order to purchase homes they couldn't possibly afford were just as responsible for the financial crisis that hit hard in 2008. (There was much hypocrisy around as self-serving home owners pleaded for help to enable them to afford mortgages they should have never taken on.)

In early autumn 2008 Gordon Brown, Britain's Prime Minister, claimed no subprime mortgages were sold in Britain and that the world's economic crisis was created in America.

Brown was, in my view, the worst Chancellor Britain has ever had. But did he really believe what he said? For him to claim that there were no subprime mortgages in Britain suggests an appalling and rather frightening ignorance of the real world. The reality is that thousands of house purchasers were encouraged to lie about their income and to borrow far more money than they could ever possibly afford to repay. In autumn 2008 the *Financial Times*, reporting that banks in the UK had lent to hundreds of thousands of consumers with impaired or low credit ratings, estimated that 5% to 8% of UK mortgages were subprime.

The whole financial mess was born out of greed. Nothing more and nothing less. The only difference between the greedy bankers and fund managers (who took millions from the system) and the greedy home buyers (who bought homes they couldn't afford) was that there were fewer of the former than of the latter and that the former were, on the whole, less hypocritical about their greed. Were people who lied about their incomes in order to obtain property they could not honestly have afforded really 'victims'?

During my years as an investor I have seen trust breakdown more or less completely. (This is not, of course, something that has happened exclusively in the world of finance. Trust is now little more than a memory in most areas of public life.) Millions of people have grown accustomed to living beyond their means and have got into the habit of lying in order to continue to do so. The over-bearing, demanding attitude of many representatives of 'authority' in our society has encouraged millions to regard the truth as an irrelevant luxury.

Trust has broken down because honesty has disappeared. When pensioners, shareholders and depositors can no longer believe anything they are told by the institutions in whom they are supposed to put their trust, can anyone be surprised at the consequences? Banks don't even trust one another these days.

Until trust and honesty return to public and commercial life the investor who survives will, I am sad to say, be the investor who remains cautious and disbelieving. Oh, how I wish it were not so.

* * *

We are all exposed to far too much information. Newspapers, magazines, television, radio and the Internet smother us with short-term, irrelevant news; we are victims of an information overload. And the information 'noise' can interfere with our ability to decide what is important and what is not. The babble, chatter and opinions of talking heads and commentators become mixed in with the nuggets of hard news we are fed.

If you doubt the importance of this, consider Ken Lay of Enron.

Mr Lay, accused of playing a major part in the destruction of his company, argued that he had so much information that he didn't know what to do with it all. He (or his lawyers) argued that he couldn't be guilty of intentionally misleading investors because he didn't know what was going on himself.

Too much information means that relevant knowledge is often harder to spot and use to advantage. The dramatically increased use of spin by politicians and businessmen, and the reduction in the integrity of journalists, mean that the quality of information made available has gone down, while the quantity has gone up.

Television and radio offer only entertainment and are, at best, useful only because they enable us to see what people are being told. On the whole, the Web offers only prejudice and propaganda. (Keep an eye on magazine covers, though. When they promote a new investment theme it is usually time to sell and get out. This is, in my experience, particularly true of the *Economist*, *Fortune* magazine and *Business Week*.)

If you are to understand what is really going on you need to distill, to get rid of the rubbish, and to produce wise conclusions based on the important facts. Easier said than done.

* * *

Immediately after the Battle of Waterloo a carrier pigeon took the news of Napoleon's defeat to Nathan Rothschild who went to the stock exchange, sold enough shares to create a small panic and then, when shares were falling, used every penny he had to buy shares. The bull market which followed Wellington's victory lasted ninety nine years.

* * *

Research suggests that human beings tend to become more confident (but less accurate) as they process increasing amounts of information.

Too much information produces a strange mixture of too much confidence, confusion and edginess. Among investors this mixture results in overtrading. The confident, but nervous and confused investor buys and sells more often than is good for their investment health. In the end they will be eaten by trading costs. Besides, it is, in my experience, much harder to try and work out where the markets are going in the short-term than it is to work out where they are likely to go in the long-term.

* * *

It is, in my view, important to retain an overview of what the markets are doing, and how other people are responding to the news they are receiving. It is, after all, the actions and reactions of other investors (professional and amateur) which decide what happens to share prices. The markets are influenced not by reality but by what other people perceive to be reality. It is only by understanding geopolitics and the psychology of the market that you will understand what drives the market and be able to use common sense and understanding to zig when everyone else is zagging.

Too much information is bewildering noise. I believe in making fundamental decisions based on human nature and geopolitics.

I read all the time. But most of it is general stuff. And I read political books and newsletters (which are more likely to be independent) as well as newspapers and magazines. On the whole I recommend that you take great care with the Internet which has become a sacred sanctuary for nutters, price manipulators, idiots, shysters, spin doctors, quacks, hoaxers, mountebanks, charlatans, fraudsters and flimflam artists.

* * *

We all need information, of course. But we need good stuff; reliable facts which enable us to make thoughtful appraisals.

In order to spot potential investment opportunities you should try to follow what is going on in the world by reading whatever you can. I read publications with a left-wing bias and publications with a right-wing bias. If you want to beat the market, you need to know what everyone is being told. You need to have access to information that will help you find the truth.

Trying to find out what is going on by using the ordinary mass media will do you little or no good at all. And learn to take note only of financial journalists you have reason to trust.

If you read all the advice provided by investment professionals you will end up exceedingly confused. They contradict one another all the time.

If you were to ask 100 doctors how to treat appendicitis there would be differences but there would be significant similarities too. If you were to ask 100 lawyers a specific legal question you would get largely similar replies. There would be variations but not massive, diametrically opposed viewpoints.

The existence of huge variations among investment professionals shows that investing is not a science.

Read as much as you can, and keep your wits about you, and you can beat the professionals. But be aware that too much information can ruin your life and damage your prowess as an investor. Much information (and most comment) is meaningless at best and misleading at worst.

* * *

Don't take financial advice from television programmes, bank managers or people you've met in the pub. Don't take investment advice from people who inherited their money or won it on the lottery. Don't take investment advice from anyone who isn't considerably richer than you are and who hasn't earned their money (or a good chunk of it at least) through their investments.

* * *

I asked one well-known investment newsletter writer/publisher why he didn't sell back issues of his newsletter to his subscribers. (This is a well accepted way of boosting income among non-financial newsletter publishers). The well-known newsletter writer/publisher told me that he couldn't do that because if he did his readers would be able to check out how badly his previous recommendations had done.

Another investment newsletter writer was exposed as having been paid a huge fee by at least one of the very small companies he was recommending in his publication. Naturally, the price of the company shares had risen as his subscribers had bought them. The newsletter writer won four times. He received money from his subscribers. He received money from the company he recommended. He received money from buying and selling shares in the company he recommended. And, of course, he was able to attract new subscribers by pointing out to them how successful his recommendation had been.

The only people for whom it all ended in tears were the subscribers who bought the recommended shares and who were doubtless still holding them long after the newsletter writer had banked his fee.

* * *

When we see a queue outside a restaurant or cinema we may draw the conclusion that the restaurant serves good food or that the cinema is showing a good film. But there is another possibility. Maybe the queue started because the restaurant or cinema opened late and a few people who had bookings had to wait outside. And what if the last person in the queue is there only because he thought that the presence of a queue must mean that the restaurant serves good food or that the cinema is showing a good film? And what if the person in front of him in the queue thought the same thing? (Clever restaurateurs sometimes ensure that there is a queue at their door in order to take advantage of this phenomenon.) Much the same thing happens in investing. People see a share price go up, read approving comments from journalists and want to join in.

* * *

When you read news about a company in a newspaper or magazine, or hear it on television or radio, remember that it may have been manufactured by a public relations agency. Most investment news isn't news at all. It is propaganda. And information is of no use at all unless you can use it to help you draw useful conclusions and predict the future.

* * *

Most parts of the media focus on what has been happening, not on what is about to happen or what might happen. As an investor your job is to try to 'read' the markets so that you can predict what is going to happen next. It is the future, not the past, which decides what will happen to your investments. But it is much easier to study the past (by looking at charts, for example) than it is to try to predict the future (by strategic thinking).

* * *

What use to you is the information you obtain? You must always know that. I have a friend who looks at the gold price every half an hour. He isn't a trader. He is (or was at the time) holding gold for the long-term. So, apart from adding to his ulcer, what was his work doing?

* * *

Beware when famous investors share their views with the world. Are they doing so because they have investments which they are talking up? Maybe they want you to buy in order to push up the price. And maybe when you have bought they will, quietly, sell.

* * *

When you purchase an investment keep all the cuttings, notes and so on which you have used to help you make your mind to buy. Put the cuttings and notes into a folder and look at it whenever you review that particular investment. It's often easy to forget why an investment was bought.

INVESTMENT TRUSTS (AND UNIT TRUSTS)

'The sense of responsibility in the financial community for the community is not small. It is nearly nil.'
JOHN KENNETH GALBRAITH

Looking for a share that will survive, pay good dividends and increase in value is like looking for a needle in a haystack. You may find the needle. You may just find a lot of straw. It is much easier, safer and (in the long run) probably more profitable to invest in the haystack rather than try to find the needle. And one of the best ways to invest in the haystack is to buy shares in an investment trust. Although the costs are higher than a tracker fund there are times when an investment trust can make a wise choice.

Investment trusts are companies listed on the stock exchange which make a living by buying shares in other listed companies. The directors or managers of the investment trust company choose what shares they buy and they are allowed to borrow funds in order to increase the size of their company's investments (known as 'gearing up'). The share price is decided by supply and demand.

Investment trusts are quite unlike unit trusts. And in my view they are far better value. Indeed, I never put money into unit trusts or open ended investment companies (also known as OEICs). I consider the costs and expenses to be far too high. Performance isn't too hot either. Most unit trusts fail to beat the stock market But they charge well and pay their investment bosses well too.

But those aren't the only problems with open ended unit trusts. Another big problem is that if people take money out of a unit trust the managers have to sell some of the underlying stocks in order to find the cash. Incidentally, open ended funds such as these are known by the name 'mutual funds' in America.

When you buy a unit trust you can only buy or sell through the fund manager and you can only do so at a set point during the day. The unit price always reflects the value of the underlying assets. If there is a run on a unit trust (if a lot of investors want to sell) the company will have to sell its underlying investments in order to obtain cash to pay its investors. This sometimes means that heavy selling pushes down prices still further. (It is because of investors redeeming investments in unit trusts that stock markets which are falling sometimes fall even faster and may crash.) In times of crisis it may be difficult (or impossible) to sell your unit trust shares. On the other hand, because investment trusts are traded on the stock market, you can buy or sell their shares whenever the market is open.

In the UK most investors buy unit trusts rather than investment trusts simply because the rules allow unit trusts to advertise and to promote their shares with great enthusiasm but don't allow investment trusts to advertise in the same way. To this must be added the fact that financial advisers can earn big commissions for recommending unit trusts whereas they don't get paid a commission for recommending an investment trust.

Investment trusts have several big advantages over unit trusts. Here are facts you should be aware of if you are considering investing in investment trusts:

1. From time to time some will trade below their underlying net asset value. When this happens you can buy the shares owned by the investment trust at a discount. It is not at all unusual for investment trusts to sell at a 10-20% discount or even more. This happens because the net asset value of the portfolio is determined by the shares the manager has bought for the investment trust whereas the share price of the Investment Trust is determined by what investors are prepared to pay for those shares. When this happens you can, if you buy shares in an investment trust, benefit enormously. If the discount narrows or disappears your shares will become more valuable – regardless of what happens to the underlying portfolio. Incidentally, it is worth remembering that investment trust prices can also rise above the net asset value of their constituent shares. When this happens the investment trust is said to be trading at a premium. I don't recommend buying investment trusts when their price is at a premium to the value of the underlying portfolio.

2. Investment trusts can borrow money to increase their returns. This means that if the manager believes that share prices will rise he can borrow money to buy more shares. Naturally, there is a downside to this. If share prices fall then the borrowing (known as leverage or gearing) means that the investment trust will lose money faster than it would if it hadn't borrowed money to buy additional shares.

3. Investment trust costs are much less than unit trusts. Unit trust fees usually include a 5% entry charge, an annual fee of up to 2% and another exit fee when you sell. Investment trusts, on the other hand, are like ordinary shares. You pay your stockbroker a fee and the usual difference between the buy and sell price. But these costs are likely to be much lower than the costs of buying and selling unit trusts. The annual charge on an investment trust is usually less than 1% a year. I consider the advantages of investment trusts over unit trusts to be huge. I invest quite a lot in the former and virtually nothing in the latter. Don't ever buy into a unit trust. If you do, you do

not own shares in the companies which make up the trust. You own a part of the unit trust. If there is a panic then the unit trust will have to sell off shares in order to pay back the shareholders. They will have to do this even if it means selling out at distressed prices. An investment trust is better (because you effectively own shares in the investments which the investment trust holds). If you trust your own judgement it is, of course, better still, to create your own portfolio so that you own your own shares. One or two companies may go bust through greed, incompetence or dishonesty. But you are unlikely to lose everything.

4. If you are considering investing in companies based outside the country where you live then I recommend using an investment trust specialising in the country you are interested in. Buying individual shares in foreign countries can pose a number of difficulties. For one thing it can be difficult to keep up with news (let alone prices). And dealing with dividends paid in a foreign currency can be a complication. Finally, foreign taxes can be a nuisance. Even if you can put them against your own country's taxes it still means wasting time on filling in another tax form. I have done well with relatively short-term investments made abroad but my best long-term foreign investments have been ones made through investment trusts. At the start of the 21st Century I bought shares in investment trusts specialising in China, India, Russia and New Zealand. All of these had done exceptionally well by the start of 2008 when I sold most of them.
5. You can find out what shares an investment trust is holding by looking at its annual report or its website.
6. Investment trusts are also a good way to invest in a sector which you think is likely to do well. There are, for example, good investment trusts specialising in mining companies and property companies. It can be much easier (and safer) to invest in a specialist investment trust if you want to put money into a sector which you think is likely to do well in the future.
7. Sadly, investment trust managers have now started to give themselves the sort of performance fees (also known as incentive bonuses) that hedge fund mangers have enjoyed for some time. There is no logical reason for this and the evidence shows that investment trusts where the managers have an incentive bonus do worse than investment trusts where they do not. Grant Thornton, an accountancy firm, studied five year performance data for 48 investment trusts. The 24 investment trusts which had incentive schemes beat their benchmarks 53% of the time, whereas those without incentive schemes beat their benchmarks 59% of the time. All you can do is to ask, and maybe check out the annual report, to see if there is such a scheme in operation. If you have a choice then I suggest that you avoid investment trusts which pay such fees.

8. Investment trusts make life easy for investors. If you invest in ten separate property companies, for example, then you have ten separate companies to watch. And there will be ten sets of dividends. Occasionally, one of your chosen companies will be taken over. There will be mail to sort through and documents to read. And there will, of course, be unavoidable tax liabilities – which might well come at an inconvenient time. Putting money into an investment trust which has holdings in your chosen ten companies (and maybe a few more in the same area) can certainly make life easy and allow you to spend your time studying investment strategies rather than ploughing through dull paperwork. Plus there is the advantage that you won't be liable for tax when your investment trust buys and sells shares.

LEVERAGE [AKA 'GEARING']

'If you owe the bank £100, the bank controls you; but if you owe the bank a million pounds, you control the bank.'
JOHN MAYNARD KEYNES

A lever is a tool which enables you to turn a small amount of strength into a great deal of power. Using leverage means making a small amount of money do a lot of work. If you try to lift a large object you can do so more easily if you use a lever. Similarly, if you have a small amount of money and want to make a big profit you may be able to do so by using leverage. The snag is that using financial leverage is very dangerous. If things go well you can make a lot more money. If things go badly you can lose a lot more money. Leverage is the same as gearing. Which is, of course, the same as debt.

> *'If it isn't the sheriff it's the finance company. I've got more attachments on me than a vacuum cleaner.'*
> JOHN BARRYMORE

Using leverage is the way the hedge funds make vast amounts of money. If they have £10,000,000 to invest they use financial instruments, such as futures, to enable them to buy far more of whatever it is they want to buy than they could possibly afford if they simply invested their cash. So, for example, they buy a futures contract which might give them 10 or 100 times the purchasing power of the funds they have at their disposal; their £10,000,000 enables them to benefit as though they owned £100,000,000 (10 times) or £1,000,000,000 (100 times) of the stock or commodity they wanted to buy. The upside is obvious.

Let's assume they have bought copper and leveraged themselves up by a factor of 100. If the copper doubles in value the hedge fund will make 200 times its initial investment – instead of merely doubling its money. You can make huge profits using leverage.

There is a downside, of course.

If the price of copper goes down then the leveraging works against the hedge fund. If the copper price goes down just 1% they will lose all of their initial investment, because only 1% of the money they invested was really theirs. And if the copper price halves they may lose billions.

Investment bankers and hedge funds used leverage a great deal to make themselves rich in the latter part of the twentieth century and the early part of the twenty first century.

Both groups used leverage a great deal because they had nothing to lose and a great deal to gain. They were both gambling with other people's money to make themselves rich. Investment bankers used leverage because their bonuses depended on their making huge profits. And using leverage helped them make ever bigger profits. If the worst happened and their gambles didn't come off then the money they lost belonged to the bank. Their only loss would be that their bonuses would be cut.

I don't ever use leverage or gearing. And I don't recommend that you do either. There were a number of causes of the banking crisis which hit the world in 2008, but the problem wouldn't have happened without leverage. Banks failed because they borrowed too much money and then invested it unwisely. Individuals who borrow too much, and then spend or invest their borrowings, are just as vulnerable as the banks proved to be.

Theorists claim that there are two types of debt: good debt and bad debt. Good debt brings in money (e.g. it is considered good to borrow to buy a property if the rent exceeds the interest). Bad debt takes out money (e.g. if you borrow to buy a house to live in or to buy a car).

I think all debt is bad. All debt sucks and can be a great cause of pain. For the last part of the 20th Century and the first part of the 21st millions of people saved too little, borrowed too much and spent everything they could borrow.

Lives were built on debt. And ruined by it.

I try to avoid companies which are heavily in debt. They may make lots of money if things go well. But if things go less than well they could lose everything.

And I never borrow money to buy stocks (known as buying 'on margin'). You can make much more money if you borrow to invest. But you can also lose much more.

LIQUIDITY

'Liquidity is a coward; it disappears at the first sign of trouble.'
POPULAR SAYING

A company has a decent liquidity if it is fairly easy to buy and sell shares in it. If a company's shares aren't widely held or traded very often the liquidity may be low. If a company's shares are liquid you will be able to sell them easily. If a company's shares aren't liquid you may have difficulty in selling – and may find that when you try to sell you will move the price against you. (In other words the very act of you trying to sell your shares will reduce their price.)

LUCK

'Although men flatter themselves with their great actions they are not so often the result of great design as of chance.'
DUKE DE LA ROCHEFOUCAULD

Don't confuse skill with luck. If you put twelve people into a room and invite them all to toss coins there will, eventually, be one player who gets a dozen tails all in a row. If you ask that lucky player his secret he will blush and tell you that it was all about special timing, special flicking and a good deal of practice. He will lower his eyes and talk about writing a book to explain his skill more fully. He will never admit that it was just luck and statistical inevitability that led to his success.

When you lose money, don't blame it on bad luck. Don't moan that you have been victimised. And when you make money don't assume it's all down to your genius. Whining won't rescue your investment portfolio. And hubris will endanger your future success by encouraging you to become over-confident.

It is safer to assume that everything bad that happens is a result of your own incompetence and that everything good that happens is a result of good luck.

Acknowledge to yourself when your success is a result of good luck. (As an investor you will have more than your fair share of bad luck – even though this is, of course, impossible. You will be quick to blame bad luck when you lose money so be prepared to credit good luck when you make money, or avoid losing it.) I first started investing in the stock market in the mid and late 1960's when I was a medical student. I had an active brokerage account in Birmingham and invested my earnings as a columnist and drama critic on the market. I was lucky, picked some good stocks which were booming and did quite well. (I did well enough for the stock broker to offer me a job.) When I qualified as a doctor and started working in hospital I closed my broker's account because I didn't have time to deal. This was fortunate for it enabled me to miss the horrible bear market of the early 1970's.

MISSION STATEMENTS

'Execute their aery purposes.'
JOHN MILTON

Public companies exist to create value for the shareholders. That's it. The job of the directors and staff is to care for the shareholders. The other things that companies do – things such as providing jobs, serving the community, satisfying the customer and so on – are all subservient to the primary purpose and are morally less important. Company mission statements should, if they are honest, be simple: the company's primary task is to make a profit and to make money for shareholders.

However, these days most companies are run for the benefit of the directors, executives, employees, pensioners and taxpayers. Shareholders, the owners of the company, are at the bottom of the list. They and their interests receive little or no protection. Sadly, shareholders have been betrayed by institutional money managers who are the ones who are supposed to represent their interests at annual general meetings. (Individual shareholders usually hold their shares through nominee accounts and are, therefore, deprived of the right to attend and speak at company meetings. Fund managers, who should represent their own shareholders, are usually more interested in protecting the interests of directors and executives.)

It is true that a company which treats its staff well, and which is good to its customers and the community, will almost certainly do better than one that doesn't do these things. But these should not be the company's primary motives. It is clearly also important that companies should treat former employees well – and should provide them with good pensions. But shareholders should (but do not) always take priority over both employees and pensioners. Shareholders are often pensioners too. Sadly, their rights are often forgotten, ignored or suppressed.

I don't have much faith in companies which have fancy mission statements which witter on about the community and the environment and providing a pleasurable working experience for staff. It is the job of governments to worry about communities and the environment. It is the job of the company to make money for the shareholders. That is the company's sole purpose. I like companies which care for the environment, the staff and the community. But those things should not be the purpose of a company.

To summarise: the people who work for a company are working for the shareholders. Many of them seem to forget this.

MOMENTUM INVESTING

'An investor who is seriously eager to make money doesn't have to watch the markets every day. He just has to make, once in a while, a good investment decision on the trends that will last for a number of years.'
MARC FABER

The principle behind momentum investing is pleasantly simple (as, indeed, are most of the people who practise it). Its aficionados look for an investment which is rising in price and they then buy some for the ride. Momentum investing is, in fact, just a smart name for 'jumping on the bandwagon'. Momentum investing involves spotting trends and jumping on them. It can be very profitable on a short-term basis. But it can also be very risky, it can run up lots of expenses and, worst of all, it takes a lot of time and effort.

Of course, momentum investors sometimes practise their technique in reverse: selling investments which are falling in price.

But the usual technique is to look for an investment (usually a share) which is going up in price and to buy some in the belief that the share will go up some more before it stops or goes down.

Momentum investing does work well from time to time (particularly during a bull market when more or less everything is going up). But when it goes wrong (as it does) then the losses can be significant. A share which has soared is quite likely to plummet back to earth again. And it is quite likely to do this quickly. One or two investors decide that the price has gone high enough and so they sell. Their sales bring the price down a little. And the other momentum investors all ring their brokers to sell their shares. The result: pandemonium as thousands of small, momentum investors clamour to flog their shares. Inevitably, the price plummets (and may then become a 'good buy' for value investors).

As you have probably guessed, the tricky part about momentum investing is managing to get out when other investors have stopped buying. Most investments rise in a jerky sort of way, rather than a nice, smooth mountain slope. And investors who are buying because a price is rising (rather than because of any underlying value) need strong nerves to sell out every time the price rise is interrupted. To be successful the momentum investor has to get out just as other people stop buying and just because other investors start selling. This doesn't sound easy and it isn't as easy as it sounds. I've tried momentum investing and it can be exhilarating and profitable when it works. But it's real, pure gambling rather than investing.

Momentum investors like to refer to themselves as 'players'. I have a much better name for them: lemmings.

NET ASSET VALUE (AKA BOOK VALUE)

'Nothing ever becomes real till it is experienced.'
JOHN KEATS

The total assets of a company when liabilities, charges and provisions have been deducted are known as the net asset value or the book value. The net asset value (NAV) per share is obtained by dividing the company's NAV by the number of ordinary shares in existence. Asset values are sometimes given including and excluding intangibles such as the value of brand names. Tangible assets are much more interesting to value investors. If a company sells for 50 pence a share but has a NAV of 80 pence per share (of tangible, realisable assets) then it's probably a good buy. It is still possible to buy shares which sell for less than their NAV, and I have done so several times in recent years. It always seems slightly naughty (the phrase 'taking candy from a baby' springs to mind) but it is invariably profitable and I have never found the taxman unwilling to take his share of the loot.

With companies, the underlying value often lies in the property the company owns. So, consider Useless Components Ltd. The factory isn't making any money and its shares are very cheap. But, the company owns the freehold to a large factory which could easily be replaced by a shopping centre or a housing estate. And the freehold, which is valuable, is not included in the company's accounts at its real value. In fact the property hasn't been revalued for 30 years. The shares in the company could be worth far more than their price.

Finally, remember that intangible assets (things such as brand names and patents) are less valuable than tangible or hard assets (such as buildings and land) simply because their value may vary and it may, in difficult times, be hard to find a buyer.

NEW COMPANIES

'The new-issue market...is ruled by controlling stockholders and corporations, who can usually select the timing of offerings or, if the market looks unfavourable, can avoid an offering altogether. Understandably, these sellers are not going to offer any bargains, either by way of a public offering or in a negotiated transaction.'
WARREN BUFFETT

Don't invest in a small start up unless you are closely involved in the company and know exactly what is going on. The offer will probably be structured to benefit the founders and the banks who have advised them. And why wouldn't it be? Can you really imagine that someone will work his fingers to the bone creating a new company and then hand over shares in the company to complete strangers at a knockdown price?

If strangers are offering you shares in their new company it is because they cannot get the money anywhere else. Neither their bank manager nor their friends and relatives will lend them money. Why should you? If you want to give your money away find a more deserving cause.

Don't buy shares in new issues or untraded shares or initial public offerings (IPOs). When a small company comes to the stock market it will always be because the directors and shareholders believe that the time is right for them to sell some of the shares they hold in their company. They know more about their company than anyone alive. And, despite all the hassle and the enormous cost, they want to get out because they think the price they are getting for their shares is a good one. For them. Why on earth should you be daft enough to buy the shares they are selling? What makes you think that you know more about their company's prospects than they do? The only other people (apart from the initial shareholders) to make money will be the bankers arranging the IPO. Generally speaking investments made in such companies are a flop for several years. Shares in newly floated companies tend to underperform the market by an average of 15% in the years after their initial public offering. Shares underperform because the directors of the company usually choose to float at the best possible time – when their company is doing unsustainably well. You can't blame them. They've worked hard for years and they want their big pay day. The banks arranging the offer will cream off any other profits which might be available. And if the directors (who have created the company) sell a lot of their shares there is always the risk that they will totter off with their 'winnings' and sit on a beach somewhere – leaving the company and your investment to wither.

You might also be invited to invest in a private equity fund or a venture capital fund.

Private equity specialists are people who buy a company, usually using borrowed money, then cut costs in order to find the money to pay for the loans they've taken out. They reorganise the company, sell off assets, pay themselves huge fees and then flog the whole miserable mess back to the public.

Venture capitalists use their money to support very small businesses. They work on the basis of 'win some-lose some' and make their money by taking a huge equity stake in the companies in which they invest. If you are offered a chance to invest in either of these I suggest you run to the nearest railway station and give your money to the first beggar you see. You will feel better, you will have done something useful with your money and you have as much chance of seeing any of it again. If venture capitalists or private equity buy-out specialists are prepared to cut you in on a deal then you really don't want to have anything to do with it.

If there is any real chance of profit in the world of private equity or venture capital (both of which invest in small, troubled or cash-strapped companies) the professionals will do everything they can to avoid sharing the profit with you. If they're inviting you to the party it probably isn't a party you want to attend. None of these people sit down and say to one another: 'There's a huge amount of profit to be made here. We ought to invite some ordinary investors to the feast.'

PENNY STOCKS

'One a penny, two a penny.'
NURSERY RHYME

A penny stock is a low priced share – usually speculative. Some investors think that if a share costs 5p and they can buy thousands of them for very little outlay then they will make money when the share goes up. This isn't really true. The spread on penny stocks can sometimes be ruinous. So, for example, you may pay 5p per share if you are buying but receive only 4p per share if you are selling. The big spread on such shares means that the share has to rise a great deal for you to make a profit. And there is no rule that says that a share costing 5p ever has to cost £2.50.

PENSIONS AND RETIREMENT

'And don't rely on the state – why do people trust this manifestly untrustworthy institution?'
PAUL HAM

A typical 65-year-old has a life expectancy of around 20 years. Half of all 65-year-olds will live longer than their life expectancy – longer than 20 years. Some will live to over 100.

You will need quite a lot of money to look after yourself for that length of time. If you have a pension provided by a sound employer who is guaranteed not to go bust then you are in a good position. But I do have a couple of warnings. First, no employer is guaranteed not to go bust. Even big, safe companies might not survive in the future. And you should not assume that your pension will survive if your employer does not. Second, even the Government may have difficulty in meeting its pension commitments in the future. Taxpayers are going to become increasingly upset at having to pay for pensions for civil servants.

Here are some things you should know about pensions and retirement:

1. The retirement age of 65 was fixed by Chancellor Otto von Bismarck of Germany. He decided civil servants could collect a pension when they reach 65. The average German citizen died at the age of 63 at that time so he wasn't giving a lot away. He wasn't the meanest of the mean. That prize goes to the Japanese official who set the official retirement age at 55 when life expectancy in Japan was 43.
2. For every five years you delay starting a pension plan you will probably have to double your monthly investments to achieve the same retirement income. Young people who put all their income into servicing a mortgage they cannot afford, and put nothing into a pension fund, are facing a bleak future. It isn't safe to rely on property prices providing a pension. House prices cannot possibly rise enough to pay for everyone to have a pension. Who is going to buy all the expensive houses? Don't regard your house as your pension. The value of your house rises and falls. Individual houses may be difficult to sell. Volatility for individual houses is high. Neighbourhoods change.
3. Means-testing programmes in the UK mean that if you are British and do not have a solid gold pension plan you have a clear choice: you can either save very little and trust the Government to look after you in your old age (since Government pension programmes aren't funded but are Ponzi schemes this means that you will be reliant on future taxpayers to keep you fed and warm) or you can save as much as you can so that you are independent in your later years. If you are planning to rely on the State you

should be aware that the laws of supply and demand will undoubtedly mean that State supplied pensions will be much smaller in 10, 20 or 30 years time than they are today. I think it is pretty safe to say that State pensions will be insufficient to pay for a half-way decent standard of living in the future.

4. A Ponzi scheme is a fraudulent investment operation that involves paying returns to investors out of money raised from subsequent investors, rather than from genuine profits or from the savings of the original investors. Ponzi schemes were named after originator Charles Ponzi, who operated in 1903. Such schemes work well because the early investors – who get good returns – usually keep their money in the scheme. They do well out of it. The people running the scheme send out statements showing investors how much money is being made and so people keep investing. In the end, the scheme collapses as investment slows and the promoter has difficulty paying out the high returns. Investors become suspicious and the promoters of the scheme usually disappear with what money is left. Sometimes, the scheme is exposed because the assets that are supposed to exist have been paid out as the 'profits', 'interest' or 'pension'. Politicians use illegal Ponzi schemes when setting up Government pension programmes because they are enormously popular with electors. Instead of putting aside some of the tax paid by each worker (in order to create a sound, pension fund) politicians rely on each new generation to pay the pensions of each retiring generation. All the money paid in tax is spent. It's fraud, of course, but no one seems to care.
5. You will need enough money in your retirement fund so that you can live on no more than 5% of your retirement pot (in other words, the interest). If you need to take out more than 5% of your investment pot per year the pot will shrink and as you get older there will be less and less money available. How much does that mean that you will need to have saved for your retirement? That's easy. Multiply the amount of money you would like to have as an annual income by 20. Oh, and don't forget to allow for inflation too.
6. Formal pension funds aren't necessarily the best way to save for your retirement. There are some tax advantages to be had from saving in an authorised pension fund but the rules which govern when you can take your money, and how you can take it, are stringent to say the least.
7. The figures available a few years ago showed clearly that a man with a pension fund of £80,000 will have a 10% shorter life than a man with a pension fund of £100,000. A man with £500,000 in his pension fund could expect to live 10% longer than the man with £100,000 in his pension fund. Why the difference? That's simple, I'm afraid. The retiree with a little more

money can afford to eat and keep warm. And he can also afford to pay for private medical treatment when he needs it.

8. I have always put as much money as I could afford into pension funds. I started doing this when I was a medical student (and was earning money by writing articles and columns and by investing on the stock market). One of the pension funds I trusted with my money was Equitable Life. Over the years I noticed that the pension fund managers didn't seem to me to be doing terribly well and so as soon as it became possible I took my money out of Equitable Life and put it into a fund I could manage myself. I'm delighted to say that I'm much happier with the results I've obtained by managing my pension myself than I would have been if I had left the task to the professionals. My investigations and observations suggest that most people would be better off managing their pension fund themselves than entrusting their money to the professionals.
9. The biggest mistake investors make is in holding a high proportion of their wealth in shares of the company for which they work. When Enron went bust many of the employees had their savings in Enron shares and most or all of their pension funds in Enron shares. On the day Enron went down they lost their jobs, their savings and their pensions. (The boss of Enron had been encouraging employees to buy shares in the company at the same time as he'd been selling his shares.) So, if you have a company pension scheme, do not allow your pension fund to be invested entirely in shares of the company for which you are working. Many dot.com employees had all their wealth tied up in the company for which they worked.
10. In the past money used to be passed down from one generation to the next. In the future this will be reversed. The days of children expecting and receiving an inheritance from their parents are almost over. In another generation children will have to spend their own money looking after their parents.
11. The rules governing pensions are horrendously complicated. Politicians have repeatedly promised to simplify things but inevitably this has meant that things have got worse, rather than better. Moreover, politicians have given themselves the freedom to alter the rules as and when they like, even retrospectively, and to interpret the rules as they see fit. The chances of the rules being the same when you retire as they were when you began your pension plan are non-existent.
12. Investment advisers sometimes recommend that older savers take their money out of shares and put it into bonds or cash deposits. I think that this is dangerous. It is a myth that older people should hold fewer shares than young people. It is often argued that the proportion of shares you

own should be equal to 100 minus your age. But I believe that alternatives (bonds, cash) have their own risks. (Cash can be lost if a bank goes bust and may be hurt by inflation). The real problem is that people at 65 may live another 30 or 40 years. They need their savings to beat inflation.

13. It is possible to buy index-linked gilts from the Government. These gilts are designed to grow slightly faster than the rate of inflation. Although the rate of inflation that is used is the Government's (rather than the real rate of inflation) these are an excellent investment for pension funds.
14. Annuities are bad if you die early but good if you die later. (But if you die early what you get out of your annuity is probably the least of your problems.) People whose homes aren't burgled transfer money to people whose homes are burgled and similarly, people who die early lose but those who live longer win. In the future, annuities are likely to go down for healthy pensioners. In the wonderful old days, all pensioners who bought annuities got the same deal. People who had looked after their bodies, and who were lucky, lived longer and received more money in the end than people who died early. But today the companies providing annuities are offering more money to smokers, the overweight and the chronically ill. This means that the money available for the healthy and able-bodied will be less. Those who eat carefully, don't smoke and drink in moderation will be forced to live in more penurious circumstances unless they ensure that their pension pot – the sum available for an annuity – is large enough.
15. Don't build your retirement plans around emigrating to France and running a boarding house. If you do the chances are that you will end up having to come back to UK and take a job as a school crossing attendant. (And don't buy a retirement cottage near to a convenient airport serviced by a cheap-flight airline. By the time you retire the chances are that the airport will have been closed, leaving you with a 300 mile car journey.)
16. It's worth remembering that the modern concept of retirement did not really catch on before the 1930's when it was brought in to convince older workers to retire in order to open up jobs for young people. Most of the people retiring were doing physical jobs which required brawn and strength rather than wisdom and experience. This happened during the great depression in the USA in the 1930's. Today, most people have jobs which require thought rather than action and there is not a great deal of logic in retirement these days. Most retirees miss their work and feel useless and unwanted for many of the 30 years they spend visiting the public library and riding round the country on coach trips. So, don't ever retire. If you already have retired then you should consider unretiring. If you are planning retirement from a full-time job look for small part-time jobs to take up.

Today retirement causes misery because millions simply don't know what to do with themselves. Poor pensions mean that many are now living in penury. Retirement is an unnecessary anachronism. Much wisdom and experience are wasted.

17. In recent years many companies have effectively become huge pension funds. They exist not to make money for shareholders but to run pension funds for past and present employees. Such companies will be in big trouble if the market falls because then the value of their pension funds (invested in equities) will fall and the companies will have to put more of their earnings into the fund in order to obey the law. There are many companies in existence which owe so much in pensions to present and past employees that they are effectively worthless as investments.
18. A survey conducted by the Clydesdale Bank showed that of 1,000 people questioned more than 60% dreamed of a lottery win to pay for their retirement. I hope that you share my horror at this attitude.

PORTFOLIO MANAGEMENT

'The ideal investment portfolio is divided between the purchase of a really secure future income (where future appreciation or depreciation will depend on the rate of interest) and equities which one believes to be capable of a large improvement to offset the fairly numerous cases which, with the best skill in the world, will be wrong.'
JOHN MAYNARD KEYNES

You can put your spare money (or savings as they are known in the industry) in an old shoe box under the bed. You'll know how much is there and you'll be able to count it whenever there isn't anything decent on the television, or whenever you feel like cheering yourself up.

But there are some disadvantages to keeping your money in a box under the bed.

First, the government may change all the notes. They do this from time to time and you will feel (and look) more than a trifle suspicious if you have to push a wheelbarrow of old notes into your bank and ask them to change them into the new stuff. The chances of the bank not calling PC Plod round to ask you where the money came from are approximately nil. The chances of you being able to produce an explanation that will satisfy PC Plod are roughly the same.

Second, mice will eat your money. Or it will go mouldy. Or it will be burnt up in a fire. Paper money is very vulnerable and all these bad things can easily happen to it if you leave it in a box under your bed.

Third, a nasty person will break into your home and take your money. If they know that you have money hidden away and they aren't very good at games like Hunt The Slipper they may tie you to a chair and do nasty things with matches and golf clubs to encourage you to tell them to look under the bed.

Fourth, your money will be worth less next year than it was worth this year. And the year after that it will be worth even less. While it is sitting under your bed snoozing your money will not earn anything for you. And inflation will eat up the purchasing power of your money so that by the end of every year it will be worth less than it was at the start of the same year. Your money will be shrinking just as surely as if mice were eating up a chunky percentage of it every month.

If you're going to invest your money and make it grow you will need a plan.

When he got stranded on his desert island, Robinson Crusoe began with a plan. You too have to have a plan. You need to know what your aims are. And you also need to have some idea how you are going to achieve them. Without ideas, aims and a plan you won't get anywhere.

The most important decision investors have to make is not which share to buy but how to allocate their assets. A collection of assets is known as a portfolio and it is, of course, perfectly possible to have sub-portfolios within the main portfolio. The main portfolio may contain shares, property, bonds, cash deposits and gold. The share portfolio may contain oil company shares, bank shares, investment trusts and so on.

The aim of creating a portfolio is to provide diversification and to protect your savings from dramatic changes in the economic world. Uncorrelated assets usually (but not always) provide some protection.

Asset allocation is crucial to good portfolio management. Generally speaking, most bank shares do much the same (there will always be one which does better than the rest and one which does worse than the rest) and the same is true for retail shares, utilities, building companies and so on. Most property values go up and down together too.

Long-term studies, conducted by people with a lot of time on their hands and a talent for using calculators, have concluded that 85% of investment success is due to asset allocation. Other researchers have shown that 40% of the return difference between one fund and another is explained by differences in asset allocation. The other 60% of the difference between funds is explained by timing, the specific securities that are chosen and the differences in fees and expenses.

Picking the right variety of assets to buy is where you need to have an overview; to be able to see the wood rather than the trees. And you need to remember that investment is an art more than a science. (If it were a science you'd be able to invest according to strict formulae. But, despite the claims of many, there are no such formulae.) Investing alone, and taking personal responsibility for making sure that your hard earned money is preserved, and grows, means you can bet against the herd and invest in companies, sectors or countries you believe in.

The two investments most people think of when they think of making money out of money are property and shares. More people become really, really rich through investing in property than through anything else (often because they buy crummy buildings in crummy locations, do them up and then wait for the area to become fashionable) but in the long run the average investor in shares has, in the past, done better than the average investor in property.

The advantage of property over shares is that you can see what you've bought. You can touch it. You can go inside it. And, if you have a tenant, you should get some rent, though you may have to go round and collect it yourself. If you've borrowed money to buy the property the rent might even cover the interest payments. (Although I don't really approve of borrowing to invest, most of the people who have become multi-millionaires through property have done so because they've borrowed up to their eyeballs to fund their property buying sprees.) The downside of investing in property is that property is illiquid (it may take years to sell a building and to get your money back) and it needs a lot of looking after. You have to pay rates and insurance and your building will probably need painting from time to time. Toilets and gutters get blocked too and unless you're prepared to deal with these problems yourself you will need to pay an agent and a man with a wrench to do the work for you. There's also the problem that there are likely to be spells in between tenants when your building is empty and earning you nothing. Unless you are very rich your money will only buy you one or two properties with the result that most of your wealth will be tied up in one or two specific investments. If the neighbourhood goes downhill then you could end up losing money.

> *'The first rule is not to make mistakes. The second rule is not to forget the first rule.'*
> WARREN BUFFETT

With shares you don't get anything you can touch. You probably don't even get a certificate. But shares do give you a chance to diversify much more easily.

You can spread your risk much more widely than you can with property. And you can, of course, invest in property by buying shares in property companies. You can buy and sell shares easily – usually just by picking up the telephone – and if you pick the right companies you should receive regular dividends without having to go round and threaten a tenant with a big stick. In the long run the capital gain from shares should beat the capital gain from investing in property. The downside of investing in shares is that you have to rely on brokers and bankers and they all charge big, fat fees. (But, on the other hand you don't have to deal with lawyers and estate agents.)

'I believe now that successful investment depends on three principles: a) A careful selection of a few investments (or a few types of investment) having regard to their cheapness in relation to their probable actual and potential intrinsic value over a period of years ahead and in relation to alternative investments at the time. b) A steadfast holding of these in fairly large units through thick and thin, perhaps for several years, until either they have fulfilled their promise or it is evident that they were purchased on a mistake. c) A balanced investment position, namely a variety of risks in spite of individual holdings being large, and if possible opposed risks (for example, a holding of gold shares among other equities, since they are likely to move in opposite directions when there are general fluctuations).'

JOHN MAYNARD KEYNES

Property and shares are not, of course, the only two places where you can put investment money.

Here's a summary (in no particular order) of the other main possibilities:

a) bonds and gilts

b) national savings

c) precious metals (including gold, silver and platinum)

d) stuff (including art, books, stamps etc.)

e) cash

You should look through the variety of investments you can choose from and select for yourself an appropriate mix that will suit your aims and ambitions.

Once you have devised a portfolio, and made a number of investments, you need to remember that it is the overall success or failure of the portfolio that really matters, rather than the success or failure of individual investments. If your portfolio is properly diversified, your successful investments should more than cover the losses of your unsuccessful investments. But don't diversify too much. For example, if you end up with a mass of separate shares you might as well buy an index fund. Your portfolio will almost certainly not do any better than the general market, your wealth will not boom even if your strategies are proved correct and your expenses will be too high. In addition, if your portfolio is too large you will spend most of your time on portfolio administration. There will be little time left for strategic thinking or for finding new investment opportunities. In the world of finance (as everywhere else) crises are normal. The more complex your portfolio, the more likely you are to have to deal with problems and the less time you will have for having ideas. So, try to keep your portfolio simple enough so that whatever happens you will still have some time left to enable you to think clearly about what is happening.

> *'When a man does not know what harbour he is making for, no wind is the right wind.'*
> LUCIUS ANNAEUS SENECA

When you start to create a portfolio you have two choices. You can either give your money to an expert and ask him to manage it for you. Or you can decide to create a portfolio yourself.

My advice is that you should not give your money to the experts. They probably don't know any more than you do. And they certainly won't care as much about your money as you will. Most important of all, the money you will save by managing your portfolio yourself is likely to increase your portfolio's performance dramatically. Most portfolio managers will charge at least 2% or 3% of the sum under management. That 2% or 3% saved can increase your performance from, say, 6% to 8% or 9%. Those are dramatic improvements which can, over just a few years, make a spectacular difference to the success of your portfolio.

And creating a portfolio isn't as difficult as most people imagine. Many investors have been served well by a simple portfolio consisting of 40% gilts, 40% equities and 20% gold. (But, be warned, such a portfolio could prove disastrous in a major bear market.)

One sensible investment strategy is to use passive funds (such as equity based index-linked funds) as the foundations of the equity part of your portfolio, and to then add active funds or shares in an attempt to boost your portfolio performance. Today, this is known as the core/satellite approach. When I first devised this scheme privately in the 1980's I described it as the 80:20 approach because I put 80% of my investments in solid, fairly boring investments and the other 20% into more risky investments. It has become extremely popular.

Here's my advice about creating, and managing, an investment portfolio. I've added advice from one or two other voices.

1. First ask yourself a question: Why are you investing? You must know the answer to this. What do you want to buy or spend money on in the future? How much money will you need? Know your limitations. Be selective. You can't possibly know everything there is to know about every possible investment. Specialise. You will do better if you specialise in areas where you have some knowledge, or in areas in which you are genuinely interested.
2. You might feel that it is wise to create, at the heart of your portfolio, a lifestyle reserve containing enough money to keep you in basic comfort should everything else go 'bad'. This reserve should be invested in index-linked Government bonds, tax exempt National Savings and gold. With such a reserve behind you, you might feel that you can be a little more aggressive with the rest of your portfolio.
3. You may want to rebalance your portfolio occasionally. Otherwise there can be dangers. So, for example, if you start with 50% of your portfolio in equities and they do very well you could end up with 75% of your portfolio in equities just as the market peaks. If, however, you take the extra percentage of equities and put it into an asset class that has done poorly (bonds or property, for example) you could well be nicely positioned to take advantage when that asset class does well. At some point investments that go up tend to go up too much. And then they come down. Rebalancing your portfolio is a way to avoid this danger. (On the other hand, you may prefer to stick with the investments which have done well for you. This is what I usually do.)

> *'Study general conditions, take a position and stick to it.*
> *Wait without impatience.'*
> JESSE LIVERMORE

4. If you ever feel that your portfolio has grown stale – and you have lost your edge – don't be afraid to sell everything and start again. The costs will be painful. But at least you will have the chance to get rid of all your old investments and recreate a new portfolio.

> *'Life is frittered away by detail...simplify, simplify.'*
> HENRY DAVID THOREAU

5. Don't allow your portfolio to determine the way you feel about the investment climate. If you have a lot of shares in your portfolio it is easy to allow your hopes to become expectations – and to continue buying shares.

Try to remain dispassionate. And always be prepared to change your mind and to take a loss when it is wise to do so.

6. General investment success has nothing to do with luck. If your portfolio of investments consistently do badly it is because you have failed to 'read' the investment climate properly. Maybe you should, after all, consider asking a professional to look after your money for you. It is particularly important to do this if your investments produce a notably worse return than you could have obtained from giving your money to a fairly average portfolio manager. (These days most banks provide portfolio management services.)

> *'What is your money doing tonight?'*
> NEWSLETTER OF THE SELF-HELP ASSOCIATION FOR A REGIONAL ECONOMY IN GREAT BARRINGTON, MASSACHUSETTS, USA

7. A well-diversified portfolio will always have winners and losers. Try to keep your eye on the overall picture rather than on individual investments. And do not allow yourself to be suckered into spending too much time on tiny investments which will have little or no real effect on your overall financial situation. Many investors spend as much time worrying about small investments (in which they have 1% of their wealth invested) as they spend worrying about big investments (in which they may have 20% of their wealth invested). This is obviously dangerous.

8. Losses do a great deal of damage to a portfolio. A big loss will damage a portfolio more than a big gain will benefit it. If your portfolio goes up 50% one year and down 50% the next year you will end up 25% down. (You start with £10,000. At the end of year one you have £15,000. At the end of year two you will have £7,500. That's a 25% loss on your original capital.) If you need to sell something it is usually wise to sell an investment that is doing badly and to keep your winners.

> *'Experience is the name everyone gives to their mistakes.'*
> OSCAR WILDE

9. Try to think of your investment portfolio as an integrated whole. If you have a good, well-balanced portfolio you won't need to keep checking it or keep changing the contents. You can spend more time at the beach. If you make investments then some of the time you will make bad investments. No investor in history has ever been successful every time. The important thing is to concentrate not on individual losses (or gains) but to look at the overall profitability of your portfolio.

10. Don't ignore or reject bad news that affects your portfolio. If you fall in love with an investment theory and things go badly you must reassess your viewpoint. Maybe you made a mistake. Maybe you were given bad advice.
11. Nothing produces average results more reliably than holding a huge portfolio of investments. Too much diversification may increase your safety but it will also reduce your profitability. A broadly based portfolio will not enable you to beat the market. A more specialised portfolio may be a little bit riskier but it will give you a better chance of beating the market.
12. When planning a portfolio you should think long term. Do not expect your chosen investments to rise suddenly or in a smooth line.
13. Remember: if you create a portfolio deliberately designed to make you rich you may become rich. If things go well you may become very rich. But if things do not go as planned you may become poor. If things go badly you may become very poor. This is because bigger profits usually come from greater risks.
14. I don't think it is a good idea to regard your main home as part of an investment portfolio. It's reasonable to include other homes (holiday homes, houses or flats which are rented out) as part of your portfolio, but your main home is where you live. (And people who borrow money on their main home and then spend it on stock market investments are taking a bigger risk than I would feel comfortable with.)
15. At any one time there will almost certainly be some parts of your portfolio that are doing badly. That is why you have a diversified portfolio. You should expect some failures and disappointments. You need to reconsider your investment strategy only if your portfolio is doing badly overall.
16. Measure your success over a 12 month period – not less – or you will make the mistake the professional money managers make, and end up making too many changes in a desperate attempt to deal with short-term moves.
17. A major global economic downturn tends to damage every form of investment. During the bear market and credit crunch crisis of 2008 just about every possible type of investment lost money. Shares went down. Property when down. Commodities went down. Bonds went down. Gilts went down (as investors bought them for safety). Gold and other precious metals went down. Even the investors who were in cash and who (perhaps rather smugly) thought they weren't losing money were, in reality, losing money hand over fist because inflation was eating away at the purchasing power of their savings.
18. Once you have developed your investment plan, and worked out a real strategy which makes sense to you, try not to fiddle with it too much. You

don't need to review your investments constantly. Make quarterly reviews of your finances. Be critical. Imagine you have to report to a board of directors. How are you doing? Would you give yourself a bonus? Or would you merit firing? But don't tinker too much. Banks and brokers want investors to review their holdings frequently so that they churn their portfolios and pay big dealing commissions. But most so-called experts aren't rich, or ever likely to be. Don't abandon your plan just because of an opinion from someone who doesn't agree with your well-thought out view. Make firm decisions and try to stick with them. I spend several hours each week thinking about my investment strategy in general (and my specific investments in particular) but I don't buy or sell investments every week. I look at individual share prices once a week at the most but I do try to keep an eye on what is happening to exchange rates, interest rates and the prices of major commodities (such as oil and gold) on a daily basis. You can't buy shares and forget them. You need to keep an eye on things. But you don't have to sit hunched over a trading screen all day.

19. The key to good investing is to do well when things are going well (when the markets are rising), but not to lose too much money when things are going badly. If you can do this then you will, of course, almost certainly beat the market. Sometimes, when things are bad, just not losing too much money is all you can hope for. And if investment portfolios are shrinking everywhere and you are holding onto your capital then when things change (which they assuredly will) you will be in a far better position than most to take advantage of the next boom. When do you know that the bottom has arrived? When absolutely everyone is filled with gloom and despair about the future for companies, shares and investments of every hue. When the vast majority of investors have capitulated the brave are buying.
20. Don't put money you might need in a hurry into illiquid investments. If you put all your money into buying a little shop you could be in trouble if you need to sell the shop in a hurry. Similarly, if all your money is invested in silver cow creamers you could find yourself being stuffed if you have to find cash in a rush.
21. If you are investing in individual shares, you should not hold fewer than 20 stocks. If you don't have enough money to spread it around 20 stocks then wait until you have. If you invest in too few stocks then the risk of your portfolio being damaged by a single failure is, inevitably, greater. But you should not invest in too many shares either. Warren Buffett suggests that investors should have only 20 shares in their share portfolios and that when investors want to add a new share to their collection they should get rid of an old one to make room for it. If you have too many separate holdings in your portfolio you will become confused. Some investments

will demand more of your time than they deserve. And other investments will get forgotten. The costs, effort and general risks will hold you back. To beat the market you need big, well thought out positions that you can watch carefully.

22. Doing nothing is sometimes the right thing to do. When there are problems our instinct is to do something. In investment, as in medicine and goalkeeping, that might not always be the right thing. In medicine, doctors who interfere too soon, and who forget that the human body can often heal itself, can frequently do more harm than good. In football, when a goalkeeper is trying to save a penalty he will probably dive to the right or the left. He stays still in the centre of the goalmouth just 6.3% of the time. But the penalty taker is likely to hit the ball straight at the middle of the goalmouth 28.7% of the time. So, to play the percentage game, goalkeepers should keep still and stay where they are far more than they do. Don't just do something, stand there. But they don't. It is embarrassing to do nothing and have to pick the ball out of the net. Goalkeepers feel better if they've tried and failed. Penalty takers should kick the ball straight ahead since that gives them by far the best chance of scoring. But most don't because it looks as if they haven't made a decision on where to place the ball. Research shows that trading activity rises when markets fall. Investors feel they have to do something to protect their money, or to make back their losses. Most of the time, of course, they simply make things worse.

23. Keep your expectations realistic. During the 1980's and 1990's many investment portfolios returned 15% a year. Some managed considerably more. These were exceptional years. Over the long-term the average return is half this. Investors did well during those years because falling inflation pushed up company profitability. They also did well because the stock market became chronically over-valued as increasing numbers of investors began to believe that such returns could be obtained indefinitely. Investors whose expectations remain too high are likely to be disappointed. And in chasing results they are likely to lose money.

24. I am an investor and not a trader and so I try to think at least a year ahead. I don't make investments expecting to make a profit within weeks or even months. (But I don't object if I do.) Investors who aim for instant gratification are, in the end, invariably disappointed.

25. It pays to own things that pay you to own them. Properties that pay rent. Bonds which pay interest. Shares which pay decent dividends. Even if the value of your investments goes down you will still be earning money.

26. When looking at possible investments it is well worth remembering Jim Slater's Zulu Principle. The idea is very simple. 'The idea,' says Slater,

'came from a four-page article about Zulus in *Reader's Digest*. Anyone who read it would have immediately known more about Zulus than most other people. If they were then to have visited the local library and read all the available books on the subject they would certainly have known more about the subject than anyone in their town or county. A visit to South Africa with a few months spent on a Zulu kraal, followed by reading all the available literature on Zulus at a South African university, would without a doubt have made them one of the leading experts in the world.'

It's a wise observation.

'By investing a disproportionate time in the subject, almost anyone could become an acknowledged authority on it,' says Slater.

Naturally, the same principle can be applied to investing.

Most investors are unfocused. They thrash around wildly, following tips here and fashions there. They know a little about a lot but they don't know very much about anything in particular. It is hardly surprising that in the end they lose money.

If you concentrate your effort on a relatively small area (or a few relatively small areas) then you will know more than most people. And, as an investor, you will do better than most people.

27. I think it's wise to treat the various parts of your investment portfolio in different ways. Money in your pension, and money you have on deposit for emergencies (a problem with the roof, an illness, a dying motor car) needs to be treated with more caution than money which you are prepared to invest and want to grow.

28. Your mix of shares, bonds, property and other assets should always be appropriate for your goals and for your financial and emotional ability to sustain losses. How you handle money depends on the amount of security you want, the amount of risk you are prepared to take, the amount of income you need from your money, how easily you want to be able to access your funds and the time you are prepared to spend on looking after your portfolio.

29. All great investment portfolios are run by individuals who think for themselves. It's one area of life where eccentricity can be a virtue. Don't be afraid to be original. But remember: running a portfolio isn't about flaunting or satisfying your ego. Running a portfolio is about preserving capital, generating capital and generating income.

> *'Put all your eggs in one basket and watch that basket!'*
> MARK TWAIN (MR TWAIN, AKA SAMUEL CLEMENS, HAD CONSIDERABLE EXPERIENCE OF MONEY SHARKS AND, WHEN IT CAME TO MATTERS OF FINANCE, KNEW WELL OF WHAT HE WROTE. HE REALISED THAT ALTHOUGH DIVERSIFICATION MAY MAKE INVESTORS FEEL SAFE IT DOES NOT ALWAYS PROVIDE THE EXPECTED LEVEL OF PROTECTION. INVESTORS WHO PUT THEIR MONEY WHERE THEIR HEART IS ARE OFTEN BETTER SERVED.)

30. Managing a successful personal portfolio is like running a small, private investment trust or, perhaps even more, a small, private hedge fund. You need to create a mix of investments which will protect your wealth from a wide range of threats – including inflation. Mix sectors and strategies for protection and profit. Imagine you are running a small investment trust of your own with the minimal aim being the preservation of your capital (measured against inflation as your only benchmark) and your optimal aim being to grow your capital a little each year.
31. I keep a list of possible future investments. It's just a file of cuttings and notes. Whenever I spot something which might suggest a new investment possibility I cut it out and put it into the file. Every couple of weeks I look through the file. I throw out things that don't seem such a good idea. And I keep collecting information on investments which might prove worthwhile.
32. Don't overtrade. Overtrading will destroy your portfolio performance.
33. Here are the things you need to think of when creating a portfolio:
    - Your objectives. (Why are you creating a portfolio?)
    - Your time horizon. (How soon do you want to meet your objectives?)
    - How much risk are you prepared to take? (How well will you deal with losses?)
    - How much money have you already got to invest?
    - How can you add to this sum?
    - How will you allocate your assets?
    - What individual funds or shares will you choose?
    - What tax considerations do you need to be aware of?
    - How do you want to diversify your portfolio?
    - How much income do you want to take from your portfolio?
34. Many experts recommend that investors should sell specific shares (or other investments) which rise in value and become a larger part of a portfolio than originally planned. I understand the theory behind this suggestion but I don't believe it is necessarily always wise to fine tune a portfolio too often or too much. Tuning a portfolio involves selling investments which have done

well and which may continue to do well, in order to purchase investments which might not prove so profitable. And, of course, there will be costs.

35. Keep careful records of all your investment transactions. You will need such records for the taxman, of course, but you should also keep them for yourself. Without them you won't be able to tell whether or not your investment plans are proving profitable. I keep basic information in a small hand-held PDA. I actually use an old-fashioned Psion 3mx which I happen to think is still the best discrete, portable computer ever made. And I know what all the buttons do. Occasionally, I try out something new but I've not yet found anything as good. I don't put my personal investment information on a device which has Internet access or which can be used as a telephone. I like my private information to remain private.
36. At least one big investment house advises clients who have less than £2 million to invest not to hold shares directly. Another investment house says that £5 million is the minimum. Both claim that if your wealth is less than this then all your equity investments should be in unit trusts or investment trusts. I can understand why they say this. It is clearly good for business. But it is rubbish. The banks argue that investing in specific shares is risky. But an investment in a major blue chip company is probably safer and less volatile than an investment in a unit or investment trust which specialises in the shares of small companies in an emerging market. Anyone who has £20,000 or more to invest has enough to create a small but well diversified portfolio without relying exclusively on unit or investment trusts.
37. What you gain or lose in a day or a week is irrelevant. Try not to take too much notice of short-term gains or losses. If you do, there is a risk that you will become too confident during bull rallies and too despondent during bear troughs and will, therefore, take your eye off the long-term prospects for your portfolio. A successful investment strategy requires a long-term approach. (By long-term I mean at least a year and generally five years or more.)

> *'There are only three rules on investing: first, never lose any money, second, never lose any money, and third, never lose any money.'*
> WARREN BUFFETT

38. Deduct your expenses, the inflation rate and the taxes you have to pay from your rate of return to find your profit.
39. Most investors spend more time thinking about which telephone to use, or which shoes to buy, than they do before making an investment or starting a pension. Learn to spend more time on the big stuff and less time on the little

stuff. I have known too many people who spent their lives saving pennies through thrifty shopping but losing pounds through bad investments.

40. Finally, don't let your investing become too serious. Investing money, and making it grow, is a means to an end. But for too many people investing, and making more money, becomes an end in itself; a macho, self-assertion that is regarded to begin with as a game (to see who can make most money) and that turns into a war (with the aim being to defeat all the other competitors and to end up with as much of the money as possible). This is dangerous. It's why many investors hold onto investments for far too long. They are unwilling to sell losing investments because when you sell a loser you have to admit, both to yourself and to whatever part of the world might be interested, that you made a mistake. Many investors allow their investments to become personal; they are constantly searching for signs of evidence which confirms their prejudices instead of, more wisely and far more usefully, looking for signs of evidence which might question their prejudices.

POUND COST AVERAGING

'Share prices rise when there are more buyers than sellers. They fall when sellers outnumber buyers. The consensus view is not always right but the actions of many usually tell a stronger story than an individual view. However, the best investment profits go to those who anticipate change and that means investors often need to swim against the tide.'
ROBERT COLE

Diversification in time is as important as any other form of diversification. Currency-cost averaging (or pound-cost averaging) enables investors to avoid investing everything at the top of the market. If the market rises the investor gets more shares for his money. If the market falls he gets less. Over time things balance out.

Pound-cost averaging means investing the same, fixed amount of money in a fund or a share at regular intervals (once a month or once a quarter for example). If you do this over a long period it will reduce your risk of investing your money at a time when prices are temporarily and optimistically inflated.

When you average down you buy more of a share at a lower price. So, if you have bought 1,000 shares of Tiddlywinks International at £10 per share and the price goes down to £5 a share you can average down by buying more shares at the lower price. If you buy another 1,000 at £5 per share you will own 2,000 shares and will have paid £15,000 for them all. This means that your average price will be £7.50 per share. I believe that if the price of a share goes down while the fundamental values of the company remain the same then the share must be a better buy than it was when you first bought it. On that basis I will usually add to a position if the price falls but the fundamentals remain sound.

On the other hand, to average up is to buy more of a share at a higher price. If you have bought 1,000 shares of the Bilbury Beer Company at £5 per share and the shares go up to £10 a share you might, if you still think the shares are cheap, buy another 1,000. You will now have bought 1,000 at £5 each (total cost £5,000) and 1,000 at £10 each (total cost £10,000) so you will have 2,000 shares at a total cost of £15,000 which means that each share you own will, on average, have cost you £7.50.

The conclusion is simple: if you have money to invest, drip feed it into the market a bit at a time. Markets do crash (sometimes without warning or explanation) and if you've invested all your money the day before a crash you'll feel a little sick.

PRICE EARNINGS RATIOS

'A cynic is a man who knows the price of everything and the value of nothing.'
OSCAR WILDE

The price/earnings ratio (known to its friends as p/e ratio) is probably the commonest way of deciding quickly whether a share is fairly priced, under priced or over priced. The p/e ratio is found by dividing the share price (p) by the earnings per share (e). When the sum is done using the last set of company results the p/e ratio is known as 'historic'. When the sum is done using an earnings forecast (known technically as a 'guess') the result is a 'prospective' p/e. The p/e tells you the number of years that you would have to hold the share for the company to achieve earnings that match the price you paid for it. So, for example, if a company's shares trade on a p/e of 10 it would take 10 years for the cumulative earnings per share to equal the price you paid for the share.

The problem with a historic p/e is that last year's results don't necessarily tell you what this year's results are going to be like. Just because a company did well last year doesn't mean that it will do well this year.

The problem with a prospective p/e is that one of the important figures used (the earnings) is a guess and quite likely to be wrong, very wrong or so wrong that its laughable. Prospective earnings are based on someone else's guess. If you are going to make investment decisions made on prospective p/e ratios you might as well hire an astrologer. Some companies have no p/e ratio because they have no earnings. (This was true of most companies in the dot.com boom.) I don't usually buy shares in companies which have no earnings.

The p/e ratio can be useful for providing a quick guide to a share's value and it is a particularly useful way of assessing a share's price in comparison with other shares in the same sector. A high p/e may suggest that the market as a whole is positive about the company's future prospects. A low p/e may suggest that the market is gloomy about the company.

The p/e ratio of the whole market can be useful too. A study by Yale University showed that in decades where the p/e ratio was 20 to 25 the subsequent returns were close to zero. On the other hand, other academics and students of the market have claimed that there is no link between p/e ratios and the way the market goes.

Here are five things you should know about the p/e ratio.

1. The p/e ratio plus inflation should not be more than 20.
2. The p/e ratio can be a useful way to compare a specific company with the market as a whole (both in the past and the future) and with other companies in the same sector.
3. Small companies tend to have a higher p/e ratio. This is partly because small company share prices tend to include a bid premium and partly because small companies tend to grow faster than large ones.
4. During the 1990's investors became accustomed to buying and holding shares with enormously high p/e ratios. 'Life is different because of the Internet,' was one of the most popular arguments.
5. Historically, there have been reasonably long periods when p/e ratios have stayed below 7 or 8.

PROPERTY

'Never invest in anything that eats or needs repairing.'
BILLY ROSE

The property boom of the late nineties and early noughties was, in part at least, a result of fear and greed. Millions bought houses not just as somewhere to live (they could easily have rented if they simply wanted a roof over their heads) but because they wanted to get rich, or because they feared that prices would keep rising and they would be unable to afford anything at all. They didn't seem aware that house prices could actually go down. They didn't know that for most of the latter part of the 20th Century and for all the early part of the 21st Century Japan was in a serious slump because of an absurd housing boom which had taken place. House and land prices collapsed and stayed down because they had risen too much in previous years. Speculators had driven prices ever upwards. Japanese house prices rose by 51% between 1985 and 1991. That sort of price rise was clearly unsustainable and driven by something more complex than normal market forces.

Now consider what happened in America. In the peak years their house prices jumped by 90% between 2000 and 2006.

And Britain?

Well, between 2001 and 2007 house prices in Britain leapt by 118%.

Banks encouraged reckless spending by throwing money at would-be buyers. And then, in their search for greater and greater profits Wall Street bankers discovered the joys of securitisation. They repackaged ordinary loans into bonds and then sold the bonds on to banks in Europe. As the number of good mortgages ran out (there is, after all, a limit to the number of solvent would-be home owners) banks started lending more and more money to people who never stood a chance of paying it back (the sub-prime market). This pushed up house prices still further and convinced everyone that making money out of property was as easy as falling off your wallet. European bankers became the marks; merrily gobbling up all the rubbish the American banks could produce. By autumn 2008 it was clear that European banks had more writedowns than American banks (even though the primary problem started in America). Wall Street successfully exported more than half of its financial toxic waste. (Make no mistake, the credit crunch which led to so much damage in Europe and the rest of the world was made in America.)

It wasn't difficult to predict that Britons would suffer the worst housing crash the modern world had seen.

In my book *Gordon is a Moron* (which was published in the summer of 2007) I wrote that: 'lenders have become absurdly aggressive – almost forcing barrowloads of money on borrowers and in so doing have laid the foundations for a serious crash. Banks are lending 120% of the cost of a property. Mortgages can be obtained for five times earnings – instead of the traditional three times earnings. Mortgages can now be obtained for periods in excess of half a century. There is now an industry of people selling fake pay slips so that people can persuade their mortgage lender to let them have a bigger loan than they might otherwise think wise. If you're unemployed but want a fake pay slip to show that you have a £50,000 a year job with a blue-chip company you just type 'duplicate pay slip' into an Internet search engine and choose your 'discreet and confidential' adviser. Then, take your evidence to the bank and come away with a loan for a quarter of a million pounds.'

In that book I also wrote: 'Looking at the figures dispassionately it seems that by mid 2007, property in Britain was between 20% and 30% overvalued by every possible sensible criteria. But this doesn't mean that if house prices fall they will fall by 20% to 30%. When markets get out of kilter, as they do from time to time, and as they have under Gordon Brown's direction, the correction which invariably ensues always goes as far in the other direction. So, if house prices are overvalued by (say) 25% then the chances are that house prices will fall not by 25% but by 50%. And it means, just to rub it in, that if a house is currently worth £300,000 then it will, when the crash finally teeters to a conclusion, be worth £150,000. If a buyer can be found.'

People who buy land or houses always comfort themselves with the thought that real estate always goes up in the long-term. And they remind themselves of Mark Twain's remark about land being a good investment because they're not making any more of it. But the original Americans didn't do too well out of their land holdings. And nor did the Aztecs or the Incas. Besides, how long is long-term? In the long-term we're all dead. And in the long-term shares tend to be a better investment than property. In 2008 it was revealed that £30,000 invested in a UK equity income fund 25 years earlier would, by 2008, have been worth three times as much as £30,000 invested in property.

In recent years many people have come to regard their home as a source of a pension. It's always seemed to me that this is a dangerous supposition. House prices are unpredictable and can move around more than most people realise. It can be difficult to sell a house and if you are assuming that your home is going to be your pension you may find yourself forced to sell up for less money than you had hoped to obtain in order to sell the house at all. You may also find yourself moving into a strange home, and a strange area, when you are old and frail. In bad economic conditions real estate values can fall dramatically. (By dramatic I mean over 50%.)

Property has some advantages over shares. For a start you can touch a building. It's there. It's real. It's difficult to steal. When the markets are crashing and banks are going to bust there is something rather comforting about knowing that some of your wealth is invested in something tangible. You can use a building in a way that you can't use a share. You can decide what you do with it (within the inevitable restrictions imposed by the authorities). You can live in it, work in it or rent it out to other people. Even if it falls down the land on which it is built will almost certainly have some residual value. Shares can become worthless. It is very rare indeed for a building to become worthless. (Though if you don't have the right sort of insurance and your building injures someone then you could find yourself wiped out financially.)

Owning a building has lots of plus points, but shares also have some advantages over property. You don't have to pay taxes every year on shares that you own. You don't have to insure them. And you don't have to keep repairing them. Shares just sit there quietly and let you get on with your life. And if you need your money you can (usually) sell them quite quickly. You may not get the price you want, but you will be able to find a buyer to take them off your hands. A property can stick on the market for months or years.

You can, of course, always get the best of both worlds by buying shares in property companies.

Here are some things you should know about property:

1. When people buy a house they often have a survey done to make sure that the building is sound. The idea is that the surveyor will spot serious problems which might make the property worth less than is being asked for it. This makes good sense. But, in the long run, the physical structure of a property has very little impact on the way its price moves. Dry rot and woodworm are important but other factors, which probably won't be considered by your surveyor, are likely to have a far greater impact than the property's future value. The time in the housing cycle when you are buying will have a huge impact. If you buy at the top of the cycle then it could be ten years before you can resell the house and get your money back. And environmental factors are crucial too. If the council decides to build an incinerator in that nice field across the road the value of your property will plunge. If travellers decide to set up camp in a lay-by outside your house then the value of your property will go down. If the village shop closes and the local bus company stops providing a service then your house price will probably fall. If a river is diverted and land in your area starts to flood you may find it impossible to get insurance. It is the big issues, not the small ones, which decide the future value of your house. It's the same with investments. If you buy shares in a retail company when the country is booming then you will probably make money. If you buy shares in the same company at the start of a recession then, in the short to medium term, you will probably lose money. What is happening outside is crucial. In the case of a house the important factors can be global, national or local.

2. Price and value are distant relatives. Don't ever trick yourself into thinking that the two are one and the same thing. The price an estate agent asks for a house isn't its value. The price an auctioneer puts down as the reserve for a piece of furniture isn't its value. And the price you pay for a share isn't its value. Price and value are two different things. Occasionally, they match. But most of the time they don't.

3. When buying property as an investment it is, as with most things in life, a good idea to stick to what you know. If you have always lived in one small town, and you have bought and sold a couple of properties there, then your knowledge of the property market in that town will probably be greater than your knowledge of the property market in a town a thousand miles away. Use your local, specialist knowledge to help you. And do your research before trying your hand as a property entrepreneur. Encouraged

by television programmes showing how easy it is to make money out of property, lots of people now try investing (and dealing in property) without doing any real research or acquiring any real knowledge. Doing this is arrogant. It's like turning up at Wimbledon with a tennis racquet in your hand and expecting to win without ever having played before. When buying property to make a profit look for potential. Can it be split into more than one property? Pick an area which is accessible and which is likely to become more fashionable. The decor doesn't matter much except that if it is ghastly you have an opportunity to knock something off the price.

4. Keep your home separate from your investments. If you have decided to buy your own house or flat, that's great. Owning your own home can offer you security. And, over the long-term, you will probably do very well out of it financially. But I think it is a mistake to do as many people do and to regard their home as an investment; a potential source of profit and a pension fund. There are only two times when you should regard your home as an investment: when you are buying it and when you are selling it. The rest of the time you should think of it as somewhere to live. Don't use your home as a source of easy cash by borrowing against it. (In 2008 it was revealed that most people had so little equity in their homes that they were less than two pay cheques away from homelessness.) And when you come to sell your home try to forget the happy times you've spent living in it. The new buyers are buying a piece of real estate, not your memories and they will bid accordingly. When you are selling a house don't be unnecessarily stubborn if your buyer offers you a lower price than you think it is worth. Think of the cost of retaining your home – and the lost opportunities.

5. If you are buying a property always research the area thoroughly. Not for nothing do professionals all agree that location is the key to making a property a successful investment. What are the neighbours like? What's the traffic like? How about road and rail links? How easy is it to get to (and away from) the area? Buy in the best area you can afford. And only buy property you like.

6. To assess the value of the property look at the potential rental yield. If the rental wouldn't cover the interest on a mortgage then the chances are the property is overpriced. And beware of debt. Borrowing money can be a good thing when prices are rising. It isn't such a good idea when prices are falling.

7. The people of the Caroline Islands used 12 foot round blocks of stone as money. They didn't have much trouble with pickpockets. And if they saved up enough money they could build a house out of their money without having to go to the bank.

RECESSION

'Markets discount the future and hence should forecast, rather than follow, real economic performance.'
IAN RUSHBROOK

Recession is theoretically defined as a period of time (which can change according to who is assessing whether it was a recession or not, but is usually defined as two quarters or sometimes a year) when gross domestic products actually falls. Most recessions come as complete surprises to all the experts, the vast majority of whom are usually still enthusiastically predicting positive growth long into the recession.

The first important thing to remember about recessions is that markets rise and fall according to investors' sentiments rather than according to reality. Talk about recessions can make investors exceedingly nervous and this can become severely exaggerated. The result is that when the 'R' word is widely used in the media, investors tend to start selling everything they can. Naturally, they usually sell their good stocks first so that they can take profits (and avoid having to admit their mistakes).

The second thing to remember is that recessions dramatically increase volatility so that news tends to excite or depress investors. Gloomy news sends the markets crashing still further. Good news sends the markets soaring. And, during a recession, there is usually a lot of financial news around. Even quite trivial incidents can sometimes seem terribly important.

The third thing to remember is that recessions tend to affect a few people a lot but they don't tend to affect most people much at all. One study conducted during the UK recession of the early 1990's showed that 83% of the gross fall in profits was accounted for by just 10% of firms. Astonishingly, four out of every ten firms saw their profits rise during the recession. Recessions can, in some ways, be very specific in their effect. The problem is that it can be difficult to predict which companies are likely to suffer and which are likely to gain. Sometimes, only directors and executives really know whether their company is strong enough to survive. And sometimes even they are too blind to accept the truth

'It's only when the tide has gone out that you can see who's been swimming naked.'
WARREN BUFFETT

Just how we all survive a recession depends, of course, upon our personal circumstances. Someone who has a government job is less likely to be vulnerable than someone who is self-employed or who works in a growing industry in a vulnerable area. Pensioners, who are receiving inflation-proofed, solidly-held pensions are unlikely to suffer a great deal.

REGULATORS

'The ten most terrifying words in the English language are:
'I'm here from the government and I'm here to help.''
RONALD REAGAN

Regulators are highly-paid civil servants who are employed to protect your interests and to ensure that the financial services industry provides a decent and honest service for its customers.

Sadly, although civil servants have proved adept at feathering their own nests (by building up their departments and increasing their pay) they have proved woefully inadequate at protecting the interests of investors. (As I write this the Financial Services Authority in the UK has 2,665 highly paid members of staff and a budget measured in hundreds of millions. At the height of the British Empire, Britain managed India and 250 million Indians with 900 civil servants. Just before the First World War, The Home Office managed Britain with a staff of 28.)

> *'Despite its claims to the contrary, the Government pays little heed to private investors, favouring its friends and sponsors in business.'*
> 'INVESTORS CHRONICLE'

Do not expect regulators to protect you from crooks or charlatans. And do not expect justice from the regulators if you feel the need to complain. Regard the regulators as just another bunch of useless pen pushers. In addition to securing the maximum level of compensation for themselves, regulators only have one other skill: they are very good at thinking up excuses to explain away their egregious incompetence. Bottom line: forget about being protected by the regulators. They are in the business of protecting themselves. You are on your own.

RISK

'If you risk nothing, you win nothing.'
NAPOLEON BONAPARTE

The saddest words in any language are: 'If only...', 'It might have been...' and 'I wonder what would have happened if...'.

Make two lists.

On the first list write down all the investment errors you have committed and which you now regret; the mistakes you know that you have made and which you now wish you could have avoided. On the second list write down all the errors of omission you have made; the things you haven't done but which you now wish you had done.

Whichever list is the longer will tell you a great deal about yourself – and will, perhaps, give you a hint about how you should conduct your life in the future.

If your first list is the longest then maybe you are being a little reckless – and taking too many risks. But if the second list is the longest (and many people are surprised to find that this is the case) then you should perhaps be taking more risks.

If you are going to take risks successfully you need to be able to assess the bottom line with some degree of accuracy. Only when you know the bottom line will you be able comfortably to take chances that you might otherwise avoid.

Constantly ask yourself: 'What is the worst that can happen?' 'What will/could happen if I do/don't do this?'

Whenever you are taking a risk find the bottom line: what is the worst that can possibly happen. You may be surprised to hear that there are not many risks which can make the sky fall in or stop the world going round.

Most of us regard risk taking as both hazardous and unnecessary. And many people would say that they try to avoid risks whenever they can. Some people probably seriously believe that they are wise in constantly doing all they can to eradicate risk from their lives.

But taking risks is a necessary and unavoidable part of life. Every decision worth making is potentially dangerous. There is a risk in every venture you undertake – personal, professional or commercial.

Every time you get out of bed or walk out of your home you are taking a risk. Every time you make an investment you are taking a risk. (Despite words such as 'guaranteed' there is no such thing as a safe investment. Even a government bond can be risky if the government falls.) Every time you begin a new relationship or a new business project you are taking a risk. It is impossible to live without taking risks.

But what you can do is to make an attempt to quantify the risks before beginning any new venture. Only when you have quantified the risks can you make a sound judgement about whether or not an individual risk is worth taking. You must put risks into perspective.

> *'The game of professional investment is intolerably boring and overexacting to anyone who is entirely exempt from the gambling instinct; whilst he who has it must pay to this propensity the appropriate toll.'*
> JOHN MAYNARD KEYNES

One of the great tragedies of life is that we tend to take fewer risks as we get older. We become more wary of danger and more aware of the things that can go wrong. The danger is that a preoccupation with safety may reduce the possibility of success.

Investors are often encouraged (or even advised) to take fewer risks with their money. It is widely accepted among financial advisers that older investors should have a much smaller proportion of their investment portfolio in shares and more of it in bonds or cash. One suggestion I've often heard is that investors should have their 'age' in bonds and similar investments. So, an investor who is 30-years-old should have 30% of their money in bonds and 70% in equities, whereas an investor who is 70-years-old should have 70% in bonds and 30% in equities.

I disagree with this philosophy.

We should take more – not less – risks as we get older. After all, as we age we have less to lose. Regularity, habit and commonsense tend to paralyse. In reality, not taking risks is sometimes the riskiest and most dangerous option. When we're older we really need to maximise our income from investments. (We probably won't have a wage and health costs can be enormous.)

The security and comfort which ordinary people enjoy has always been achieved because exceptional individuals have been prepared to take risks.

You should learn to take risks which have the highest possible upside and the lowest possible downside. In order to succeed you have to be able to assess risks accurately. You should learn from your own mistakes but (and this is just as important) you should also learn from other people's mistakes. Knowing the bottom line leads to confidence which leads to success. You should be aware that most people who get rich do so by taking risks rather than by being enormously skilful. And for every individual who gets rich by taking risks there are others who become poor. If you are going to take risks then you should decide what part of your wealth you are prepared to lose in order to gain.

Investments are not necessarily safe just because you feel comfortable holding them. Some of the most disastrous investments I've ever made have been (in theory) the safest and the ones I had least reason to worry about. There are two reasons for this.

First, institutions lie about the security of the investments they sell. (As, for example, some did when selling zero dividend preference shares). Second, it is easy to feel comfortable about holding an investment which is popular with the crowd simply because a lot of other people are holding it. In practice, however, the fact that a lot of people hold an investment does not make it a safe investment. On the contrary, crowds can show remarkably poor stock-picking skills.

And the advice and information upon which we rely can often be of doubtful value. Companies are given credit ratings by specialist credit rating agencies. So, a company which is believed to be particularly safe might be rated AAA. A company which is considered riskier might be rated BBB. There are a number of different levels of rating available.

During the banking problems of 2008 it became clear to me that these credit ratings were not entirely reliable. I use them sometimes as a vague guide but I don't trust them. I prefer to make my own judgements – using what information is available – when classifying investments. I make mistakes. But they are my mistakes. And I know I made them honestly.

The truth is that risk is unavoidable. If you leave your money in a bank deposit account there is a risk that the bank will go bust and you will lose all or part of your money. If you put your money into government bonds there is a risk that the value of your savings will deteriorate because of inflation. If you have money you cannot avoid risk, whatever you do with it. There is as much risk in doing nothing as there is in doing something. Whatever investment you choose there is risk. Even if you put your money under the bed (or in a safe deposit box in the bank) there is the risk that inflation and taxes and charges will destroy the value of your savings. There is no escape from risk. All you can do is try to maximise your opportunities while keeping your risks to a minimum. Opportunity can only be found where there is risk.

Managing risk is crucial. If you can't, don't, or won't manage your investment risks, you will lose all your money and your investment career will be over. The bigger the potential profit the bigger the risk. But this does not necessarily work in reverse. If you take a big risk there will not necessarily be a chance of a high profit. Investing is basically about balancing risk. To do it successfully you need to understand more about geopolitics and psychology than company accounts.

* * *

Your savings need to grow at least 10% a year gross in order to cover tax and to beat inflation. Growing your money at 10% a year will, however, only maintain your money at its previous level. Since making 10% a year is difficult it is clear that maintaining your wealth (let alone growing it) involves a good deal of risk.

* * *

Everything we do is a gamble. We gamble every time we make a decision. We use our instincts and our ability to survive to help us predict what is likely to happen in different circumstances. Every intention leads to action which leads to a result which either leads to satisfaction or dissatisfaction.

You need to assess your intentions and the various actions you can take in order to increase the chances of a satisfying outcome. You have to understand risk – its dangers and its virtues – and how you can make it work for you.

1. Begin by defining your general goals. What do you want out of your money? What is your money for?
2. Then put your goals in order. Decide how much of your available effort you will allocate to each one. How much of your wealth do you want to use to satisfy each of your goals?
3. Assess the upsides and downsides of each goal.
4. List all the ways in which your goals may be affected by external factors. Some of those factors will be specific, some will be general.
5. Who will help you meet your goals? Which advisers can you recruit? Where can you find help? How much can you trust the people you consult?
6. Are your hopes achievable or do they depend on unreal hopes or expectations?
7. Is there a Plan B?
8. How do you think your future life might change? How can you put yourself in a good position to prepare yourself for these changes?
9. How many other people's actions affect you? What are they likely to do? What will you do when they do A? What will you do when they do B?
10. Remember that the returns generated by an investment are directly proportional to the risk of losing your shirt. And there is as much risk in doing nothing as there is in doing something. Whatever investment you choose there is risk. Even with money under the bed (or in the bank) there is the risk that inflation and taxes and charges will destroy the value of your savings. There is no escape from risk. All you can do is try to maximise your opportunities while keeping your risks to a minimum. And remember: opportunity can only be found where there is also risk.

SAFE INVESTMENTS

'An economic franchise arises from a product or service that 1) is needed or desired; 2) is thought by its customers to have no close substitute and 3) is not subject to price regulation. The existence of all three conditions will be demonstrated by a company's ability to regularly price its product or service aggressively and thereby to earn high rates of return on capital. Moreover, franchises can tolerate mismanagement. Inept managers may diminish a franchise's profitability, but they cannot inflict mortal damage.'
WARREN BUFFETT

Warren Buffett's 'franchise' investment may be as close to 'safe' as you can get. But the fact remains: there is no such thing as a truly safe investment.

My four worst ever financial mistakes have involved investments that were promoted as safe. I had a pension investment in a life assurance company called Equitable Life which was supposed to be as solid as a rock. It exploded in a most unrock like fashion. I had shares in Railtrack, the blue chip company which was nationalised by the Government. I had investments in permanent interest bearing shares. They were supposed to be boring and reliable. When the building society banks imploded they turned out to be as dodgy as a wallet full of nine bob notes. I had zero dividend preference shares in a variety of split capital investment trusts which were promoted as particularly suitable for nervous widows and orphans. They imploded as a result of some very sharp practice and some very lax regulation by the Government. (I did at least receive compensation for some of my losses. This would have been more exciting if the Government hadn't chosen to tax the compensation.)

Today my idea of 'safe' investments isn't the same as that of the 'experts'. I've grown rather suspicious of traditional 'safe' investments.

Here's a lesson I learned.

When I was a GP I discovered the 80:20 rule. In general practice this rule says that 20% of the patients will be responsible for 80% of the work.

The same rule can be accurately applied to many areas of life. In investing I have found that 20% of the effort put into managing investments results in 80% of the profit. Conversely, 80% of the effort results in 20% of the profit.

I utilised the 80:20 rule in two ways.

First, I recognised that I would never understand or acquire even a useful, working knowledge of 80% of the investment opportunities which are available. Many are arcane, technically convoluted and extraordinarily risky. So, I decided to concentrate my efforts on the 20% which are understandable, useful and potentially profitable.

Second, I decided long ago that I could use the 80:20 rule to minimise my long-term losses and, at the same time, maximise my long-term gains. My theory was simple. I would put 80% of my money into safe investments and I would invest the other 20% more aggressively. The theory seemed to me to be a good one. The 'safe' money would sit quietly in a corner, collecting interest and growing. It would need no attention. The risky money would be used more aggressively. I would buy investments that were risky but that would, if they survived and grew, make me a lot of money. If I wanted to invest in oil I would do it aggressively. Instead of buying a blue chip such as BP I would buy something more heavily exposed to changes in the price of oil. This would enable me to gear up my exposure while at the same time limiting the downside. If I lost the lot then I would still have the 80% and the interest that was compounding away quite nicely by itself. But if I did well and the 20% of my money that I was using to invest riskily increased satisfactorily then I might make a lot of money.

I put my 80% in AAA bonds, gilts and zero dividend preference shares. This was the secure portion of my money and its job was to maintain my capital position through steady growth. My overall aim was to maintain my capital and match inflation after five years.

And I put 20% into warrants, capital shares and small companies. I deliberately picked high risk shares that promised a good return. I knew that I might lose this portion of my money in a major bear market. But I also knew that I could make big profits from these investments if I was reasonably lucky. And whatever happened my safe 80% would just carry on collecting interest and growing. I would have full exposure to the equity markets without risking all my capital. And once I had set up the investments I would be able to leave them to run more or less by themselves. I was pleased with my plan. When I mentioned it to brokers and bankers they were horrified – not because they didn't think it would work but because they realised that if my plan became popular they would be out of business.

My initial 80:20 plan failed.

And it failed for a reason I had never expected.

It failed because the 'safe' part of the plan, the 80%, let me down. The risky part of the plan did well. It grew well in ordinary times and very well in bull markets.

But the initial 'safe' investments I had made, and which I had left to sit quietly by themselves, ran amok.

And so I abandoned that version of my splendid 80:20 scheme. Today, the 'safe' part of my portfolio contains gold, shares in big oil companies and utilities and solid investment trust shares as well as gilts. And for me it works very well.

And I'm delighted that I did because if I had been invested that way during the credit crunch of 2008 I would have lost vast amounts of sleep and money as corporate bonds, preference shares and deposits in banks and building societies were endangered.

I learned two valuable lessons.

First, there is no such thing as a safe investment. Nothing is safe.

Second, as in many other areas of life, it is the stuff you don't expect to give you trouble that will give you trouble.

Good lessons.

And you get them for free.

Don't forget them.

SECTORS

'An investor who is seriously eager to make money doesn't have to watch the markets every day. He just has to make, once in a while, a good investment decision on the trends that will last for a number of years.'
MARC FABER

You don't need to pick shares to make money. You're better off picking sectors. It is nigh on impossible to decide, when looking at companies within the same sector, whether company A or company B will do best in the short, medium or long-term. There are many variables affecting individual companies which do not affect sectors. And yet the factors which affect sectors must inevitably affect individual companies. It is clear, therefore, that picking individual companies is much harder than picking sectors. It is much easier to say (for example) that mines will do better than banks in the next twelve months than it is to say that mine A will do better than mine B.

I am a macroeconomic, geopolitical, sector investor. I choose sectors, and then buy shares in those sectors, rather than choosing individual shares as a 'stockpicker'. I pick sectors to invest in according to how I think they are likely to thrive in the future. In practice, this means that if I think the oil price is likely to go up I will buy shares in companies operating in the oil sector of the stock market. If, on the other hand, I think builders and construction companies are set to do well I will buy a basket of shares in the building and construction industry.

I do this because I have made much bigger returns by spotting trends, finding strengths and weaknesses, and going with sectors, than I have by buying individual shares. Doing this probably involves more strategic thinking but less ploughing through annual reports and reams of statistics. Very few investors can pick stocks that will do better than average. I have had some successes with stock picking. But I have also had some failures. Individual companies are far more susceptible to far more unpredictable events than are whole sectors. I have been far more successful in picking sectors than picking stocks.

If you are buying one share in a sector because you believe that sector is likely to go up, then you might be better off spreading your money among many or all of the shares in the same sector. If one share in a sector goes up there is a good chance that they will all go up. On the other hand, if one falters, because of a specific problem affecting that company, the others will probably keep going up. The only way you will do better with just one share is if that share rockets out of proportion to the others.

I feel that there are several advantages to selecting sectors rather than individual companies.

First, you get a chance to really back your beliefs. If you get things right you could make a lot of money. Conversely, of course, if you get things wrong you could lose a lot of money too. Stockpickers are always going to win some and lose some. And so they are much more likely to end up just matching the index.

Second, by selecting sectors and buying a number of shares within your chosen sector, you reduce the risk of deliberately investing in individual companies which are run by crooked or incompetent directors. It is extremely unlikely that all the oil, retail or banking companies are going to be run by crooks. It is perfectly possible that if you pick out half a dozen shares several of them will be run by crooks.

Third, if you invest in sectors you don't even have to bother picking individual company shares at all. You can invest in sectors by buying shares in investment trusts. If the sector does well the chances are pretty good that a specialist investment trust will do well. And you can reduce the risk by investing in several investment trusts in your chosen sector. Because the investment trusts will be run separately you won't be adding an extra layer of fees onto your investment, you will simply be spreading your risk. Investment trusts are an excellent way to invest in all sorts of sectors – including, for example, mining or property. They are also a good way to invest in individual countries (such as Russia, India, or China) or in investing in regions (such as the EU, North America or emerging economies).

Fourth, many sectors are cyclical. You can make money by buying as the sector starts to go up and then selling a year or two later when you believe that the situation has changed. Do not, however, make the mistake of chasing after 'hot' sectors. By the time everyone else is investing in a sector it is almost certainly too late for you to get involved.

Fifth, individual share rises and falls can be due to unpredictable events (the boss may do something stupid or dishonest, there may be a fire in a plant or a specific product may suddenly become unfashionable). On the other hand, however, macroeconomic factors are a big influence on the returns you are likely to get from sectors. Picking individual shares depends on researching accounts and company reports. This sort of information is widely available. It is, therefore, extremely difficult to 'beat' the professionals if you are using precisely the same information that they are using. On the other hand the prices of whole sectors are based on expectations and geopolitics and so it is much easier for the individual investor to win. There are, in my experience, fewer surprises for the thinking investor who puts money into sectors rather than particular shares. Surprises bring volatility with them and, for the investor seeking a quiet life and a steady gain, neither is a good thing.

SELLING (AND KNOWING WHEN TO SELL)

'Cut the weeds, cultivate the flowers.'
PETER LYNCH

Some people don't like to admit this, either to themselves or others, but the point of owning shares (or, indeed, any other form of investment) is to make money. The profit can come from dividends or (in the case of bonds or bank deposits) interest, or (in the case of property) rent, but it can also come from capital growth.

Sometimes an investment is worth holding onto for years. Shares in a good company can produce regular and even substantial dividends and modest capital growth for decades. A well-located property can produce rent and capital growth for generations. Holding an investment for a long period makes life considerably easier and dramatically reduces costs by cutting out transaction costs completely. (When you sell an investment you obviously have to pay the costs involved in selling the investment but you also have to pay the costs involved in buying something else.)

But these days the return from most investments tends to fall off after a while. Companies stop growing or start declining or are taken over and lost in some huge, unprofitable conglomerate. Some of the companies which were stock market stars in the 1970's are gone. If you'd bought and held their shares you would now be left with nothing. Remember this when you are told to buy some good shares, put them in a drawer and forget about them.

And so you have to consider the tedious business of selling.

Knowing when to sell is just as difficult as knowing when (and what) to buy. Controlling losses is a key to making a profit. In any portfolio there will always be some investments which lose money. The trick is to take full advantage of the gains while keeping the losses to a minimum. Big losses can ravage a portfolio. If 90% of your investments are modest winners one big loser can still wreck your final results. The corollary to 'letting your profits run' is the phrase 'sell your losers early'. If you sell an investment quickly when it is falling you can protect the overall success of your portfolio. Selling, not buying, is the key to profits. Knowing when to sell is just as important as knowing what and when to buy.

Here are my thoughts based on the simple rules I try to follow:

1. Cut your losses and let your profits run. Generally speaking, I try to sell losers rather than winners. Most people sell investments that have done well rather than investments that have done badly. It's much more fun to sell something that produces a profit. It makes you feel good. And it saves you worrying about losing the profit you've made. Selling losers is depressing. Once you've crystallised the loss you know for certain that you aren't going to recover the money. But my advice is: sell your losers and keep your winners. Most investors do the opposite. They sell the shares that do well and they keep the shares that do badly so they won't have to admit to themselves that they made a mistake. They hold onto the losers in the hope that they will go back up to where they were. Similarly, if the market crashes most investors sell their winners and keep their losers. And if they need cash they sell their winners and keep their losers. (The losing shares that investors hold onto usually underperform the winners that they sold.) If you sell your winners and keep your losers your investment results will almost certainly be dismal. If a portfolio does well, and beats the market as a whole, it is usually because of the spectacular rise of one or two really successful investments. If you sell a share because it has gone up 50% then you will make 50% profit (before costs and tax) and that is very nice, thank you, and rather better than a loss. But if the company has gone up 50% then it might go up 500%. And you don't need to be a wizard at maths to know that a 500% rise will have much more impact on your portfolio than a 50% rise. Selling winners and keeping losers is stupid. But it is one of the stupidities that gives wiser investors an edge.
2. Here are some of the signs which suggest that it might be time to sell an investment:
    - The company's competitors are having problems.
    - The directors are selling shares. This is particularly relevant if several directors are selling lots of shares. (If just one director is selling it could be that he is buying a new house or acquiring a new wife – though these excuses are probably overworked.)
    - The finance director has suddenly resigned. This can damage the share price because the new incumbent may well uncover all sorts of problems. Naturally, he will want to get the problems into the accounts quickly so that he looks good a year down the line.
    - The nature of a share changes. So, for example, a growth share in telecoms may become a utility.

- There are big legal problems likely to affect the company. So, for example, if a company's major product faces legal challenges it is probably time to sell the share.
- If the company releases its financial results at odd times (between Christmas and New Year) so that the bad news exposure is limited. There is always a reason for this.
- If the boss comes up with lame excuses for missing targets. Blaming the weather is, for example, a weak excuse. The weather affects everyone. And since we get weather every year a good company should be prepared for all eventualities.
- There are too many Ferraris and company jets.
- If you bought a share because you thought it would recover, remember to sell it when it has recovered.
- If the fundamentals which inspired your purchase change noticeably.
- When the company issues its first profit warning. If there is one warning, there will probably be more. Profit warnings rarely come alone. If a company issues a profit warning there will probably be another and the price will probably fall again. You might like to sell after the first warning.
- A sharp increase in the trading volume in the stock suggests that people who know things might be dumping the shares.
- There is a change of accounting policy. This can suggest underlying problems since changing the accounting policy is an easy way to produce some fake profits. For example, an airline which suddenly decides not to depreciate its planes can easily turn a loss into a profit.
- There has been a change of year end. This is a classic way to cover things up. What are the directors covering up?
- The dividend is omitted or cut. This can be a bad sign.
- If the share price drops by a predetermined figure (say 30%).
- The boss of the company spends too much time at parties. If the Chief Executive spends more time in the social columns than on the city pages it might be a good idea to dump the shares.
- Finally, I believe it is time to sell when everyone is recommending the share. When the brokers all agree that a company is a 'buy' and the newspapers are agreed that an investment is a 'sure thing' it is time to sell. I say this not through cynicism but because when a share has been promoted widely there will probably be no one left to buy it.

3. Before deciding whether to sell or keep a share ask yourself this simple

question: would I buy this now? If the answer is 'no' then you should probably sell. If the price falls and you don't want to buy more then you should, perhaps, consider selling. You should not hold an investment if you would not buy it.

4. Try not to sell too soon. Baron Rothschild said he was rich because he always sold too soon. But maybe he would have been richer if he'd held on a little longer. The big profits usually come from holding really successful investments for fairly long periods.

> *'If one investor sells high, another must buy high.'*
> WARREN BUFFETT

5. If the price of a share doubles and you are feeling nervous, consider selling half. This means that you've got the remaining half in your portfolio without any cost. If the price doubles again sell another half. And so on. This approach enables you to have your cake and to eat it. You can't lose your original stake but you can still participate in future growth. This approach also helps you to keep your portfolio balanced. If one share soars then it may eventually take up too much of your portfolio.
6. Listen to your intuition. Sell if your intuition tells you a share is going to fall. Always listen to your intuition. The more you do this the stronger your intuition will become.
7. Some investors sell every May and then buy their shares again in October. There is sound statistical support for this seemingly crazy approach to investing. The evidence suggests that if you stay invested in equities between 31st October and 30th April each year but keep your money in cash for the rest of the time you will do much better than you would if you simply left your money in shares all the time. No one really knows why this should be. One explanation is that the economy is more volatile in winter. Another is that investors get depressed during the winter and so are careful with their money, whereas during the brighter, summer months they are more optimistic and so take unreasonable risks. Neither of these theories is mine, incidentally and I disclaim responsibility for them. I don't follow this investment philosophy. It sounds like a lot of trouble and I have a suspicion that the dealing costs I would incur (and the taxes I would pay) would destroy any advantage I might enjoy.
8. Selling failures early is good because it enables you to avoid over-dealing to try and make up for big losses. Selling losers also frees up time and energy.

Most investors spend most of their time on the investments which are doing badly. Fretting over a share which is going down means wasted time and missed opportunities.

9. Don't be afraid to hold onto shares (or other investments) which are doing well. The 'buy and hold' philosophy is old-fashioned and out of favour but the people doing the sneering are, by and large, the people who make their living out of selling you new ideas or taking a profit from you when you deal. (Remember too that newspapers and magazines depend upon advertisements from banks and investment companies so they tend to encourage constant trading too.) One of the best-known maxims in investment is 'you can't go broke taking a profit'. There are many variations on this. In a way it's perfectly true. A lot of people have become exceedingly rich by taking profits too soon. It is impossible to time the market and impossible, therefore, to be sure that you sell your investments at the very top. But if you always sell every investment which shows a profit you will never be really successful. Really good investors (the ones who make a lot of money) usually do so because they have found a good investment and held it for quite a long time.
10. Don't sell a share just because you have been holding it for a while without it going up a great deal. If the company is paying good dividends then you are still making money out of it. Are you sure you can find a better, safer home for your money?
11. When you sell a share forget about it (unless you are intending to buy it again). Don't mourn your losses. Let them go. This way lies madness. Don't look back. If you sell a share (either for a profit or a loss) don't keep looking to see how it is doing unless you intend to buy it back again. And, if you sell a house, don't curse yourself every time you see it being sold for more than you paid for it.
12. If you are unhappy with an investment sell it now. Don't wait. Don't say that you will only sell if you get a certain price. Sell now.
13. Look at your portfolio just before the end of the tax year. If you have a capital gains liability and you have any investments which are losing money consider selling the losers to reduce your tax liability.
14. If you think things are turning bad and your investments could be in trouble, then it is probably time to sell. One experienced investor once said: 'I am prudent enough not to stand in the middle of the railroad tracks while I try to decide if the headlight I think I see is a freight train or an illusion.'
15. If the balance of your portfolio has changed dramatically because of the success of one share and the relative failure of other shares, then it might be wise to sell some of the successful investment so that you can re-establish the balance in your portfolio.

16. If you are in doubt about an investment the best policy is to be a coward. Heroic investors get no medals. They don't get much money either.
17. Don't think of the price you paid when thinking of selling a share or a house. Never think: 'I paid £5 so I'm not selling for less'. Life doesn't work this way. Sometimes investments go up in price and sometimes they go down.
18. If you have shares in an investment trust and the price of the share goes to a premium (i.e. the investment trust is selling for more than the value of the shares owned by the trust) then you should consider selling.

> *'Throughout my years of investing, I've found that the big money was never made in the buying or the selling. The big money was made in the waiting.'*
> JESSE LIVERMORE

19. Sell if the price has risen and the investment is no longer good value.
20. Sell if you have found a better investment for which you need to free the funds.
21. If you buy a share hoping for a huge profit, don't sell it immediately afterwards because the price has dipped a little. Really profitable investments are often volatile.
22. Analysts and brokers who don't want to admit that a share isn't worth buying will sometimes give it a 'hold' rating. In theory this means that the share is worth holding onto but not worth buying. In practice it means that the share should be sold but the analyst or broker doesn't want to upset the company (or risk losing future business). If a company is worth buying it is worth buying. If it isn't worth buying then you shouldn't be holding it. The minute you no longer believe in an investment (or your premise has changed) you should sell. Don't wait. Good portfolio results are obtained by selling losers before they become disasters.

> *'Never get rooted in an investment because of the feeling that it 'owes' you something.'*
> MAX GUNTHER

23. Remember: whatever you are buying, someone else is selling because he doesn't want it. You may be pleased to be buying, but he is pleased to be selling. And whatever you are selling someone else is buying. You are selling

because you think you are getting a really good price. The buyer is buying because he thinks he is getting a bargain.

24. If you own a share that everyone says is a 'winner' it is probably time to think about selling. When everyone agrees that a share is a winner there are no potential buyers left. When there are no potential buyers left the price can only fall.
25. Sell when you made a mistake in buying.
26. When dealing through a broker you may be asked if you want to put a limit on the price you are prepared to pay for a share (or a limit on the price you are prepared to accept if you are selling). On the whole I don't think limits are a good idea – particularly when selling. If you've decided to sell then you should sell. If you wait to get the price you want you may find yourself holding the share much longer than you want to.
27. It is never too late to sell something. A share, house, bond (or anything else) that has gone down 90% can still halve. Or worse.

> *'You do better to make a few large bets and sit back and wait... There are huge mathematical advantages to doing nothing.'*
> CHARLES MUNGER

28. Sell investments which lose money and which no longer have a sound strategy behind them. I hold a number of oil investments because I believe that oil is going to get considerably more expensive. But if it turns out that I'm wrong and someone invents a perpetual motion machine that runs on air I will sell my oil investments. The strategy will no longer make sense so I'll take my losses and do something else. I don't think this is likely to happen. But if it does I won't stubbornly hold on to my oil investments.
29. When markets start to turn down and people start selling it is usually not because they are frightened of the economy or some wider issue. People sell because they fear that others are frightened of a failing economy, a faltering government or a coming recession.
30. Finally, think carefully before selling. Do you really want to sell? Over the years I have discovered that most (but not all) of the properties and investments I sell eventually trade for a much higher price than the price at which I sold. Just a thought I thought I'd share with you. Do you really want to sell what you're selling? Don't be too keen to buy and sell. Judicious lethargy is often more profitable than hectic overtrading.

SHARES

'Wall Street, in theory, is the centre of the financial system which provides for the capital needs of the nation. But Wall Street is in fact a speculation centre organised for the purpose of enabling a self-selected minority of men of boundless greed and ambition to become millionaires and billionaires.'
RALPH BORSODI

All predictions about shares are based on only two things: a knowledge of the company's history and a view of what the future holds for it. That's it. The market price already allows for the first of these. Buying shares solely because of information about the company's past is, by and large, pretty pointless. The market already knows what the company did last year. The market knows what products the company has available. The market knows how much profit the company made last year. Unless the company is a small one (and therefore under-researched) any information about its past is too widely available to be of any real value. It is the second factor which is the one that matters. And yet although most analysts, investment managers and investors are very good at accumulating information about a company's past they are very poor at predicting what is going to happen to a company in the future.

I believe that investors who want to be successful should spend relatively little time worrying about a company's past but should spend most of their time puzzling over its future. An understanding of geopolitics and human psychology will help the investor far more than a desk piled high with old company reports.

In less politically correct days British newspapers used to run beauty contests. The newspapers would print a collection of photographs of beautiful young women and the readers would be invited to try and win a prize by picking the one who would be chosen by all the other readers as the most attractive.

The twist here was that the readers weren't asked to choose the girl they found the most attractive.

They were asked to pick the girl they thought all the other readers would prefer.

It was John Maynard Keynes, a great writer on financial matters, who first drew attention to the fact that the stock market works in a similar way.

You don't win (or get rich) by picking the best share. You get rich by picking the share (or shares) that most other investors choose as their selection.

If a lot of people think a company is good one, and want to buy shares in it, then the share price will go up.

> *'Though the mathematical calculations required to evaluate equities are not difficult, an analyst – even one who is experienced and intelligent – can easily go wrong in estimating future 'coupons'. At Berkshire, we attempt to deal with this problem in two ways. First, we try to stick to businesses we believe we understand. That means they must be relatively simple and stable in character. If a business is complex or subject to constant change, we're not smart enough to predict future cash flows. Incidentally, that shortcoming doesn't bother us. What counts for most people in investing is not how much they know, but rather how realistically they define what they don't know. An investor needs to do very few things right as long as he or she avoids big mistakes. Second, and equally important, we insist on a margin of safety in our purchase price. If we calculate the value of a common stock to be only slightly higher than its price, we're not interested in buying. We believe this margin-of-safety principle, so strongly emphasised by Ben Graham, to be the cornerstone of investment success.'*
>
> WARREN BUFFETT

Here are the things I've learned about selecting shares to buy.

1. Buy shares for the long-term. Buy something you believe has value (and is good value) and hold it. Take your dividends and wait. Look for companies which are producing cash and which are so cheap that even if they went out of business you would not lose money (because the value of the underlying assets would cover the cost of the shares). Look for companies which have a powerful brand, good management and a strong balance sheet. If a company looks cheap compared with a fairly conservative forecast of the cash it will generate over the coming years then the market has got it wrong and once the mispricing has been corrected you will make money. Buying shares that are good value provides an opportunity to win a lot even though the downside is that you will not lose much. There is no specific, reliable way of assessing the value of a company. There is no specific, reliable way of deciding whether or not a share is too cheap or too expensive. If such methods did exist the people who had access to them would soon have all the money. Shares cannot really be overvalued or undervalued because they have no true value. Shares exchange hands for the price one investor is prepared to accept and another investor is prepared to pay. That doesn't mean that the share is good (or bad) value. The market gives you a price. This is what you pay for the share you are buying. The value of the share is something else. Your job, as an investor, is to buy when you believe that the value is greater than the price and to sell when you believe that the price is greater than the value.

2. Many investment writers suggest that investors should set price targets for the shares they buy. 'You should,' they say, 'know in advance what price you expect your share to reach. And then, when the share reaches the price you want, you should sell.' This is, in my opinion, sheer lunacy. Picking shares that will go up is tricky enough. Forecasting the price the share will reach before you sell it requires supernatural powers.
3. One trick pony shares can be hugely profitable. But companies can go bust very quickly. If a firm relies on one thing it may be vulnerable to changes in the market. For example, a company which makes a product which could be rendered obsolete, or replaced with a cheaper alternative, is vulnerable. A company which earns all or most of its money from another company could be in difficulties if its contract is ended. Suppliers to high street stores can sometimes find themselves in trouble for this reason.
4. Unless you understand exactly what a company does and how its returns are achieved, don't invest in it – however compelling the argument to invest might be.
5. Don't buy shares in service or retail companies whose staff have been rude to you more than once. This isn't a question of revenge. If staff are rude to customers then the company is more likely to fail and the shares will crash. I don't hold shares in mobile telephone companies for this reason. If anyone ever creates and builds a mobile telephone company which looks after its customers the existing companies will fold within a year. And don't buy shares in a company which has a bad PR problem. Companies which annoy the public are annoying their customers. And that isn't good business.
6. A share that has fallen a long way can always keep falling. It can, indeed, fall until it can fall no more because it is no longer worth anything.
7. Share prices move ahead of the economy. Investors who judge their investments according to the current health of the economy will probably buy and sell at the wrong times.
8. Conglomerates have had their day. Large companies which make washing machines, television programmes, nuclear power stations and silk underwear have no point. The overheads will be far too high. The directors and executives will pay themselves far too much because of the size of the company and they will spend most of their time travelling between plants and offices (for which they will, of course, need a fleet of expensive jets).
9. The market always overshoots. When there is bad news about a company the chances are that the price will go down too far. When there is good news there is a chance that the price will go up too much. Price rises tend to be exacerbated during a bull market and price falls tend to be exacerbated during a bear market. You are likely to be buying at the top of the market

if you buy when a company has just reported excellent results and when the world seems rosy. Remember: all markets overshoot. That is how you can make money out of investing. The time to be bold is when everyone else is timid. The time to be timid is when everyone else is bold.

10. News never changes share or commodity prices. And commentators don't change prices. It is the market's reaction to the news that changes the prices. And that means it is the reaction of real people – investment amateurs and investment professionals – which changes the price. It is important to remember and to understand this. Sometimes, a piece of good news about a company may result in the company's share price falling instead of rising. Why? Simple. The market (which means investors) had expected better news and had already priced in the good news. Markets discount information. Many people who are new to investing are surprised that a company's share price may fall after it makes an announcement that its profits are rising. The reason is simple. The market anticipates reality. If the share price falls after good news has been announced it may be because investors were expecting even better news.
11. Investors often think that investing in the stock market is about picking successful companies. In fact it is more about asset allocation, sector selection and psychology. If you are planning to buy shares you should first decide the market's general direction (based, among other things, on what you think other people will think and do), then pick the sectors which you think will do best and finally the best individual stocks within that group.
12. Popular shares (the ones most people own) are often overpriced. Unpopular ones are often underpriced. If you think about it this isn't at all surprising. The price of a share depends upon the number of people who want to buy it and the number of people who want to sell it. A popular share is popular because a lot of people like it and own it. And that means that the chances are that most of the people who want to own the share already own it.
13. The odds of the stock market rising are much better when the market is low. If the FTSE 100 is at 3,000 then the chances of it going up are much better than they would be if it was at 6,000. When current returns are poor the prospect of better future returns improves.
14. Anne Scheiber retired from the US Internal Revenue Service in 1944. She invested $5,000 in the stock market. She invested mainly in large, well-known companies and she did not deal very often. When she died in 1995 at the age of 101 her $5,000 had become $22 million. A perfect example of the twin benefits of keeping your costs down and allowing your investments to benefit from the miracle of compounding.
15. Utilities (water companies for example) usually produce a steady income.

Their dividends tend to be reliable. Even in a recession people still need to make tea and wash their faces. The only snag is that utilities tend to be subject to government regulation. Despite this, I still like to have exposure to some basic utilities in my portfolio. Politicians are stupid but who will it help if they push the big water companies into bankruptcy?

16. Surprises tend to improve the performance of out of favour stocks but impair the performance of those in favour. Popular, in favour shares, respond more dramatically and badly to news of any kind. Out of favour shares do well with good news and don't tend to do too badly with bad news.
17. You have to invest for the long-term and be prepared to ride out storms and hurricanes. Shares are the best way to grow your money but only if you invest for the long-term. Between 1988 and 1998 the All-Share index of London shares rose by 166%. But in the following decade (1998 to 2008) shares stayed more or less where they were. If you'd chosen 1998 as your investment starting point then, apart from whatever dividends you'd managed to gather, you would have had the same amount of money at the end of the ten year period as you'd had when you'd started. Once you'd allowed for inflation your purchasing power would have fallen quite significantly.
18. The news always seems most optimistic right at the top of the market. And it always seems most pessimistic right at the bottom of the market. If there is good news but share prices don't go up then that suggests that shares are already as high as they are going to go. If there is bad news but share prices don't go down any more then they may well be as low as they are going to go.
19. The share prices tells you nothing about the value of a company. The share price only tells you what investors think the company is worth at that moment. Even in calm times prices move constantly. I was on the phone a few minutes ago, talking to a broker about buying more oil shares. The conversation went something like this.

    'What's the price?

    '£49.92'

    I now think about how many shares I want to buy.

    '£49.96,' says the broker, as the price changes.

    I have found my calculator and am working out how many shares I can afford to buy with the amount I wish to spend.

    '£50.03.'

    'Crumbs. It's moving quickly.'

    '£50.09.'

    'Buy 1,500 please.'

    '1,500 shares?'

'Yes, please.'

'At £50.14.'

'Yes.'

'Done. 1,500 shares bought at £50.14'

'Thanks.'

'They're back down to £50.02 now.'

20. You will sometimes see it suggested that before you start buying shares you should create an imaginary portfolio and see how it does. This is called notional trading and it is utterly pointless. The problem is that there is a huge difference between pretending to buy some shares and really buying some shares. If you want to dip your toe in the water then start your investment portfolio with a small amount of (real) money. You will learn far more about the markets and, most important of all, about yourself, by investing a small amount of real money than by investing a huge amount of imaginary money.

21. If you are going to stock pick then you need to look for quality businesses which have a regular cash flow and a solid franchise that is not likely to be superseded. There should be a good management, with a real interest in the company. The company should be paying a decent dividend and the company's income should be enough to ensure that even if profits fall the dividend will still be paid. The company should be able to maintain its cash flow for the foreseeable future. A company's underlying strength comes from its real assets (buildings, land and so on) and its intangible assets (patents, brand names). Ideally it should be difficult for customers to switch to another product or service because, for example, the company is selling a unique product or service and because you can sell it, and make a profit, cheaper than competitors. In the long run, whatever a company does someone will eventually find a way to do it cheaper or better. The existence of barriers keeping out competitors, is hugely important. Does the company have valuable patents or a supply advantage? Does it have a brand name that customers love and which inspires great loyalty? Is the company vulnerable to competition from China or India? Are high fixed costs a deterrent to potential competitors? Is the company protected or threatened by existing and coming legislation? (Many companies deliberately encourage the introduction of legislation which will make life difficult for competitors.)
    Before buying shares or any other investment you should have a clear idea of your investment theory in your mind. You should always be able to explain your investments to anyone in a few simple sentences. If you buy a share or put money into an investment trust or fund you should be able to summarise your reasons in sentences that anyone could understand. And you need to be able to explain why you are continuing to hold this

investment on a regular basis – particularly if anything changes. You should be able to explain your plans to a child. You don't actually have to go out and find and bore a child with your investment plans. It's probably illegal anyway. But you do need to be able to formulate your theory in such a way that a child could understand your logic and your conclusions. If you don't understand it, don't buy it. Forget the child. Some of them are precocious. If you cannot explain exactly what you are buying, and precisely why, to your cat, then do not buy it.

Finally, when buying a share in a company, and putting your hard earned savings into it, you should consider the company as carefully as you would if you were considering buying the whole thing.

22. Shares (and markets) reach a top when there aren't any buyers. Shares (and markets) reach a bottom when no one wants to sell. The market can be too high as a whole, and yet individual shares can be excellent value.
23. If you hold a stock, sell at the first real sign of trouble. Don't listen to explanations or excuses. Don't wait to see if the management turn things round. Don't wait for the next problem to appear. Just sell immediately and invest your money somewhere else.
24. If you play cards (whether your game of choice is poker or bridge) you will do better if you can count cards. Knowing what cards are where will give you an advantage over the other players. The same thing is true of investing in shares. In order to do well you need to be able to spot things that other investors have missed. You need to be able to work out for yourself how and why a share should be valued. Sadly, instead of 'counting cards' most investors, like most gamblers, just rely on a good run of the cards continuing.
25. When choosing individual stocks (as opposed to investment trusts) you should only buy shares which you believe can increase enormously (by at least 100%) over the next year or two. If a share doesn't have that sort of potential then it isn't worth the effort of researching it, buying it and holding it. The only exception is if the company is paying a really good, steady dividend.
26. All you and I can achieve by researching a major company in depth is to find out what the market already knows and has discounted in the share price.
27. If ever you are tempted to believe that a well-known company is too big and too famous to fail just remember Rolls Royce. At the time of its failure Rolls Royce was Britain's most famous company. When it declared itself bankrupt on 4th February 1971 British industry was shaken to the foundations. 'Life will never be the same again,' said a City broker. I remember this failure. I

was one of the investors who believed that Rolls Royce was too big too fail. I lost money but I learnt a useful lesson. Well worth the price.

28. These days more than 90% of the value of many companies is made up of intangibles – know how, brand value and a touching belief in an endless supply of future profits. As an investor I prefer to look for unfashionable companies where more than 90% of the value is made up of boring stuff like land, property and cash in the bank.
29. The fact that a company is successful doesn't mean that its shares are good value. The company may have good products, wonderful staff and excellent prospects and yet still be a terrible buy – if the shares have been bid up too high and are already too expensive.
30. You can't spread your risk by investing overseas because these days all markets tend to move together (usually following the lead set by the American market). If shares on Wall Street fall then shares in Japan, Germany, Australia and France are also likely to fall.
31. Many investment professionals (and authors of books on investing) advise all investors to keep an eye on their shares at least once a day. Once you start doing this, however, you will find that you have to keep on with it. You won't be able to go abroad on holiday unless you can get hold of a British edition of the *Financial Times* airmailed out to you or unless you have Internet access so that you can check on your share prices on line (the foreign editions of the *Financial Times* contain only a limited number of British share prices). You will end up poring over your BlackBerry on the beach, struggling to find the latest share prices for all your investments. I don't bother checking share prices every day because I know that whatever happens isn't going to make any difference. I'm certainly not going to sell everything if the market goes down with a thump.
32. When interest rates are high there isn't much point in investing in shares. If you can get 15% by leaving your money on deposit in the bank why would you risk buying shares in a company which is probably going to struggle to make a profit in a high interest environment?
33. Most people (including investment professionals) buy shares when they are expensive and sell them when they are cheap. Investors do this because it is what the analysts and fund managers and financial journalists usually advise. For example, investment money was pouring into the heavily promoted technology funds in 1999 and 2000 – just before they crashed. Around 80% of the money the American public put into mutual funds in the spring of 2000 went into technology funds. Over the next three years investors lost up to 80% of their money. They then took out their money just before technology funds recovered and doubled.

34. Investing in new technology is dangerous. Today's new, wonder product will probably be tomorrow's embarrassing memory. Product cycles are continually shortening and competition is constantly becoming more acute. By and large, new products and inventions don't make money for investors. (There are, of course, exceptions.) Most of the benefits of technological change are passed on to consumers, rather than producers (or their shareholders). The worst performing sectors in recent years have, in general terms, been software and IT hardware. Very few investors made money out of railway companies or airlines when they first started trading. New technological advances actually damage investors' prospects by destroying the market for old products. The new products are quickly superseded by new developments. The truth, I fear, is that change and progress are usually bad for investors. Despite this many investors are always ready to believe that a new piece of technology is about to change the world. If you distort simple truths in order to fit reality you will lose money. Enthusiastic buyers of dot.com shares at the end of the 20th Century argued that neither losses nor profits were relevant because 'the paradigm had changed'.
35. Share prices don't always go up in the long run. Companies go bust. And, sometimes, whole stock markets collapse to zero. In the past there have been major stock market collapses in Russia, China, Egypt and a number of Eastern European countries. And investors in Germany didn't do too well when inflation resulted in the 100 billion deutschmark postage stamp.
36. Buying shares 'when there is blood in the streets' and the vast majority of investors are swearing that they will never again have anything to do with shares is one of the best ways to get rich. But picking the bottom is difficult. It's easy to buy shares because they are a fraction of what they were trading at just twelve months previously. But then they halve in a week and you're sitting on a huge loss and needing the market to double for you to get even. The best advice is probably to wait until the shares no longer go down much when there is bad news. At that point the shares are probably at the bottom. And, unless the company goes bust, you could be on the way to making serious money. An alternative approach is merely to pick sectors which seem bombed out. Investors tend to desert whole sectors during a bear market and so it is often possible to pick up a number of bargains if you watch carefully to see what is available.
37. The market goes ahead of events and discounts future events. And so it often happens that when a company produces bad results its share price goes up. This happens because the market (i.e. other investors) had expected problems and had already accounted for the bad results in the share price. If the price rises after bad results it is because the market is relieved that the results weren't even worse.

38. If a share falls from £10 to £5 it has gone down by 50%. But if the share price then goes up by 50%, it only reaches £7.50.
39. The fact that a share is cheaper than it has been for half a century doesn't mean that it can't go lower. Cheap markets can always get cheaper.
40. As I've pointed out elsewhere, doctors, lawyers and dentists – logical and intelligent people you might think – tend to do badly as stock market investors. They usually do worse than people who throw darts at the financial pages and choose shares that way. They do worse than coin flippers too. Their problem is that they try to be logical and scientific about investing and such an approach just doesn't work. Selecting shares that will do well isn't a logical or scientific business. The stock market is about people and it is therefore unpredictable, and a mystery to those who do not understand that share prices are influenced not by profits or currencies or interest rates but by how people (other investors) react to profits, currencies and interest rates.
41. When you buy a share imagine that the stock market is about to close for five years. Can you live with the share for that long? Will it pay you decent dividends even though you are unable to sell it? And, at the end of five years, is the company likely to be worth considerably more than you paid for it?
42. The shares of small companies tend, over long periods, to do better than the shares of big companies. Academics claim that this is because they are riskier (more likely to go down and more likely to go bust). Maybe it is because there is less information about them – and the available information is less widely known. It is also a fact that analysts and fund managers spend less time examining small companies – partly because if you are managing a fund worth billions it is not going to be worth your while investing in a company worth just a few million. Small companies are usually easier to understand because their interests are more clearly defined. Big companies may have several divisions, all doing different things. One division may do well while another does badly. With a small company the results usually depend on the success or failure of a specific product or range of products. Small companies may also have a niche advantage. They may be the only people in the world making butterfly nets. There may not be much room for growth but there probably won't be too much competition either. It is easier to judge the significance of the directors involvement in a small company (where their shareholdings are likely to be significant). And it is much easier for the private investor to become an expert on the company. But, a word of warning: small companies can be very risky. Venture capitalists, who invest in very small, developing companies for a living, expect that out of every ten investments they make three will probably go bust or nearly bust, four will not do anything (their value will neither rise nor fall) and three will

do well. Of the three which will do well, one will do brilliantly well and will make so much money that the losses on the other investments will be paid for and there will be plenty of profit left over. Venture capitalists think about their investments as a whole portfolio and they measure the success of their investments by looking at the whole portfolio. Unless they want to get ulcers the size of dinner plates they don't sit around and mope if one of their investments turns out to be a turkey. The risks for small companies which are quoted on the small market are probably not as great. But there is still a much bigger chance that Exotic Lingerie For Merry Widows Limited will go bust than that Tesco will disappear from the world.

43. Create a list of shares you are interested in buying but think are too expensive. If the share price goes down (for no very good reason) then you can buy at a more reasonable price.

44. It is a myth that equities will always outperform other asset classes in the long-term. This is a myth perpetuated with great enthusiasm by financial advisers. The phrase 'long-term' is rather imprecise but it is generally taken to mean five years or longer. In the autumn of 2008 share prices in the UK fell back to what they had been in 1997. Many investors who had put money into shares in the mid 1990's or later had seen the value of their savings fall considerably over what most people would undoubtedly describe as the 'long-term'. By July 2008 the FTSE 100 was 13% lower than it had been ten years earlier. If we assume that inflation has more or less eaten up the value of the dividends received this means that investors who did as well as the market lost money. Costs and expenses will mean that most investors did worse than the market. Over a ten year period most investors who had entrusted their savings or pensions to the professionals would have done better if they'd simply put their money into gilts. A not inconsiderable number would have done better if they'd simply stuffed their savings into a sock and put them under the mattress. (This is not, by the way, a recommended investment programme for those keen to protect their wealth.)

    Things were even worse in Japan. In October 2008 the Japanese Nikkei index reached its lowest point for 26 years. Shareholders who had held onto their shares for over a quarter of a century without seeing any gain whatsoever must, by then, have surely been feeling rather disillusioned with the idea that, in the long run, equities are the best investment. The Japanese market hit 30,000 in January 1990. In October 2008 it was between 7,000 and 8,000 – the lowest it had been since 1982. Anyone who bought Japanese shares in 1990 would have been sitting on a huge loss a generation later. Just in case you thought those figures were a misprint: Japanese equity prices were, in 2008, a quarter of what they had been in 1990. Similar things happen everywhere. In America, shares in General Motors were around $5 in October 2008. They were the same price in the 1940's – 60 years earlier. The longest period of negative real returns for shareholders in Britain was between 1900 and 1921. In France, Germany and Italy shareholders had negative returns for the first half of the 20th Century.

45. Investors need an edge – macroeconomic and geopolitical, psychological or statistical. You are unlikely to get a statistical edge (there are thousands of nerds out there who spend hours every day feeding information into computers) so that leaves potential psychological, macroeconomic and geopolitical advantages. And those are really all you and I have got.
46. Long boom/bust cycles are known as secular cycles. These occur once a generation and last around a decade. A favourite promise among politicians is to say that they will eradicate boom/bust cycles.
47. Don't buy shares in 'highly admired' companies. Investment professionals will have bought tons of shares in 'highly admired' companies. And so will private investors (encouraged by their advisors and by journalists). The price is almost certainly too high. They will certainly not be a bargain. I never buy individual shares, or a sector, or shares in general when the consensus of opinion is that they are a 'good buy'. But I do sometimes buy individual shares, or a sector, or shares in general, when the consensus of opinion is that they are a 'bad buy'.
48. If you are rich and you want to be really rich the stock market probably offers you better opportunities than a casino or a racetrack. Taking risks can be very profitable and it is perfectly possible to multiply your wealth considerably by buying and selling risky shares at appropriate times. But make no mistake: this is a dangerous strategy. Even rich people should only do this with the part of their wealth that they are prepared to lose or see shrunken.
49. During the twentieth century in America there were three huge, secular bull markets that covered about 44 years, during which the Dow Jones Industrial Index gained more than 11,000 points. And there were three periods of stagnation, lasting over 56 years. During those 56 years the country made great progress in many ways but the Dow lost 292 points. If you had been invested in the bad years you would have lost money. The problem is that picking the good years and the bad years is nigh on impossible. The investor who wants to make money needs to stay invested through the bad years as well as the good ones. Judging when the market is going to go up and when it is going to go down is called 'timing the market'. In my opinion, it is not possible. Investors who try to time the market are the losers who enable other investors to get rich. The stock market's biggest rises often take place on three or four days a year. Investors who bail out of the market on

bad days often miss the good days. It is the big swings which produce the biggest profits. If you miss the market's three best days each year you will do dramatically worse than if you are invested at those times. Markets tend to have turning points when shares rise dramatically (just as they can go the other way). If you miss the turning points, and the good days, you will do badly. If you find that you can time the market please get in touch with me as soon as possible.

50. Most of the risk in buying a share is the market and sector risk rather than any risk associated with an individual share. Before buying or selling a share you should make a judgement about which way the market as a whole is likely to move and which way the sector is likely to move.
51. Remember: every time you buy a share you are saying that you know something the seller doesn't know or are prepared to take a risk others don't want to take. And when you sell a share you are saying that you know something the buyer doesn't know. When you buy a share (or some other investment) ask yourself why the person who is selling is prepared to let go of such a splendid prospect.
52. Investors follow all sorts of tips. They copy directors' dealings, they track share-price moving averages, they use complex software to help them track chart patterns, they look for complicated relationships between different factors in company accounts and they watch the positions of the planets. There are hundreds (probably thousands) of guaranteed methods for picking shares that are definitely going to rise. These methods usually involve the use of a lot of figures and a calculator. The snag is that the figures are, inevitably, historical and don't allow for the problems which inconveniently pop up from time to time. There are, for example, many newsletters in existence which charge huge sums for giving specific advice about which shares to buy. By the careful selection of times and prices they can always provide evidence proving that their method has worked brilliantly and has produced a 75% per annum rise for the last 30 years. (To which you might respond, why are these people still bothering to produce a newsletter? Why don't they just follow their own advice and get very rich?) I suspect that most of the investors who follow these tips do worse than they would have done if they'd bought a bunch of good, solid blue chip shares or a simple tracker fund and then sat in the garden.
53. Before accepting an investment tip from a journalist or your taxi driver ask yourself this one simple question: if this person knows a way to guarantee a profit why is he sharing it with me? Does he really like me this much?
54. If someone recommends an investment it is probably because he already holds it. Maybe he wants you to share his good fortune in finding a gem. Maybe he will feel more comfortable if he has someone sitting in the boat

with him. Maybe he wants you to invest so that the price will go up and he will make a profit.

55. The biggest returns come from doing what other people don't do. Most people think that their risk is low if they are doing what everyone else is doing. In investing that's a risky thing to do. If you do the same as everyone else you'll get what everyone else gets. And how many people do you know who got rich through investing?

56. The secret of getting rich slowly is to buy shares in companies which have sustainable competitive advantages; companies which are managed by smart, passionate, honest people. Buy the shares at a discount to intrinsic value. And hold the shares for the long term.

57. It is perception and expectation that drive share prices – not reality.

58. Most people think they are better than average drivers and lovers. Most people also think they are better than average investors. The truth, of course, is that half of all people are worse than average drivers, lovers and investors. So, what this means, is that many people aren't as good at these things as they think they are. There are more stupid people buying and selling shares than you might imagine.

59. Investors are perpetual optimists who believe that really good things (huge successes) will happen more than they do in real life. On the other hand they do not expect regular market meltdowns. But these are inevitable. The timing, nature, extent and cause are entirely unpredictable.

60. Don't allow yourself to become emotionally attached to any of your investments. Investors are more likely to become emotionally attached to individual shares than to investment trusts or to bonds. The share doesn't know you own it. You don't owe the share love, loyalty or friendship.

61. Buying shares simply because the price has dropped a lot is stupid. If the company is failing then buying the shares is like buying bananas because they are cheap and expecting the price to go up. The price isn't going to go up. The bananas are rotting and will be finished in another couple of days. The price will never go up again.

62. Occasionally, I find that I have sold a share that I realise I should have held. I may then have to buy it back at a higher price. One investor I know won't ever do this. He says its embarrassing and makes him feel foolish. Anyone who refuses to take action because he might feel foolish should avoid all investments.

63. Do not expect to get all your choices right. No one does. We are all wrong some of the time. If six out of ten of your investment decisions turn out well you will make a fortune as long as you dump the losers and hold the winners. Six winners out of every ten is a far better average than most

investors ever manage. This means that you will be wrong four times out of ten. Sometimes your investments will fail because your original thesis was faulty. Sometimes it will be because events changed and invalidated your original thesis. There may, for example, have been a change in interest rates or currency exchange rates. If your investment was an individual company it may have suffered from a product failure, a rise in commodity costs, new legislation or the outbreak of a price war. It doesn't really matter which. If six out of ten of your investment decisions are good ones (assuming that your money is spread evenly among them) then you will beat nearly all the professionals. If seven out of ten of your investment decisions are good ones you will be one of the most successful investors on the planet.

64. Investing can be fascinating and rewarding. And it can be fun. But do not invest for fun. Resist the temptation to regard investing as a hobby or a form of entertainment. Rent a DVD or buy a book if you want entertainment. Take up gardening or painting if you want a hobby. Don't invest in anything just because it sounds fun. Some investments rise because they seem exciting or because they offer a chance to have a finger in (for example) the entertainment business. I have seen film and theatre companies being promoted with the added attraction that investors will be invited to theatrical first nights or allowed to visit the film set. Don't be seduced by such claptrap. If you are investing you should do so in the hope of making a profit. If you want to meet actors and actresses hang around outside the stage door.

65. Don't invest because a company offers its shareholders free chocolates, cut price travel tickets or other gimmicks. Would you choose a doctor because he offered free chocolates or cut price travel tickets? Precisely.

66. If you really believe that you have found a 'winner' it may be worthwhile making an investment big enough to change your life. If you are sure in your mind that an investment idea will prove profitable but you make only a very small investment you will probably regret the missed opportunity for the rest of your life. Big chances do not come often. I don't think it is worthwhile investing less than 1% of your investment capital in any one investment. If you have £100,000 to invest and you invest £500 in a company you will, if the company does well and triples in size, increase your overall wealth by £1,000 or 1%. I don't think the overall gain is worth the time and the distraction. Every investment you make should be significant for you. If you make very small investments you won't take much interest in them individually because they won't matter.

67. The bull market of the 1990's gave many investors an exaggerated idea of what return they could expect from their investments. Anyone who tries

to get 15% return on their capital will, for quite a few years to come, be taking huge risks. And the chances are that they will lose money, rather than make it.

68. If an investment doesn't work out don't be afraid to sell it and do something else with the money.

69. A profit is only a profit when you've banked it. A 'paper' profit isn't a profit at all – it's no more tangible than a hope.

70. Nobody knows what the markets are going to do next year, next month, next week or tomorrow. If they knew they would have all the money in the world. Your views are as good (and as bad) as anyone else's.

71. When you make an investment because you believe things are likely to change in your favour, be patient. Give other investors time to catch up and start to think like you do.

72. Think of markets as manic depressive. Sometimes they are full of euphoria, and convinced that things will always be good. And sometimes they are full of gloom, and convinced that things will never be good again. The time to buy is when markets are full of gloom. The time to sell is when they are full of joy.

73. Most people suffer more pain when they lose money than they enjoy pleasure when they win money. Don't allow this to make you freeze and reject all possible investments in case they result in a loss.

74. When making an investment always have an idea of the potential downside and the potential upside. What's the worst that can happen? What's the bottom line? And what's the best that can happen? Does the possible upside make the risks worth taking? Always ask yourself: 'What if...?' Think of all the terrible things that can happen that might adversely affect the investment you are making.

75. I only make investments I believe in. I only make investments which seem logical to me. And I don't have any faith that if I tried to jump on a bandwagon I would be able to pick the moment to jump off again. Investing is (or should be) a lonely business. Don't bother joining an investment club. (How on earth are you going to find a group of people who share your own investment needs?) Keep out of chat rooms and avoid discussing your investment plans with other investors.

76. The stock market isn't as wise as people like to think it is. Investment prices are more controlled by greed, fear, hubris and rank stupidity than they are by logic or good sense. The market behaves irrationally more often than you would imagine possible.

77. When you purchase an investment keep all the cuttings and so on which

you have used to help you make up your mind to buy. Put the cuttings into a folder and look at it whenever you review that particular investment. It's often easy to forget why an investment was bought.

78. Great investors often go for months without buying anything.
79. Big profits come from being in the right market at the right time and making big bets.
80. The term 'blue chip' was originally used to describe a chip taken from a blue stone – a diamond. Then it was used to denote high value poker chips. These days it is used to describe shares of large companies which have a good record of growth and a good record of paying a regular, reliable dividend. Investors often put their money into blue chips for safety. But beware: blue chip shares are usually well-established but, like all other investments they can go down as well as up.
81. Much of what is written and said about companies relates to the rights and needs of the customers, the employees, the pensioners and the community at large. The rights and needs of shareholders are often ignored. Here's my guide to companies – specifically designed for investors.
    - The purpose of a company is to make money (through growth or dividends or a mixture of both) for its shareholders. That's it. The primary aim is not to provide employment or pay taxes or to please customers.
    - A company which cuts its research budget may make a bigger profit for a few months. But in the long run it will go into a decline.
    - If the amount by which the company's operating profit covers the company's interest payment is falling, then either the profits are falling or the debts or interest rates are rising.
    - Be wary of companies which find ways to move debt out of the accounts – sometimes into a separate company. Debts will return.
    - Be wary of companies which don't pay dividends. Managers will sometimes say they don't pay dividends because they are using the cash to reduce debts or to expand the business. But they will sometimes not pay dividends because they aren't making any profits.
    - Avoid companies which make too many acquisitions. Acquisitions are often done to give directors and management an excuse for raising their pay. Acquisitions often fail to improve profitability. And it is difficult to see whether or by how much a company is growing naturally if it is always growing artificially.
    - If a company's inventory is growing this could be a sign of problems

ahead. Is the company's merchandise unwanted? Has the company made too much of whatever it is that it makes?

- Watch out for 'extraordinary' or 'exceptional' items in the accounts. If such costs appear more than once then they may not be extraordinary or exceptional.
- If the 'accounts receivable' are rising then the company's customers may be paying slowly because they are unhappy with the company or they may be in financial trouble themselves. Either of these could be bad for the company.
- How concentrated is the company's market? If the demand for fluorescent pink socks turns sour will the company be able to produce some other product?
- Is the company dependent upon government contracts? Politicians often talk wildly about their spending plans but if the money isn't there contracts may be abandoned or altered in some way. Companies which have a spread of customers are more likely to survive.
- Is the company likely to be more or less valuable in 10 or 20 years? Or is a competitor likely to damage the company's profitability and ability to thrive?
- How exclusive is a company's market? A newspaper publisher which produces the sole newspaper in a metropolitan area will be in a strong position to withstand competition. A newspaper publisher which shares its market (or might share its market) will be more vulnerable.
- Is the company unduly dependent on a single individual and his or her skills or contacts?
- Is the company likely to suffer if commodity prices rise or if currency exchange rates alter dramatically (both of which can and do happen with astonishing speed)?
- Is the company particularly susceptible to changes in legislation? For example, employers which have a good many employees on minimum wage may suffer if minimum wage rates rise significantly.
- Are essential patents about to run out? Or are they likely to be questioned in court? Is the company involved in any litigation? (About patents or anything else). One of the many absurdities of the way regulatory authorities deal with companies lies in the fact that when employees break the law it is shareholders who suffer because it is the company – not the responsible employees – who are fined.
- Is the company generating cash? The main problem with the dot.com

companies was that most of them weren't bringing in any income. Some of them had never even worked out how they were going to make a profit. Without cash flow the money will eventually run out. A company which grows but doesn't produce any cash won't have much of a future.

- Does the company need a great deal of capital in order to survive? A manufacturing company with expensive needs is likely to require huge loans. This can be problematical.
- Is the company fighting on equal terms with companies in other countries? Or are foreign competitors subsidised by their governments?
- How risky is the company? Former building society Northern Rock got into trouble because it had a very risky funding structure. The company relied on wholesale markets for much of its funding. It borrowed money from other banks in order to lend it to customers. This was a risky business. Investment fund managers can find the answers to these questions by talking to the company's directors and executives. But with many companies it is possible to find your own answers simply by looking at the company from a distance.
- Does the company produce an essential or a discretionary product? Bread is essential. A specific, patented drug is essential. Motor cars and £500 handbags are discretionary. Whatever the product is, can it be replaced or usurped?
- Investing in companies where the 'people are the greatest asset' is a bad idea. People can walk away from a business and leave it destroyed. They can take their ideas, reputations and goodwill with them. A people-dependent company can be destroyed overnight. Property, assets, and stock give a firm a solid foundation. Factories don't walk away in a sulk because their Christmas bonus wasn't big enough. On the whole I don't invest in companies which provide services and which rely on key employees. The star employees will either want huge salaries or they will leave. I would never invest in a football club or a hairdressing salon or a boutique money manager.
- I try not to invest in companies which make donations to charities or political parties. When companies do this it is so that the boss can get a knighthood or an invitation to a Buckingham Palace garden party. If the bosses want to give money to charity or to a political party they can. But not with my money. Call me Scrooge if you like but I try to avoid buying shares in companies where the bosses give away a lot of my money.

SPECULATION

'...an investor will succeed by coupling good business judgement with an ability to insulate his thoughts and behaviour from the super-contagious emotions that swirl about the marketplace.'
WARREN BUFFETT

If you buy shares in order to participate in the long-term growth of the company concerned, you are investing. You are speculating if you buy shares solely because you expect (or hope) to be able to sell them to someone else at a higher price. Virtually all the investments made during the late 1990's when people were buying shares in dot.com companies were speculation. Most of those companies had never made any profit (and were never likely to). The only way investors could make money out of them was if the share price went up and they could sell them to some other sucker for a higher price. Unfortunately, in the end, the prices collapsed (because there were no more buyers left) and all the investors still holding shares when the music stopped became suckers.

STRATEGIC THINKING

'Thinking: the hardest work there is, which is probably why so few engage in it.'
HENRY FORD

You will never beat investment professionals by having better information than they have. Investment professionals are up to their ears in information. They are drowning in facts and figures. They have desks carpeted with flow charts, press releases and pretty, coloured graphs. By picking up a phone they can speak to the directors of a company and find out what is going on. The professionals are awash with information.

But the experts, the ones who think they know everything, and who certainly like to give the impression that they know what is happening, why it is happening and how the 'why' will affect what happens in the future, are just as confused about whether the country is going into a recession or a depression as politicians are. They have no more idea of whether we're heading for inflation, deflation or stagflation than you have. Politicians, bankers, investment advisers, brokers, journalists and commentators have no better idea of where the economy is heading than the irritable old bloke sitting in the corner of the pub with half a pint of stout in front of him. The reasons for their ignorance? Simple. First, they are too close to the action to see what is really going on. And, second, they are filled with prejudices, bias and misconceptions. They see the evidence they like, that which supports their position, and they ignore or suppress the rest. You can only beat the professionals by being wiser than they are. And, surprisingly perhaps, that isn't necessarily all that difficult.

The key to successful investing in the future will, I believe, be to look at geopolitical issues – global political changes. To be successful, investors need to think about what is happening and to look at political affairs deeply but broadly. Spotting trends – and understanding their importance – will be increasingly important. Information is only of use if you can assess its value and then use it to draw useful conclusions.

If you are to make money out of the market in general, or shares in particular, then you need to understand what you are buying. You need to have a good idea of what the company does, and the industry in which it operates. You need to understand the environment in which it works and you need to know something about its competitors. Most important of all, however, you need to understand how the world will impinge on the company you have chosen. You need to look at what is usually called the big picture. You need to be able to buy (and sell) before the crowd. To do this you need to be able to see how investors are going to behave in the future. And you must remember that reality doesn't matter as much as what people do or think reality will be. You must separate the fundamentals (and your strategy) from the noise. Investment noise is a constant distraction and irritation and will, if you allow it to confuse you and make you uncertain, result in failure and losses.

When you've found a strategy, you have to watch out to make sure that your investment plan isn't compromised by the activities of the idiots in the city who tend to spot an idea rather late and then work it to death – destroying the strategy in the process by pushing up prices. Even if you don't believe in something it matters that others believe it because you may be able to profit from their belief. The most important factor that will decide whether or not you beat the market is whether you can judge what other people are going to do. However right your predictions may be they won't matter a damn unless you know what others are going to do. You might spot a company that is bound to become mega-successful. You might have all the evidence to show that the company is absurdly undervalued. But until other investors believe that the company is undervalued they won't buy the shares, the shares will remain cheap and you won't make a profit.

It always pays to look out for new trends and big themes. Anyone who realised that China would be a booming country a few years before the boom started would have been well placed to make a lot of money.

But you have to be careful. You have to pick the right trend and you have to be sure that the company in which you choose to invest is going to be profitable.

When global warming became 'trendy' many people started looking at alternative forms of energy as an investment possibility. Sadly, many investments in alternative energy proved disappointing because, although the theory was fine, the companies often had no realistic chance of making a profit. In some cases there was no real demand for their products. In other cases the products simply weren't terribly good.

And you have to get your timing right. You have to be early enough. If you spot a trend or a big theme too late, thousands of other investors will have got there before you and the prices of the shares you might want to buy will have soared. But you have to be late enough to be able to pick companies which have found a proven path to success.

There's a lot of luck involved but the real key, I believe, often lies in spreading your money around a number of possible investments in the area in which you are interested. And then sticking with the investments which do well.

Venture capitalists, who do this sort of thing for a living, know that although most of the investments they make will fail the odd one or two successful investments will more than pay for their losses. But, for this to work, you have to hold onto your successful investments and not be tempted to sell out because you have made a small profit.

If you spot a bandwagon you've missed it. If other people are climbing on then you should be climbing off.

It is by spotting subtle changes in the way the world operates, and by analysing the effect of major shifts in geopolitical power, that the thinking investor can give him or herself an edge over other investors and, in particular, over the so-called professionals: the fund managers, the brokers and the bank analysts.

Look for long-term trends and then hold your nerve. The oil is running out. Emerging nation middle classes are becoming increasingly demanding – wanting meat on their dinner plate and a car in their garage. Inflation is rising in India and China and will soon be exported (together with television sets and bras) to the West. The world is running out of water and timber and many other commodities (both soft and hard). The global infrastructure is crumbling. And, then, there is climate change.

What effect are these likely to have on inflation, interest rates and the global and local economy? (By local I mean the country in which you reside.) Strategic thinking means always asking the question 'what next?'. So, for example, if the oil price falls what will happen next? Will the oil producing nations accept a lower price for their asset or will they cut production (and, therefore, supply) on the grounds that they know that the oil is running out and they don't want to sell it cheaply?

If you have a limited amount of time available for reading (as most people have) then I suggest you devote a large proportion of that time to reading about wider, geopolitical issues rather than individual corporate issues. If you invest in sectors, or in the wider aspects of the market, the success or failure of your investment plans will depend more on the wider issues than on the narrower issues. A broad understanding of geopolitical issues will better enable you to predict the future of the economy, and the markets, and, therefore, better enable you to protect your portfolio. No one can predict the future with 100% success. But if you have a good idea of what may happen in the coming months and years you will be far better able to plan your investments accordingly. For example, I started investing in a variety of commodities in 2003, shortly after I first became aware of the fact that these vital substances were disappearing and just as the global demand for them was increasing.

Don't succumb to 'recent events syndrome' where you put too much emphasis on recent news, and too little on major long-term trends. The latest news always appears more important than it really is because it's happening *now*. But it's long-term, major trends which have the biggest effect on your investments.

And don't trust politicians. Indeed, as an investor it is safe to rely on the stupidity and incompetence and dishonesty of politicians. They will not do sensible things (however simple) to correct substantial threats to the economy but can be relied upon to lie, cheat and make things worse.

And, remember that when making predictions you must take into account what other people will think and how they will react. However much you believe that house prices are too high they will not fall until most people agree with you. During the dot.com boom the prices paid for Internet companies were absurdly high. But it didn't matter that they were absurdly high. Prices only fell when people stopped buying the overpriced shares and everyone started selling. And then they fell quickly and the bubble was burst. Greed drives prices higher than ever seems possible to a rational mind. The key is to remember that it is perception and expectation, rather than reality, that drives share prices.

Truth is now the rarest of all commodities. Indeed, truth is now such a rarity in our world that major public decisions (including so-called democratic elections) are invariably taken on the basis of perception, rather than reality. In essence, this means that perception has become reality. It is nothing new to say that all history is biased because of the often self-serving prejudices of those who write it. The same event can be interpreted in any number of different ways. But what is new now is the fact that the present is being reported and influenced according to the deliberately guided perceptions of the electorate. And if our understanding and appreciation of the present is being altered in this way then our actions will be changed and the future changed too.

The investment professionals tend to think short-term rather than long-term. They are so laden with instant information that they spend little time or effort on strategic planning.

And many investment bankers are far more stupid than they like to think they are.

For example, the so-called 'credit-crunch' which devastated the financial markets (and the share prices of banks) in 2007 and 2008 affected Britain because so many leading bankers behaved like idiots and bought packages of mortgage debt without, apparently, having asked fairly fundamental questions about the security of the assets they were buying. The people who borrowed huge amounts of money and who had no chance of ever paying it back were reckless. But it was the hubris of bankers (many of whom had become bosses of big banks only after their building society had become a bank but who had assumed the salaries and arrogance of investment bankers) which led directly to serious losses for investors and real problems for millions. Greed, on both sides, was the driving force. Greed among the borrowers, and greed among the lenders.

The concept of expecting people to take responsibility for their actions (known as 'moral hazard') is a basic principle of human life. Without 'moral hazard' our society would break down. (Some, including me, would argue that it is indeed the scarcity of moral hazard which explains why our modern society is crumbling so rapidly.) When moral hazard functions properly there is a direct link between action and consequence. If you do something bad, dangerous or stupid then you will pay in some way. If you do something good, honourable or helpful then you will benefit.

The credit crunch that caused so much concern in 2008 was a consequence of the breakdown of the concept of moral hazard.

Many people were responsible for the chaos in the markets which affected just about every country in the world.

First, there were the greedy bankers who lent money to people who never had a chance of paying it back. These were the people who made subprime mortgages possible. Having lent out vast quantities of other people's money, the bankers then made things worse by charging massive fees to package the loans into marketable securities and to devise a whole range of new financial instruments (such as credit-default swaps and collateralised debt obligations) that hardly any of them understood. (I would hazard a guess that none of them understood the consequences of their fiscal sleights of hand.) A major contributor to the crisis was that banks knew little or nothing about the financial health of their counterparties (the banks or institutions on the other side of the transactions). Mutual ignorance led to chaos.

Second, there were the house buyers who borrowed money they never had a chance of repaying. Many of these people lied on their mortgage application forms. Most knew what they were doing. When property prices went too high because of lax lending bankers, estate agents and mortgage brokers were blamed for lending too much too easily. No one said a word about people who borrowed too much. No one pointed out that the greedy people who were borrowing money they couldn't hope to pay back, so that they could live in houses they couldn't possibly afford, deserved what they got.

Third, there were the ratings agencies who were paid by the banks to decide which companies and products were 'safe' and who seem, in retrospect, to have taken an overly optimistic view when dishing out their ratings.

Fourth, there were the official regulators who were supposed to control the banks and ensure that the financial system worked safely.

By the time the credit crunch had hit hard it had become fashionable to regard the regulators as relatively innocent bystanders but I question this rather generous attitude. The regulators (and there were, and are, a lot of them and they were, and are, enormously well-paid) were hired to protect the public. They clearly failed miserably in this.

In the end, in order to try and prevent the entire financial system imploding, the politicians had to use taxpayers' money to rescue some of the larger institutions which, it was decided, could not be allowed to fail. This was a dangerous move because it removed the concept of moral hazard from the finance industry. The biggest institutions (and their directors and executives) were rewarded for their recklessness. And the taxpayers, the very people who had lost money as their savings and pensions disappeared, were the ones who bailed them out.

In the UK, the ultimate irony of the credit crunch was that Gordon 'the moron' Brown brought disgraced former minister Peter Mandelson back into his cabinet to help deal with the crumbling economy. No politicians, journalists or commentators seem to have noticed that one of the previous occasions when he had to resign Mandelson's 'crime' had been to fill in a mortgage application form incorrectly in order to persuade his mortgage lender to let him have money they might not otherwise have been prepared to loan to him. It was, of course, precisely that sort of despicable behaviour that triggered the credit crunch. So, one of the many greedy individuals whose irresponsible behaviour had helped bring the system to the brink of total collapse was brought back, at enormous public expense, to deal with the consequences of the communal greed.

Throughout 2008, when politicians and journalists were trying to understand and explain the financial problems facing the world they failed miserably to grasp the simplicity of what had happened. There were and are two major causes of the mess the world found itself in during 2008. The second, which was temporary and local to a few countries (specifically the UK, the USA, Ireland and Spain) was the fact that house prices had been pushed up to ridiculous levels by greedy speculators. In each country this had been encouraged by greedy bankers, estate agents and mortgage brokers and aided and abetted by reckless and incompetent politicians. The first, which was global and permanent, was the rise in the price of commodities in general and energy in particular. Both these events were easy to predict by anyone with a half-way decent understanding of geopolitics and human nature, (and I did so, in both cases, well in advance of the events) and those who took the trouble to do so should have put themselves into a good position to survive financially.

Investing successfully depends on understanding the ebb and flow of human events, making decisions and then holding your nerve. And this is best done by reading widely and generally rather than by concentrating on titbits of news spread by television and radio. You can get information much more readily and with less wasted effort by reading books, newsletters and magazines (in that order).

The best way I know to beat the market is to make geopolitical predictions and then invest accordingly. Most investors (and most investment advisers) do not yet do this. This may be because they can't or because they prefer to look at the trees rather than study the woods.

Investing successfully is about tackling uncertainty and spotting a route through the many problems which influence the future. It's also about being able to put aside prejudices and the taint of cognitive bias.

Our educational system doesn't teach us to think at all. Specifically, it doesn't teach us to think about probabilities or uncertainties. Our educational system teaches us to remember what the system wants us to believe are facts. But success in life in general, and investing in particular, needs us to know how to deal with facts.

The first most important skill for any investor is, in my view, the ability to differentiate between relevant and irrelevant news. To be successful it is essential to be able to dismiss investment or geopolitical 'noise' and to focus on crucial bits and pieces of information. It is, of course, also essential to be able to interpret the information you have selected and to use the information to help you draw conclusions. There is a danger that we will collect together all the evidence that supports our thesis and then ignore the evidence that is left – the stuff that doesn't support our belief. Psychologists call it confirmatory bias. You will always find market experts who support your view. If you believe that the price of gold is bound to rise you will always find commentators who agree with you. The danger is that you will take too much notice of the people who think the way you think (and who are, therefore, reinforcing your prejudices). You should seek out and read the reasoning of people who disagree with you. Find out why they think you are wrong. If their arguments convince you that you're wrong then you should abandon your belief and look for another investment opportunity. If their arguments don't change your mind, and you still believe you are right when you have studied all the contrary evidence and all the arguments made by people who disagree with you, then maybe you should follow your judgement with your money.

You must be open-minded. Don't be pig-headed and hold to your views as events change. If the evidence in support of your investment changes then you must consider changing your investment. And always try to understand opposing points of view. If you can understand (and overcome) their arguments then you might well be right.

Second, you must remember that success in markets isn't so much about understanding facts and figures, charts and balance sheets as about emotions and dreams. Markets are driven by greed and fear (the basis of the emotions and dreams of all investors) but there is a way to give yourself an edge: a basic understanding of money, psychology and geopolitics (no more than 'basic', because too much will do more harm than good in the way that people who study economics professionally always have less understanding of the economy than ordinary people with jobs, mortgages and a good overview and no economic theory to interfere with understanding). This requires looking at big facts (is the oil running out, what will the next American President be like and which lobby group will control him?). The big questions are as difficult to answer as they are easy to ask. But all that is really needed is that rarest of all commodities: common sense.

Once you have chosen a strategy and found a good investment give yourself a chance to make decent money out of it. Good investment opportunities don't come along very often. There is no point in putting less than 1% of your investable funds into a company which seems to offer huge potential. Invest less than that and any profit you make is unlikely to make a worthwhile difference to your overall wealth and yet the effort required will add noticeably to your overall workload. A very small number of big investment calls or decisions will make the most money for you.

And know your strengths and weaknesses. This is important in all aspects of life. But it is particularly important to you as an investor. Do you work well alone? Do you need someone to steady you when you get too excited? Do you need someone to provide inspiration? The more you know about what you can and can't do, the more successful you will become at the things you can do, and the less the things you can't do will hold you back.

And listen to your instincts. If you know in your heart that an investment is going to be a bad one don't make it. If you feel that an investment could be big do some more research and thinking. And make your final decision on the basis of that research and thinking. But do be prepared to follow your instincts, your hunches and your inspirations.

There are many trends and developments which are worthy of thought.

For example, for years many big companies have aimed their marketing programmes at the young. I've heard executives of huge corporations sneer at the prospect of promoting their wares to the elderly or even the middle-aged. This has always puzzled me. The young are fickle buyers; one minute they're buying Spice Girls records, the next minute they're buying cans of lager and the minute after that they're buying nappies. And although the young have some disposable income they really don't have (and mostly never have had) much money. I've always felt that the elderly make a much bigger and far wealthier marketing target. The bonus is that the elderly are far more loyal than the young (once they've found something that they like they tend to keep buying it). The young are constantly searching for something new to spend their money on, and, in addition, they have to cope with housing costs, babies and all sorts of whimsical extravagances. The elderly may have steady incomes and they have usually paid off their mortgages. They are relatively immune to rising interest rates. Indeed, when interest rates go up they tend to become richer (since the income they receive from their savings will be enhanced). The smart city boys spotted the potential 'grey' market (and its numerous advantages) fairly recently. The snag was that, as always, they looked for ways that they (and not their investors) could make money. And so all sorts of bizarre 'get-rich-from-oldies' schemes were launched – including, inevitably, ways to make money out of nursing homes and care homes. The good thing was that they didn't seem to realise that the elderly spend money on all sorts of things other than nursing home care, stairlifts, zimmer frames and trousers with elasticated waists. The elderly have time for hobbies and they have, for example, become huge purchasers of cameras and computers. Companies which have bothered to target the elderly with advertising not specifically designed to drag in the 15-year-olds have done well.

Birth rates are falling in the West. There are more old people than ever before. This should mean that investments in companies making prams and running schools should do badly while investments in companies making hearing aids and running nursing homes should do well. But beware! Good companies making prams and running schools will probably continue to make money. And bad companies making hearing aids and running nursing homes will go bust. (Plus: when things are as obvious as this the chances are that the competition in providing goods and services for the elderly will be more severe, while the competition for the baby market will be limited.)

Will the credit crunch lead to a rise in resentment against the rich in general and bankers in particular? Will the American and British Governments get a taste for nationalisation? What effect will falling stock markets have on the real economy? Are there really plans for a world government? Will the rise of the European Union lead to a rise in nationalism in Europe? When will multiculturalism and political correctness be overthrown? Will there be more resentment of globalisation? Will the problems created by, and resulting from, the banking problem of 2008 segue neatly into the severe end-play problems created when the oil runs out (as it assuredly will)?

If you look around the world you will probably spot many exceptional investment opportunities. Africa is a nation in turmoil but one rich in numerous essential resources. The world is running out of food and the problem is exacerbated by the increase in the number of people wanting to eat meat. The developing BRIC countries (Brazil, India, Russia and China) are being industrialised at a phenomenal rate. Is America really in terminal decline? When will the Arab States replace the dollar with the euro as their currency of choice?

Selecting big strategic themes is vital. What will happen in Eastern Europe over the next 20 years? As nuclear power plants are built will there be a shortage of uranium? Is coal likely to run out? Many of the coming changes are secular rather than cyclical.

You must learn to keep your feet on the ground when assessing changes. When the Internet first appeared it was said to be the most important invention ever. This nonsense was widely promoted by people who had clearly never heard of the wheel, the internal combustion engine, electricity, the telegraph and so on and so on.

The one certainty is that politicians will betray us all. You can rely on the fact that governments won't cooperate to find a solution to the consequences of global climate change. You can rely on the fact that governments will continue to fight for oil. Was the global warming propaganda merely a ploy to get us accustomed to the oil running out? The evidence supporting the theory that global warming is a man-made scenario is certainly far more controversial than the politicians would have us believe.

Never, never, never invest on the basis of a politician's promise. Politicians talk a great deal about improving infrastructure, and they boast about improving spending on health care and education. Ignore them. Politicians' promises are easily abandoned. Companies which adapt their plans to fit in with potentially profitable opportunities which might result from political changes are taking huge chances. Don't invest in a company which will supposedly benefit from any government decision. Politicians love encouraging companies to spend money on their behalf but they never, ever do anything to help private sector companies make money. Companies don't vote and even politicians know that.

When governments fail to save money during the good times they must print more currency if they want to try and spend their way out of trouble. Their efforts are likely to result in the decline of the currency's value. (If there is more of something around then the value usually declines.) And, with a country which is reliant on imports, that pushes up inflation. (The cost of oil, minerals and food goes up.) When inflation goes up interest rates are likely to follow. (Because governments have to try to control inflation by raising interest rates). When interest rates rise the inevitable result is that money becomes more expensive to borrow: companies and individuals suffer. And thus the boom and bust scenario is firmly established.

Whenever possible politicians, and their advisers, will do the wrong thing. It's what they do best and it's one of the few things you can rely on.

Nevertheless, despite, all my scepticism, I do believe that it is possible to make helpful predictions based on an assessment of geopolitical factors. The snag is that it is usually impossible to say precisely when the predictions will come true. If you are going to invest according to your own predictions you need to do so in such a way that you will not be forced to liquidate your positions too early. And you need to be brave enough (and stubborn enough, perhaps) to stick to your views when the walls are crashing around your ears.

STRUCTURED PRODUCTS

'Anyone who believes in fairness in this life has been seriously misinformed.'
JOHN F KENNEDY

Keep things simple. Don't put money in fancy investments you don't understand. Banks now offer all sorts of weird and wonderful investments. You can, for example, buy an investment which will, at the end of five years, give you 120% of the gain in the stock market or, if the market has gone down, give you back your original investment. Sounds good? It isn't. It's designed to make money for the bank not for you. What are the snags? First, you don't get any of the dividends that you would receive if you held the shares. Second, you will have to hand over your money for five years. It will probably be impossible (or expensive) to get it back before then. Third, the return you get will be decided on one particular day five years into the future. Fourth, if the stock market goes down, or remains steady, you will only receive back your original investment. You will not receive any interest. Structured products are, by and large, designed by crooks to take advantage of the naive.

Here's a home-made way I would put together a scheme to match or beat the bank's proposal.

I would put 80% of my money into National Savings Certificates or a deposit account. This would give me ready access to my money. The interest I'd receive would mean that at the end of five years I would have over 100% of my original investment.

I would put the other 20% into some fairly high risk investment (or investments) that I had researched well and believed would do well.

At the end of five years I would almost certainly beat the bank's proposal if the market went down or stayed level. And I would almost certainly beat the bank if my investments did reasonably well.

Why would my system beat the bank?

Simple.

The bank sets up these schemes to make itself a profit. That's the difference between their scheme and mine.

And that's why I think mine is better.

Despite the evidence against them, structured products (usually known as guaranteed equity bonds) have become very popular. They sound attractive. The advertisements usually explain that if you invest some money in one of these products you will, in a fixed period of years, receive any capital gain that you might have enjoyed if you'd bought shares and held them for that period. Some products offer to give you more than the rise in shares over the period. The offer is made even more attractive by the fact that if the market falls you will get your money back. It seems as though you can't lose.

But nothing worthwhile comes free these days and financial companies don't give anything away. You do lose, of course. The people flogging these things are far more likely to make a profit than you are. Indeed, they are the only people who are really guaranteed to make money.

Most of them probably don't realise it but investors in these products are effectively gambling all their interest and dividends that the stock market will be higher on a particular day five, seven or whatever years ahead, than it is today.

Say you put £10,000 into one of these products and leave it there for five years. At a modest 5% per year that's £500 a year and so the amount being gambled, even without the effect of compound interest, is £2,500. I wonder how many of the people who invest in these products because they are 'safe' and 'guaranteed' would happily put £2,500 on Black Beauty in the 3.30 at Haydock Park?

Another problem is that many of these financial products are complex and remarkably opaque. It is often difficult to see who owns what and which organisation is ultimately responsible for underwriting the value of the investment. I suspect that there is a risk that a structured product's net asset value might be reduced if the bankers involved had their celluloid collars ripped off and the bank backing the product ended up being derated. The failed American bank Lehman Brothers backed many structured products. And it is worth remembering that the giant American insurance company, AIG (which had a AAA rating and was, therefore, regarded as about as safe as safe can be) was also associated with a huge number of financial products. Clever sounding structured funds are frequently backed by counterparties, usually investment banks, whose bonds provide the capital protection. If the counterparty goes bust (and that, as we have seen, is surprisingly likely) the holders of structured products will have to join the queue of creditors waiting and hoping to receive some crumbs from what remains.

In my view, structured products really aren't worth bothering with. Your money will be tied up for a fixed period, the charges are often high and although the advertising blurb may make the product sound appealing to those who want to have their cake and eat it (what a wonderfully absurd phrase that is) the truth is that the complex (and often difficult to understand) conditions mean that I think you would be better off dividing up your money yourself and putting 80% in something supposedly safe (such as National Savings certificates) and 20% in something riskier (such as shares).

TAX

'No man in the country is under the slightest obligation, moral or other, so to arrange his legal relations to his business or property as to enable the Inland Revenue to put the largest possible shovel in his stores. The Inland Revenue is not slow – and quite rightly – to take every advantage which is open to it under the Taxing Statutes for the purpose of depleting the taxpayer's pocket. And the taxpayer is in like manner entitled to be astute to prevent, so far as he honestly can, the depletion of his means by the Inland Revenue.'

LAW LORD, LORD CLYDE

It is our individual responsibility to ensure that we pay as little tax as possible. That is our responsibility to our families and ourselves. Governments, however, don't always see things quite that way. As far as they are concerned what is ours is theirs and what is theirs is also theirs.

Here are some thoughts on tax and tax inspectors.

- 'An economy breathes through its tax loopholes.' Barry Bracewell-Milnes
- 'In this world nothing can be said to be certain, except death and taxation.' Benjamin Franklin
- 'Every man is entitled, if he can, to order his affairs so that the tax attaching under the appropriate Act is less than it would otherwise be' Lord Tomlin
- 'A taxpayer is someone who works for the federal government but who doesn't have to take a civil service examination.' Ronald Reagan
- 'The income tax has made more liars out of the American people than golf has.' Will Rogers

- 'Income tax returns are the most imaginative fiction being written today.' Herman Wouk
- 'Why does a slight tax increase cost you two hundred dollars and a substantial tax cut save you thirty cents?' Peg Bracken
- 'The avoidance of taxes is still the only pursuit that carries any reward.' John Maynard Keynes
- 'There are two systems of taxation in this country: one for the informed and one for the uninformed.' Honorable Learned Hand, US Appeals Court Justice
- 'The trick is to stop thinking of it as 'your' money.' Tax Accountant
- 'There is no art which one government sooner learns from another than that of draining money from the pockets of the people.' Adam Smith

* * *

1. Dealing too often won't just ruin your profits through costs, it will, if you are successful, also expose you to a higher tax bill. 'Buy and hold' might be an unpopular philosophy but from a costs and tax point of view it has much to recommend it.
2. Don't bother trying to become a tax exile. Don't bother trying moving to a tax haven. And don't bother trying to avoid paying tax by becoming a PT (Permanent Traveller). Lots of people do these things. But they spend time and effort and money in avoiding paying tax and they end up living in places that no one in his or her right mind would want to call home. Some years ago I seriously contemplated moving to Monaco. I found, to my astonishment, that it really isn't as straightforward as you might think. And Monaco itself is as dull and uninspiring as a council estate. It's full of tower blocks into which are crammed thousands of miserable tax exiles. The streets may be safe (Monaco has nearly as many CCTV cameras as Britain but they do at least use them to catch the guilty and protect the innocent rather than to simply pick up unfortunate folk who have parked in the wrong place or dropped litter into the wrong receptacle) but I am willing to pay not to live there.
3. Learn about tax rates for different types of investment. These vary constantly. And are now sometimes changed retrospectively. Some investments will be more suitable for holding in a tax free environment. For example, if income tax rates are high it makes sense to put investments which produce a lot of income into a low tax account (such as a pension fund). You must keep up with the latest rules and regulations about the way investments are taxed. Some websites provide up-to-date information and there are one or two newsletters which provide excellent, up-to-date information on taxation.

4. Stay alert for retrospective tax legislation. The British Government has begun introducing retrospective legislation and it is also using its tax collecting agencies to criminalise many activities. The result must surely be that people will be sent to prison for things that weren't illegal when they did them and will be handed huge and unexpected tax bills for earnings and profits that were acquired in the past. Things are likely to get worse rather than better. EU legislation, often gold-plated by an enthusiastically compliant UK Government, will make things ever worse.
5. Don't make an investment because of the tax break. It is often tempting to do this. Back in the 1980's I made a good many investments in companies created under the UK's Business Expansion Scheme. And I put a lot of money into Property Enterprise Zone schemes. In both cases the main advantage was the tax relief on offer and I was attracted to these investments schemes because of the generous tax breaks the British Government offered me. Oh, what a simple, trusting fool I was. What I didn't realise was that the people setting up these schemes knew that it was the tax advantage that was attractive. I was ripped off mercilessly by an endless variety of sharp-suited promoters and businessmen whose most potent ability was, I am now convinced, their skill in preparing attractive looking brochures and finding the seed money to have them printed on expensive paper. The schemes took up vast amounts of time and involved the filling in of a seemingly endless supply of forms. In the end I managed to escape from the investments. I was very little better off than I would have been if I had just paid the tax. If you count the time I spent, the schemes were just another part of my education. I learned two things. First, never invest purely for the tax advantages. The people flogging the whatever it is that you are buying will know that your eye will be on the tax break and not on the fine print. Second, I learned not to trust anything I am told by scheme promoters who work in smart offices and have their photographs taken wearing expensive suits and neatly knotted silk ties. The smarter the promoter, and the more expensive his brochure, the faster I run in the opposite direction. After a decade or so (and a lot of paperwork) I worked out that I had just about broken even. In retrospect it seems to me that a lot of the investment opportunities which I had been offered had been designed with the idea of using the carrot of the tax relief to hide the shortcomings of the businesses concerned. It was a valuable lesson and since I didn't lose any money I was lucky. Don't ever invest in schemes just because of the tax relief. If the investment is any good it doesn't need to be wrapped up in tax-friendly packaging.
6. Always be aware of, and make use of, your legal tax allowances. These change all the time and you need to consult books or websites offering up-to-date information. But, for example, as I write this book every tax

paying citizen in the UK has the right to an annual capital gains allowance. Profits on some share sales can therefore be taken without any tax being due. And yet very few people use this allowance. Indeed, thousands who invest their money in legal tax avoidance schemes such as ISAs don't use their capital gains allowance – even though the tax advantages offered by ISAs are not, in my view, either as easy to access or as advantageous as this simple allowance. (For one thing, losses within an ISA cannot be put against gains elsewhere.) Could this possibly be because investment advisers and investment companies make a lot of money out of selling ISAs but no one makes money out of telling you about your annual Capital Gains Tax allowance?

> *'There is no art which one government sooner learns from another than that of draining money from the pockets of the people.'*
> ADAM SMITH

7. I am scrupulously honest on my tax form. The tax people spot check self-employed people quite often. They've investigated me twice so far. Both were full, year long investigations. And at the end of both I ended up getting money back from the taxman. Like most people who are self-employed I have enough crises and problems in my life without taking on the tax people. I like to know that if they investigate me then, at the end, I'm going to be the one getting a cheque. I keep full records and declare every penny I earn. The more bits of paper you have the more you are likely to be able to win against the taxman. On the last occasion that I was investigated I delivered the requested records crammed into a large suitcase.
8. I am constantly amazed at how many people forget that they have to pay tax on their profits. Think of the number of pop stars who have a couple of hit records, spend all their earnings and then go bankrupt when they get a bill from the taxman. If you are a successful investor you will have to pay capital gains tax too. So put some money aside.

> *'I have always paid income tax. I object only when it reaches a stage when I am threatened with having nothing left for my old age – which is due to start next Tuesday or Wednesday.'*
> NOEL COWARD

9. Part of any appreciated asset belongs to the Government, so they share the risk when you're making a profit. And the Government shares the pain

when you're making a loss. So, consider the tax man as a partner who puts up no money but shares your profits and losses. I regard the tax man as operating a protection racket. I give him money and in return he doesn't use violence against me.

> *'There is nothing sinister in so arranging one's affairs as to keep taxes as low as possible. Everybody does so, rich or poor; all do right. Nobody owes any public duty to pay more than the law demands; taxes are enforced extractions, not voluntary contributions.'*
> US JUDGE LEARNED HAND, US APPEALS COURT JUSTICE

10. Don't over estimate the intelligence of people working for the tax authorities. A few years ago I held a bond run by the bank Goldman Sachs. A payment from the bond was listed on a bank statement under the abbreviated heading 'Gold Sacs'. During one of its typically lengthy but pointless enquiries into my affairs the tax office wrote to my accountant telling him that they now knew that I was dealing in gold. Puzzled, he wrote back and asked them for more information. 'Your client is buying and selling sacks of gold,' replied the taxman, drawing attention to the reference to 'Gold Sacs' as evidence.

> *'The government that governs best taxes least.'*
> THOMAS JEFFERSON, FORMER PRESIDENT OF THE USA

11. If you become even remotely rich you will attract the attention of the tax people. This is because tax inspectors now get bonuses for every pound they gouge out of taxpayers. It is clearly easier and more profitable to target the rich rather than the poor, and it is easier to get money out of the honest rather than the crooked.
12. If, at the end of a tax year, you have made profits and are liable to capital gains tax you may be able to reduce your tax bill by selling investments which have lost money and in which you have lost faith. Selling a share (or another investment) that is below its purchase price in order to use the loss against a capital gain and so reduce your tax bill is known as 'tax-loss selling'.
13. Always understand your own accounts. For years and years I used an accountant who used to tell me how much I owed the taxman. I simply did what I was told and wrote out the cheques. One year, back in the mid 1990's, I followed his instructions and wrote out a cheque for £129,000 for my half yearly tax bill. Only when the taxman subsequently did a spot check on my

accounts did it turn out that I'd paid thousands of pounds too much. I got a welcome refund check. I fired my accountant who told me that it wasn't his fault. He said it wasn't his firm's fault either. His explanation was that his assistant had 'been using out-of-date textbooks'. I'd been paying this guy and his firm thousands of pounds for years. It seemed to me that the least they could have done was buy some up-to-date textbooks. So I got rid of him and decided to fill in my tax form myself. It's a real pain and it wastes a lot of time (though if I used an accountant I would still have to spend some time pulling together bits of paper to show him) but at any time of the year I now know what I owe and when I've got to pay it. There are no more surprises. I like it better this way.

> *'The income tax people are very nice. They're letting me keep my own mother.'*
> HENNY YOUNGMAN

14. If you work like stink all your life and save what you can from your after-tax earnings, and you carefully invest your savings, then any income you derive from those savings will be officially described as 'unearned income'.
15. Before buying shares in a company it's worth looking to see if the company is paying tax at usual corporate rates. If not, why not? It's very pleasant for a company to be not paying any tax but usually that means that the company isn't making any profits. And profits are always a good thing.

TIMING

'Nobody waves a flag at the top (or the bottom) of the market.'
MAX KING

Timing in buying is everything. If you are out of the market on the good days you will miss the huge leaps – and the huge profits that are to be made. But market timing is more or less impossible. The only way to ensure that you are invested when a market starts to recover is to have stayed invested right down to the bottom. It is being invested on the days when the big jumps take place that contribute most to market profits. All this goes against natural instinct of course. It is tempting to get out of shares when they have fallen and to keep your cash nice and safe in a bank deposit account (well, safe as long as the bank doesn't go bust and take your deposit with it). The problem with this is that it requires making two huge decisions: when to get out of the market and when to get back in again.

I deliberately sat out the dot.com boom because it seemed obvious that Internet shares were vastly overpriced long before they crashed. I could never see the logic in investing in a company which sold cat litter by mail order. (And it always seemed to me that most Internet companies were little more than mail order companies using a new method of advertising. Since I know a little about mail order I worried that such companies would find it hard to fulfil their orders – if they ever got any.)

I remember watching a television programme in which the staff of a new dot.com company (which had raised millions) were filmed sitting around waiting for their first order to come in. The company had stocked a large building with desks and computers and had recruited a huge staff force to deal with orders which they were confident would flood in. But the orders never even reached a trickle and the company went bust quite quickly. Why didn't the bosses start off by renting three desks and hiring three temporary staff members to deal with orders? Or, better still, why didn't they start out by hiring a fulfilment company to deal with orders?

I was convinced that the dot.com boom was doomed. And so I didn't invest in it. Not a penny. I could have climbed aboard for the ride. But I didn't.

I missed out on the boom and all the profits.

Throughout the late 1990's I was invested in boring gilts and pretty dull old fashioned companies – the sort which were making profits and paying dividends.

I would do exactly the same thing again.

The bottom line is simple: don't try to time the market on a short-term basis. This is what traders do; and the vast majority of them lose money. Many of them lose all their money. Moving money in and out of the market on the basis of short-term price movements is gambling and the costs, fees, duties and spreads pretty well ensure that you will lose. Knowledge, wisdom and experience will help you not at all if you try short-term trading. It's as predictable as coin tossing.

Just as I am convinced that timing the market is impossible so I also believe that the real profits are to be made by having the courage to make decisions slightly too early – when everyone else is paralysed by fear and consumed by panic. Step back, separate your actions from your emotions, try to understand at least something of the big picture, be patient and then act just before the time seems right. There's an old adage that is worth remembering: 'Be greedy when others are fearful and fearful when others are greedy.'

TRADING

'Investing should be dull...it shouldn't be exciting. Investing should be more like watching paint dry or watching grass grow. If you want excitement, take $800 and go to Las Vegas...'
PAUL SAMUELSON

Some of the most successful investors buy or sell items in their portfolios no more than once every few weeks. One of the biggest and most consistently successful fund managers in the world makes an average of one investment transaction per year for each $1.4 billion of investment funds held. The fund, worth a total of $10 billion, sold three stocks and bought just four in 2007. Study other truly successful investors and you will see that they spend most of their time looking, reading and thinking. They spend very little time on the telephone yelling 'buy, buy, buy' or 'sell, sell, sell'. Many private investors, with comparatively minute portfolios, trade far, far more than seven times a year.

When it comes to making deals, however, ordinary investors are left in the shade by traders; and, in particular, by day-traders who try to time the market by buying and selling shares within minutes or hours.

If you trade (as opposed to invest) you will be fighting the spread, the costs and the tax. Every time you trade you lose money in these three ways. And, worst of all, you have to time your trades so that you get out somewhere near the top and get in again somewhere near the bottom. There are plenty of traders who make short-term profits but traders who succeed in the long term are as rare as hen's teeth.

Not many professionals beat the market as stock pickers. The few who do are long-term holders not traders. Before you start trading individual shares think hard about this. What makes you think you are different – and better? (You may well be different and better but you should know why.)

If you're thinking about setting up as a trader here are some things you should know.

1. The more you trade the more you risk making mistakes. Everything you buy must at some point be sold so if you buy and hold a share you are exposing yourself to the risk of having to take two decisions. Every decision is a potential mistake. If you buy shares in the Flimsy Lingerie Company and then sell those shares and buy shares in the Hand Carved Wooden Clog Company you are doubling your number of potential mistakes. Remember: every investment decision is an opportunity to make a mistake. The fewer decisions you make, the fewer mistakes you will make.

2. You cannot make money by trading because, as an amateur, you will never be able to react faster than the professional market makers to a

surprise announcement. If the President of the USA announces the start of another war you will not be able to react as quickly as the professionals. This means that there really is no point in even bothering to listen out for surprise announcements. Indeed, since prices are often pushed too far down immediately after such an announcement you may well be better off (in all ways) if you don't know what is going on in the short-term. I believe that private investors only have an advantage over professional fund managers when it comes to making decisions based on long-term strategies.

3. Jesse Livermore was the greatest and best known trader of all time. Warren Buffett would probably be at the top of any expert's list of great investors. When Livermore killed himself he was nearly broke. Throughout the latter part of the 20th Century, and early part of the 21st Century, Warren Buffet was consistently one of the richest men in world.

4. Don't waste money buying computerised trading systems. These rely on charts, relative strength signals, volumes, moving averages, the price of turnips and heaven knows what else. The providers usually claim that if you use their system you will make huge amounts of money. You will, they say, have access to as much information as the professionals.

I have three points to make.

i. Most professional investors don't even beat the index. There is no point in trying to match the professionals.

ii. If these systems really worked would anyone sell them? Or would they just keep them and make billions for themselves by trading?

iii. Such systems cannot possibly work because by providing the same information to everyone who wants it, everyone will try to make the same trade at the same time. Any advantage will be rapidly lost.

Sorry to be a party-pooper.

6. Women investors do significantly better than men investors. There is one big difference between the two that explains the variation: men trade, on average, 45% more than women. The extra costs (inspired by over-confidence perhaps) result in a disastrous performance.

> *'For investors as a whole, returns decrease as motion increases.'*
> WARREN BUFFETT'S SUGGESTED FOURTH LAW OF MOTION.

7. Overtrading can damage your wealth. Even if your costs are low you will lose money through the 'turn' (the difference between the buying price and the selling price) and through taxes. Between 1986 and 2005 the S&P 500 grew at an average rate of 11.9% per year. But the average investor

managed only 3.9%, thanks largely to over trading which ate up profits through commissions, taxes and bid-to-offer spreads. A study of 66,000 households with brokerage accounts showed that the 20% of investors who trade least actively significantly outperform the 20% who trade most actively. Another survey showed that during a bull market investors who had a portfolio turnover of less than 1% a year had a net return of 18.5%. On the other hand investors who had a turnover over 20% had a return of 11.4%.

TRICKSTERS AND SWINDLERS

'Men have been swindled by other men on many occasions. In the autumn of 1929, men succeeded in swindling themselves.'
JOHN KENNETH GALBRAITH

Every year a considerable number of investors – many of them experienced – lose money to 'boiler room' tricksters. The typical victim is male, around 60-years-old and has some experience of investing. The average loss is around £20,000. A boiler room is the name given to an operation that offers investors a 'special' opportunity to buy shares in an investment that cannot lose. The shares are usually in a foreign company, and boiler room operatives usually work in offices outside the country where the investor is situated. (This enables them to avoid local regulators. By the time a heavy-footed policeman eventually knocks on their door they will be long gone. You will be in country A, the policeman will be in country B, the money will be wandering between country C and D on its way to country E and they will be in country F or, possibly, country G.)

Boiler room scams can sometimes take some months to reach the end play. The tricksters often start by offering investors a few small, apparently real profits. And then they go for the 'kill'. Boiler room scams can be avoided quite easily. Never invest in anything that has been offered to you by a stranger – by telephone, mail, fax or e-mail. After all, why would a complete stranger offer you a foolproof way to make money?

Boiler room operatives aren't the only ones of whom you need to be wary. Don't respond to people who write or ring you with specific investment prospects. They will tell you about huge once-in-a-lifetime opportunities and you may suppress the thought 'Why are they offering this to me?' and if you do you will lose your money. They will be patient, 'grooming' you for months with gentle telephone calls or e-mails, preparing you nicely before pouncing with the investment bargain you no longer have the strength to refuse; the property that has suddenly come onto the market at a fraction of its real value, the electronic gizmo that will be worth millions, nay billions, once a few tiny flaws have been sorted out.

Be paranoid about your money. Be very wary of people offering you financial advice. Be very wary of people offering you a partnership or a chance to invest in their idea – the one that they guarantee will make you a millionaire in months. Be very wary of people offering you a way to get rich quickly. Be very wary of people whose promotion for their get rich scheme involves photos of their splendid home and their expensive motor car.

Be wary of tipsters who send you letters offering you a chance ('a limited opportunity to a few special, discerning people') to take advantage of a brilliant new investment programme.

There are all sorts of ways to part people from their money. I have a filing cabinet full of examples and many of them are brilliant in their design and execution. The best are often the simplest. The trickster writes to 2,000 people (whose names and addresses he has bought) and tells them about his share dealing programme. As a gesture of goodwill he sends you the name of a share he recommends. It will, he says, go up. You don't buy, of course. A month later he writes again and points out that the share price rose dramatically. You remember the tip. You curse your stupidity in not following the advice. He offers another recommendation. You put it to one side. A month later you receive a third letter. He points out that the second share rose too. You could have made a fortune. And now, having proved his skill as a tipster he comes in for the kill. He offers you a subscription to his share tipping newsletter. It's normally £499 a year. Or £799 a year. Or whatever. But if you subscribe now it will cost you just £149. You write a cheque but the investments he recommends never seem to work. How does he do it? Simple. When he wrote to you recommending the share whose price would rise he also wrote to another 2,000 people telling them that the share price would fall. Whatever happened to the share price he had 2,000 would-be customers. And then he split the 2,000 into two halves. To 1,000 he sent the name of a share. It will rise, he announced. To the other 1,000 he sent the name of the same share. It will fall, he promised. One group of 1,000 was impressed. And to those he sent the offer. Softened up, impressed, many of them wrote cheques.

The best scams are the simplest.

There are a lot of people out there who will cheat you. Some will do it illegally. But the cleverest and most effective will do it entirely legally. I am being entirely realistic (and not in the slightest bit contentious) when I tell you that you will be cheated by lawyers (of all varieties), accountants and bankers. The more money you have the more you will be cheated. You can't stop this happening. All you can do is minimise your losses. And one way to do this is to make it clear that if they steal too much from you then you will take your business elsewhere. Sadly, you can't beat these people (any more than you can, by and large, beat the police, the planning authorities, the tax people or the government) and you probably can't change them either.

* * *

Confidence tricksters who make predictions are sometimes very skilful at promoting their own strengths. Unfortunately, they invariably share a single weakness: an inability to predict both time and event successfully. Most of those who make predictions for a living can assure you firmly that the stock market will go down at some time in the future. And most can tell you, with commendable certainty, that August 3rd will be a Monday in 2015, a Wednesday in 2016 and a Thursday in 2017. The problem is that they can't combine the two skills and tell you the precise date when the stock market will crash – or, indeed, the date when it will go back up again. You can, therefore, safely ignore the specific prognostications of those who claim to be able to forecast the future with great accuracy. If there is ever anyone with a genuine skill in this area you will soon be able to identify him: he will have all the money in the world.

* * *

'Do you want to be rich? Send a SAE and £10 to the following address.' (Advertisement)

You send £10 to the address.

And a week later your envelope returns. Inside is a slip of paper with the following words printed on it.

'Do as I did.'

* * *

People are not rational when it comes to money. Professionals are just as guilty of behaving stupidly as amateurs. Ponzi schemes and pyramid schemes suck in the professionals just as often as they suck in amateurs.

Greed, fear and irrationality are commonplace. People are invariably keen to follow the herd rather than plough their own furrow. How else can one possibly explain the popularity of Bermuda shorts, Mohican haircuts and safety pins through the nose?

People can, and do, act with astonishing stupidity. They will, moreover, believe that they are behaving sensibly when they are patently behaving like idiots. This is just as true of their behaviour when handling money as when deciding on a hair do or preparing to spend £500 on a new pair of shoes.

Don't respond to any scheme that offers you a chance to get rich with no work and no risk. Many of them are pyramid selling schemes. Some are unsustainable, illegal Ponzi schemes where the capital investment from the latest members is used to pay interest to the original members (most government pension schemes are Ponzi schemes as I explained earlier in this book). Some involve fool-proof ways of betting on horses and winning. Some are stock tipping services that sound very, very convincing and often cost a lot of money. Some involve selling a course explaining how you can sell things by mail order. (The most successful mail order courses of all time are the ones which tell people how they can make money by explaining how to make money by selling things by mail order.)

Be watchful and sceptical. There are more tricksters and hucksters and grifters out there than you can possibly imagine.

And, when (not if) you are tricked, don't blame the trickster. Don't waste too much time or energy blaming the bankers, brokers or politicians who took your money.

Every investor on the planet loses money to fraudulent or dishonest schemes. Most of them, the biggest, are organised by big banks or investment houses or governments.

Frauds, cheats and thefts are as much a part of investing life as they are of any other aspect of life. Things aren't fair. Boo hoo. Even the best and most successful investors have occasional losses. Learn from them.

If you blame others for your losses you will never learn from the losses. Only by accepting your share of the responsibility will you benefit.

Don't get too angry when you make a mistake or get conned. The important thing is to use the experience as a learning experience. There is no point at all in getting upset with them (or yourself).

Like many cautious investors I avoided dot.com companies at the turn of the millennium, and kept well away from telecom shares. I can't quite remember the South Sea Bubble or the tulip fiasco but in my nightmares I can still hear the growling bear of the early 1970's.

Despite my caution I've had my mistakes. I took out a solid, safe, boring pension with Equitable Life. I bought zero dividend investment trust shares – according to advisors, brokers and commentators everywhere the safest way to plan for the future. And, looking for a good solid blue chip investment, I bought shares in Railtrack. This turned out to be a painful and expensive triple whammy. The Equitable Life investment turned out to be about as reliable as a papier-mâchè bicycle in the wet. And the part of the investment trust industry specialising in zero dividend investment trust shares showed itself to have about as much credibility as a Labour party spokesman.

I'm not whingeing about this.

The only thing to be done in these circumstances is to ask: 'What have I learned?'

I didn't learn anything much from the Railtrack fiasco. I didn't trust politicians before they stole my money and I certainly won't ever trust them in the future.

But I've learned not to trust anyone in the investment business. Never again will I trust an investment company, an insurance company, a pension company, a broker or an advisor.

For a career in investment banking the primary requisite seems to be the talent to be able to lose vast amounts of other people's money (preferably managing to siphon large quantities of the stuff into your own pocket as you do so) without losing any sleep or turning grey. This is not a rare talent (if talent is the right word) but it is one so richly rewarded that the lucky few who obtain these jobs have more in common with lottery winners than with employees of more prosaic establishments.

And that's the sad truth. It is a jungle out there and as private investors you and I are on our own. Other people do care about your money as much as you do. But only because they're desperately keen to get their sticky fingers on it. And the worst and most effective confidence tricksters in the business are the ones working for the establishment.

VALUE INVESTING (AKA CONTRARIAN INVESTING)

'Without Contraries is no progression.'
WILLIAM BLAKE

You are a value investor if you try to buy shares which seem cheap. This can be because the company concerned has assets per share which are worth more than the share price or simply because the company's dividend yield or p/e ratio suggest that the share is underpriced.

Value stocks have historically outperformed the market in general and growth stocks in particular. Over time value stocks produce 2% more than growth shares. That's a lot. Small cap value shares tend to do best of all.

Value stocks may be cheap because they aren't performing or are performing below their potential earning power, are suffering from poor management, are going through some sort of crisis caused by geopolitical factors, have debt or are considered risky. Investors buy them (despite whatever might be wrong with them) because they suspect that the market has got it wrong and that the shares have been beaten down to an unreasonably low level. Of course, shares may be good value simply because other investors have been concentrating on other shares and have missed the opportunity. Value investors expect to buy unwanted shares cheap because they are unwanted, unattractive, underowned, undervalued and underloved. Misfortune has, perhaps, made the share unpopular. The ideal 'value' share can be purchased below the asset value so that even if the company goes broke there will be value left in the shares.

To be a value investor you need to have a strong conviction about a share. You need to believe that there is underlying value that has not been spotted by other investors. If you buy shares in a good business when the shares are cheap you can, if the business is re-evaluated, either keep the shares (a good investment which you bought below cost and where the dividends will keep rolling in) or, if you know of something better to do with the money, sell them and take a profit and pay whatever taxes may be due.

When looking for a 'value' share that has been cyclically mispriced you should look for a company which is earning lots of cash and has a strong market position. Such a company may, if the share is available at a low price, be a good long-term investment.

Value investors are sometimes also known as contrarian investors (and vice versa). Value investing is rewarding over medium and long periods. Buying high yielding unwanted shares which are in a good but unfashionable business sector can, over the medium and long-term, be enormously profitable.

VOLATILITY

'Lethargy, bordering on sloth, should remain the cornerstone of an investment philosophy.'
WARREN BUFFETT

Volatility measures the degree to which the price of a share or some other asset varies; it is the size and frequency of the fluctuations in the price of whatever is being examined. It is a measurement of how rapidly, and unpredictably, a market changes. If a price goes up and down a lot then it is volatile. Traders try to make money out of volatility by buying when a price is low and selling when it is high. (Another good way to lose your money is to play poker with men who have ponytails and wear dark glasses.) Nerdy people who have inky fingers and nothing better to do with their lives measure volatility by finding the average of the high-low ratio of a share price for the past five years.

Volatility frightens many investors but without it there would be fewer chances to buy bargains. A wildly fluctuating market means that there will occasionally be great opportunities to buy.

Share prices are more volatile than fundamentals and markets are more volatile than the economy as a whole. This may be because investors overreact to bits and pieces of news. And sometimes they worry about things which don't actually happen. Investor psychology has a greater effect on share prices than basic information about the company's activities.

One of the causes of volatility is the fact that prices always overshoot. Investments (whether they are shares or houses or coffee beans or paintings by Van Gogh) become more and more expensive. They go up far above any possible conception of fair value. And then a leaf falls off a tree or a bank clerk sneezes in Panama and everything goes into reverse. The same investments which were soaring will now plunge. And they will plunge far below a reasonable assessment of their value.

Electronic trading is largely responsible for these huge swings in prices. Once the market has established a trend the computers kick in with their momentum strategies and prices surge upwards, ever upwards. The banks' independent analysts, just following what the computers are doing, try to justify the new prices (whether they are high or low) with all sorts of gobbledegook research.

Volatility then becomes even more extreme when investment managers and hedge fund wizards suddenly have to sell shares in order to raise money to pay investors who want their money back, to pay interest on loan payments or to satisfy margin calls. Since the poorer stocks in their portfolios may well be unsaleable they end up selling the good stocks – which then also plunge in price.

Volatility varies enormously with different asset classes. If you look at the 30 years covering the 1970's, 1980's and 1990's the figures show that in its best year (1979) gold rose by 126.5% but in its worst year (1981) it fell by 31.6%. Silver was even more volatile. It rose by 267.4% in 1979 and fell by 46.4% in 1981. Commodities as a whole also showed some extraordinary ups and downs. Their best year was 1973 when they went up by 57.7% and their worst year was 1981 when they declined by 46.4%. Shares and real estate weren't as volatile as gold and silver but they were just as volatile as commodities as a whole. And even long-term government bonds, which averaged a return of 9.5% throughout this 30-year period, produced some amazingly good years and some horrifyingly bad years. In 1982 long-term government bonds rose by 40.4% but in 1994 they fell by 7.8%. If you buy government bonds at the wrong time you stand to make a thumping great loss that can take years to overcome.

Volatility isn't the same thing as risk and when markets seem unstable I think it is important to remain calm. If you believe in your methods you should think of the medium and long-term and accept the volatility as just another facet of market behaviour.

Many investors are tempted into overtrading by market noise. They react to variability rather than to deep seated trends.

The best way to avoid this temptation is, perhaps, to avoid the temptation to over-monitor your investments. This is especially important if you are a long-term investor. When volatility is high there is a great temptation to trade too much. And that can be costly both in terms of expenses and in terms of the fact that you may well be 'out of the market' on the one or two big up days.

Here's a story which illustrates the hazard of over-monitoring your investments. It revolves around the use of computers, which can cause far more comprehensive trading chaos than you might imagine. The 'fat finger' syndrome, whereby a trader's digit adds a few noughts to a trade and, as a result, breaks either his own bank or someone else's by buying a hundred million shares when he intended to buy a few thousand, is now well-documented. But that's a simple keyboard error.

It isn't difficult to find other, rather more sophisticated, examples of the sort of chaos computers can cause.

In September 2008 it was reported in the *Financial Times* that a single mouse click had very nearly grounded United Airlines, the world's second largest airline.

Here's what happened.

A reader looked at the website for the *South Florida Sun-Sentinel* newspaper and found an article about United Airlines's bankruptcy which had originally appeared in the *Chicago Tribune*. That single page visit triggered a chain of events which resulted, less than a day and a half later, in the crash of United shares from 12 dollars to 3 dollars in a matter of minutes, and then back up again almost as quickly.

The visit to the *South Florida Sun-Sentinel* website resulted in the article appearing in a list of the paper's most read stories.

What happened next seems to have been that an electronic Google programme swept through the newspaper's website for news stories and found the story about Universal Airlines.

The article was indexed and appeared on Google's news pages. There was by then no date line on the story.

The news item was then spotted by an employee of a distressed-debt investment newsletter who wrote and published a summary of the story which ended up in a report sent out on Bloomsberg's service.

At 10.44 a.m. United Airlines were trading above $12.

By the time trading was halted at 11 a.m. the shares were down to $3 each.

And even a week later the shares were still almost 15% down.

It's difficult to know what lessons to draw from this.

But one lesson is that constantly looking out for news items can damage your wealth. If you'd been holding United Airlines shares and had panicked and sold them when they were down to $3 you could have lost a lot of money. If you hadn't known about the story because you'd slept through it you'd have missed all the excitement and you would have saved yourself a lot of money.

PART THREE

VERNON COLEMAN'S 100 LAWS OF MONEY

'I forget what I was taught. I only remember what I've learnt.'
PATRICK WHITE

1. In investing, as in many areas of life, things are never completely different and yet things are never quite the same.
2. The financial markets (and in particular equity markets) move ahead of the real economy. In other words, markets anticipate economic trends, rather than responding to them. Indeed, the markets are more likely to influence the economy than they are to respond retrospectively to what is happening in the real world.
3. Most people hate losses more than they love gains. This is a leftover instinct from our Stone Age days when the downside from misfortune far exceeded the upside from good fortune. (Breaking a leg while out hunting meant certain death. But catching an animal merely meant temporary respite from hunger.)
4. Risk and return go together like Laurel and Hardy. If you want a big return you have to take a big risk. If you take a small risk you will probably get a small return. This isn't always true, of course. But not many things *always* happen.
5. The entire financial industry exists to sell things and to make money out of you. If you don't understand – and remember this – you will be cheated, tricked and conned. You are the only person interested in making money for you. Everyone else is interested in making money from you.
6. If you're going to add value to your investments then someone else has to lose money. That's the way it works. Adding value to your investments is a zero-sum game. In order to add value you must know or understand things which most other investors do not know or understand. And you must be able to think independently and think conceptually. You will also need the confidence to go against the crowd. Remember, that you will be competing with highly paid professionals who are equipped with hugely expensive resources.

7. Successful investing involves anticipating change, not reacting to it.
8. You should always be able to explain your investments to anyone in a few simple sentences. If you buy a share or put money into an investment trust or fund you should be able to summarise your reasons in sentences that anyone could understand. And you need to be able to explain why you are continuing to hold this investment on a regular basis – particularly if anything changes.
9. Don't expect the authorities to protect you. They will not. Don't expect compensation when you are deceived. You will probably not get any.
10. If you are uncertain about what is going to happen, it is sometimes wisest to do nothing. This is often difficult to do and may require some strength of will.
11. You can gain even when you lose. If an investment goes wrong and you lose money, study what happened. Did you do something wrong? Were you just unlucky? Be brutally honest with yourself and you will learn from your losses.
12. You must never panic. If you panic you will sell at the wrong time and lose money. The best way to avoid panicking is to make sure that you don't put yourself in a position where you are ever going to feel uncomfortable or under pressure.
13. In the world of investing there are no rules and the only constant is change.
14. If anyone tells you that an investment is a 'no brainer' let them invest in it. They're the ones with no brain.
15. The big mistake investors make is in becoming over-confident. Once you have had a success it is tempting to put that down to your natural genius. On the other hand, if you have a failure that can be dismissed as 'bad luck' or 'unforeseen circumstances'. Over-confident investors tend to trade too much. Don't make the mistake of thinking you are brilliant because you get something right. The chances are that you will screw up next time. The trick is to minimise your losses and to be able to get it right again.
16. Don't take money too seriously. It's only money. In the end the taxmen and the lawyers get it all anyway.
17. Deceit, corruption and disappointment are secular not cyclical.
18. Investing is an intellectual and emotional challenge.
19. Investing is like tennis and golf. At the top level the winners are the ones who make the fewest mistakes.
20. Every investor has a unique risk and reward profile. An investment that is perfect for one investor may not suit another.

21. Buy things when nobody else wants them. And sell when everybody does want them.
22. Buy investments because you want them, not because someone has sold them to you.
23. Markets can behave more irrationally than you would possibly believe. And they can do it for longer than you would possibly believe too.
24. Expect the unexpected. However much you know you will never know more than a tiny percentage of the relevant facts. The only constant in our lives is change. And the only thing that will always happen is the unexpected. The things you are expecting hardly ever happen (and because you are expecting them they are probably already discounted). It is the things you aren't expecting which will threaten your investment and change your life.
25. Big investment opportunities are rare. When you spot one, and you are sure, you have to seize it with both hands.
26. To make long-term gains you need to minimise your losses.
27. Listen to what other people are saying. But do so not because you want to follow their investment advice but because you want to know what they are saying (and probably doing).
28. It may sound silly but you should listen to your instincts when making investments. Don't fight your superstitions or your prejudices. If you have never liked a company or a country or an asset group, find somewhere else to put your money. If you fight your instincts, your prejudices and your superstitions you will never be comfortable. And instincts, prejudices and superstitions are not infrequently based on fact.
29. It is not true that everything that goes up must come down. Nor is it true that everything that goes down must come up.
30. Avoid the idea that things cannot get worse for a company, a sector or a nation. Things can always get worse.
31. Cut your losses in stocks you no longer believe in and, as long as you have faith in the companies, let your profits run. That is probably the most important truth to follow
32. Make your investment choices according to what is happening and not according to what you think should be happening.
33. People are not good at predicting disasters (or any aspect of the future). When something unexpected happens most people tend to overreact. Always be prepared to change your mind if the facts change. But try to do so calmly.
34. Know your weaknesses as an investor. Do you tend to react too much to small items of news? Do you listen too much to what other people say? Are

you afraid of losing money? Are you afraid of making money? Do you feel guilty about having money? Until you know yourself, you will not make a competent investor.

35. Many people regard money they've earned with their sweat as being in some way different to money they've won, inherited or received as a bonus of some kind. They will treat the first sort of money with more respect than the second sort of money. This is illogical. Money doesn't know where it has come from.
36. It is easier to lose money than it is to make it.
37. With the possible exception of education there is no such thing as a safe investment. And for an education to be an investment it must result in the acquisition of a skill or talent that is permanently useful and/or readily saleable.
38. Try to find investments which offer you a chance to make money without too much of a risk of losing it. Heads you win, tails you don't lose very much.
39. If you want to make big money you have to be far enough ahead of the crowd to feel uncomfortable.
40. Only accept investment tips from people who love you.
41. Make sure your money works for you, and not the other way round.
42. If you are to be a successful investor you must know what you want from your investments. And you must know what you are prepared to risk in order to get what you want.
43. People with government jobs usually have a long history of failure. The people with the biggest jobs are usually the ones with the longest history of the greatest failures. This is true for all countries.
44. It is the unexpected things that will affect your investments most dramatically. The events you are expecting will probably have a relatively mild effect. Unexpected, small incidents can often produce a quite disproportionate response.
45. You need to free your mind from distracting noise (irrelevant, short-term information) and from distracting, egotistical notions (such as the idea that selling a losing investment is a sign of failure).
46. If a combination of talent, experience, hard work and a bit of good fortune bring reward to just about every walk of life why should investment be an exception?
47. Battles are won one bullet at a time and investment portfolios are built one decision at a time.

48. Whenever you find yourself facing an investment problem the answer is to focus on the solution rather than the problem.
49. If you want to beat the market you have to outthink the majority of other investors (both professionals and amateurs). That is as easy as it sounds. If you are daunted by that prospect you may succeed. If you are not daunted you will probably not succeed.
50. You will look after your money better than anyone else will.
51. Most of the people who manage investments for a living are complete fools.
52. Act on your convictions. Your convictions (unlike those of the analysts and professional managers) are honest and objective.
53. Don't be stubborn. If you have made a mistake, admit it to yourself and move on.
54. Don't believe anyone who is not a billionaire who tells you that he can predict interest rates and exchange rates.
55. It is possible to be very successful by being right 30% of the time, as long as you hold your winners and sell your losers.
56. If you go with the crowd (buying what everyone else is buying) you will be no more of a success than everyone else. And most investors (amateur and professional) do worse than the market.
57. Markets are illogical and inefficient.
58. You will hardly ever buy at the bottom and sell at the top. But you can hope to sell higher than you buy.
59. Do more of what works and less of what doesn't.
60. Once you have decided on a course of action – stick to it.
61. Traditional investment rules all rely on hindsight, whereas it is forecasting and predicting skills which count. Identify and understand your investment strengths and then invest accordingly.
62. It isn't information that matters in the world of investing: it is knowing how other people will respond to the available information.
63. Don't fall in love with your investments. It's the most difficult trick of all. The investments you own don't know that you own them. They won't care (or be hurt) if you sell them.
64. Just because everyone else is behaving stupidly, and you are behaving sensibly, does not always mean that you will make more money than them.
65. Don't trust anyone but yourself. And be wary of yourself.
66. Buy today what you think others will want to buy tomorrow.

67. If it sounds too good to be true then it probably isn't true.
68. Now is always the most difficult time to make an investment decision.
69. What is money for? Regularly ask yourself this question.
70. If you buy an investment which everyone else agrees is worth buying then you are probably paying too much. This is true for every investment you can think of – including bonds, shares and property.
71. Never take investment advice from anyone who isn't a self-made millionaire and/or considerably richer than you are. What does the guy in your local bank know about investments? If he is so good why isn't he rich, rather than sitting behind a desk telling you what to do with your money?
72. If you aren't prepared to take small losses you will probably have to accept big losses.
73. You can either eat seeds or you can plant them. Money is like seeds.
74. Never allow yourself to become too optimistic. Remain pessimistic about your investments and you will watch them more carefully – and be less likely to lose money.
75. Investments should be for the long-term. Unless there has been a major event causing you to rethink the reason for buying and continuing to hold you should not monitor your portfolio too often. Prices of shares and other investments move on a daily basis. But these movements are often irrelevant. However, it is important to understand that things move faster than they used to and although 'buy and hold' used to be a wise philosophy it is an approach which needs to be tempered. Consumers' tastes, markets, geopolitical forces and technologies change – all these things mean that buying and holding any investment can be dangerous.
76. Interest rates which are high can always go higher. Exchange rates which are low can always go lower. Interest rates which are low can always go lower (until they reach 0%). Exchange rates which are low can always go down until one of the currencies is worthless.
77. Investors should focus. Tiger Woods doesn't try to win the Wimbledon tennis championship. The more you focus the better you will do.
78. The only constant in our lives is change.
79. Above average returns are usually a reward for taking risk. Investors who do particularly well are usually taking big risks. They may do well for several years. But then they may have a bad year. In the long run they will be successful investors only if their good years far outweigh their bad years.
80. Develop your instincts and learn to listen to them. The fundamental philosophy behind my book *Bodypower* was that we should all learn to 'listen to our bodies'. We can know our bodies better than anyone else ever can. As

far as investments are concerned no one knows as well as you do what risks you are prepared to take. No one else knows what makes you comfortable. Just as you are the best medical adviser you will ever have so, too, you are also the best financial adviser you will ever have.

81. Investing in the belief that 'the market will eventually come round to my way of thinking' is doomed to failure. You may be right that the market is wrong. But it does not necessarily follow that the market will correct itself. Ever. Why are others ignoring what you know? What do they know that you don't know? What other factors (some known and some only predictable) might you and they have missed?
82. Seek out opinions that contradict your own. Use them to test the soundness of your own strategy before making an investment decision. Look at both sides. Situations are rarely simple.
83. Before investing try to read as much as you can written by those who think that your planned investment is foolish. If you can understand and counter their arguments your thesis and conviction will be stronger.
84. Keep six months income in cash. Who knows when the roof is going to start leaking, the car is going to fall apart or the taxman is going to send an unexpected demand for money. If you have some cash you can deal with these problems. If you don't have any cash available you may have to sell investments at a terrible time.
85. Don't expect your chosen investment to rise immediately after you've bought it. You might have to wait a while for the rest of the market to realise that you're a genius and that they want to make the same investment decision that you've made.
86. Past performance does not guarantee future success. Indeed, if past performance is based upon styles which have gone out of date there is a chance that past good performance will guarantee future failure.
87. You won't go far wrong if you buy what most people are selling. Successful investment is largely about courage.
88. Learn as you go. If you take notice as you get wealthier you will be able to do it all again (and quicker) if everything goes bad.
89. Nobody – nobody – knows for certain what the markets are going to do next year, next month, next week or tomorrow. If they knew they would have all the money in the world.
90. However much you know you will never know more than a tiny percentage of the relevant facts.
91. Always be prepared to ask dumb-sounding questions when planning an investment. You can't afford not to ask them. Asking dumb questions

requires courage. That's why they are worth asking.

92. Before investing, always work out the worst case scenario. And give yourself an exit strategy.
93. Always remember why you are investing. The aim is to make money. Do not feel shy or embarrassed about this. If your aim is to make the world a better place, put your money to work in some more direct way.
94. There is no single rule for successful investing. If investing was easy everybody would follow the rule and everybody would be rich.
95. If it sounds too good to be true – don't buy it. If you don't understand it – don't buy it. If you don't understand how the seller can make money – don't buy it.
96. Find an investment with the minimum downside and with a good possible return. Make as big an investment as you dare so that you can make a big profit. Do this rarely, when you are convinced that your investment choice will do well.
97. When markets are in turmoil it is vital to keep your emotions out of your decisions. Fear, panic and greed have no place in rational decision making – though they are the forces which drive most investors, most bankers and most politicians. Rational thought, based on an understanding of the larger picture (which includes the interaction between geopolitical events and human nature) is the only basis for investment success.
98. Find an investment approach that matches your personality; your fears, your hopes, your needs.
99. You can only beat the professionals by being wiser than they are. And that is easier than you might think it is.
100. The key to successful investing is to look at geopolitical issues and to spot global trends, and to understand their importance to other people.

'We've had some good centuries and we've had some bad centuries.'
A WISE FAMILY INVESTOR.

For a catalogue of Vernon Coleman's books please write to:

Publishing House
Trinity Place
Barnstaple
Devon EX32 9HG
England

Telephone	01271 328892
Fax	01271 328768

Outside the UK:

Telephone	+44 1271 328892
Fax	+44 1271 328768

Or visit our website:
www.vernoncoleman.com